Resiliency Enhancement

Resiliency Enhancement

Putting the Strengths Perspective
Into Social Work Practice

Edited by Elaine Norman

COLUMBIA UNIVERSITY PRESS   NEW YORK

Columbia University Press
Publishers Since 1893
New York   Chichester, West Sussex

Copyright © 2000 Columbia University Press

Library of Congress Cataloging-in-Publication Data
Resiliency enhancement : putting the strengths perspective into social work practice :
edited by Elaine Norman.
   p. cm.
  Includes bibliographical references and index.
  ISBN 0–231–11800–7 (cloth : alk. paper) — ISBN 0–231–11801–5 (pbk. : alk. paper)
    1. Social service — Psychological aspects.   2. Resilience (Personality trait)
  I. Norman, Elaine.

HV41 .R47 2000
361.3′2′019 — dc21   00–022727

♾

Casebound editions of Columbia University Press books
are printed on permanent and durable acid-free paper.
Printed in the United States of America
c 10 9 8 7 6 5 4 3 2 1
p 10 9 8 7 6 5 4 3 2 1

Contents

Resiliency Enhancement

1 Introduction: The Strengths Perspective and Resiliency Enhancement — A Natural Partnership

Elaine Norman

Social workers and other people in the helping professions have grown tired and disillusioned with the traditional disease model that has dominated their professional practice for many decades. The traditional disease model, borrowed from medicine, highlights injury, pathology, victimization, and learned helplessness. Bubbling to the surface is the felt need to sprinkle some hope into the incessant focus on problems and maladjustment, stress and adversity. Momentum has developed to concentrate professional practice on coping rather than on risk, on opportunity rather than on fatalism, on wellness and self-repair rather than on illness and disability. In other words, a change from a medical damage model that focuses on curing illness to a health model that concentrates on promoting health (Rutter 1989; Weick 1986; Wolin and Wolin 1993). In social work this change in model and emphasis has been dubbed "the strengths perspective" (Saleebey 1996).

A strengths outlook is not new to social work, but until recently it has remained in the background, taking a back seat to the field's fascination with the three Ds: dysfunction, deficit, and disease. The push to change the field's predominant paradigm from pathology to strength began in the early 1980s. Weick (1983) strongly advocated the "growth-task model" of human development, emphasizing the idea that all people have an inherent push for growth and that a focus on the tasks of growth fit well with social work's interest in client empowerment. Continuing this theme Weick (1986) suggested a "health model of social work." Believing that healing — either biological, psychological, or social — is an inherent capacity of the human organism, she advocated that social work attempt to mobilize the innate self-correcting mechanisms of individuals and environments in order to stimulate healing.

In a further attempt to persuade the field to move more urgently toward a strengths perspective Weick and her colleagues itemized the ways in which they saw the current deficit- and problem-focused orientation of social work to be counterproductive (Weick et al. 1989). It disheartens clients by stressing their inability to cope. It isolates clients by setting them apart from others who do not have their problems. It stigmatizes clients by seeing "the problem" as a lack or inability in the person affected. Treatment is directed toward overcoming the deficiency at the heart of the problem rather than at an appreciation of positive attributes and capabilities. The authors graphically describe the helping encounter as "an emergency room where people come to be patched up" (352). They call for a qualitatively different context for social work practice, one that emphasizes the positive. "Rather than teaching people evermore sophisticated formulations of their problems [social work can help] people learn to recognize and appreciate [and use] their strengths" (354), thereby enabling them to take control of their own lives and solve their own problems.

With the need for a new way of working with clients made increasingly clear the question becomes how do we actually put the strengths perspective into daily social work practice? Illustrations have recently begun to appear in the literature. Cowger (1994) detailed a plan to include strengths in the assessment process. His strengths assessment would look for mobilizable competencies, ways to build client self-confidence, and to stimulate hope. Rapp (1998) describes a first attempt to include the strengths model in case management with the mentally ill. He enumerates several useful strengths-related concepts, and attempts to codify methods derived from them for use by case managers.

Suggesting that the field must look at clients "in the light of their capacities, talents, competencies, possibilities, visions, values and hopes," Saleebey has recently become a prominent spokesperson for the strengths perspective in social work (1996:297). His edited book *The Strengths Perspective in Social Work Practice* (1997) presents the latest thinking in the field about the paradigm. In it he clearly states that at present the strengths perspective is just that—a perspective, "a way of thinking," an approach to practice. The monumental task of developing ways to put this way of thinking into everyday social work practice remains. Both Howard Goldstein (1997) and the author of the present article see *resiliency* as the attribute, the concept, the process, that epitomizes and operationalizes the strengths perspective. In fact, resiliency enhancement is probably the most reasonable way that social work can put the strengths perspective into practice.

What Is Resiliency?

When a pitched baseball hits a window, the glass usually shatters. When that same ball meets a baseball bat, the bat is rarely damaged. When a hammer strikes a ceramic vase, it too usually shatters. But when that same hammer hits a rubber automobile tire, the tire quickly returns to its original shape. The baseball bat and the automobile tire both demonstrate resiliency. Resiliency is the ability to bounce back from, or to successfully adapt to, adverse conditions. When we talk about human beings rather than inanimate objects, resiliency is usually defined as "successful adaptation under adverse conditions" (Luther and Ziegler 1991:8), or as the factors and processes enabling sustained competent functioning even in the presence of major life stressors (Masten, Best, and Garmezy 1990).

Resiliency combines the interaction of two conditions: *risk factors* — stressful life events or adverse environmental conditions that increase the *vulnerability* of individuals — and the presence of personal, familial, and community *protective factors* that buffer, moderate, and protect against those vulnerabilities (Jessor 1993; Kumpfer 1993; Masten, Best, and Garmezy 1990; Rutter 1987). Individuals differ in their exposure to adversity (vulnerability) and the degree of protection afforded by their own capacities and by their environment (protective factors). A person's ability to recover, to adapt, or to bounce back to a normal condition (*resiliency*) varies over the person's lifetime, as well.

This chapter will enumerate those individual and interpersonal protective factors that have been found in the research literature to increase a person's ability to cope with stressful life spaces. Since they have the potential to lead to resilient outcome they will be called *resiliency factors*, or just simply resiliency. Enhancement of these resiliency factors can be a primary step in operationalizing the strengths perspective in social work practice.

There are several important considerations to keep in mind when thinking about resiliency:

1. *It is not a fixed attribute of individuals.* Rather, a resilient or adaptive

outcome is a process of interaction between environmental and personal factors. If circumstances change, outcomes may be different (Kumpfer 1993; Luthar 1991; Richardson et al. 1990; Rutter 1989).

2. *Adversity is additive over time.* The larger the number of factors stressing an individual, the more likely maladaptive, rather than resilient, outcome will result (Cowan et al. 1990; Garmezy 1985; Masten, Best, and Garmezy 1990; Rutter 1979; Werner 1990).

3. *Resilient behavior does not necessarily indicate good emotional health.* Resiliency is measured by observable behavioral criteria. At least two studies, one of highly stressed adolescents (Luthar 1991), and one of concentration camp survivors (Moskowitz 1983), indicated that behaviorally resilient individuals can clearly be emotionally troubled.

Resiliency Factors Noted in the Research Literature

In the past few decades a body of research results has accumulated that begins to describe a common core of personality characteristics and environmental protective factors that enable highly stressed individuals to maintain competence and control in their lives. The results of these research efforts have shown that psychological and/or dispositional attributes have proven to be adaptive and that emotional ties, cohesiveness, and interpersonal socialization have been shown to be protective. A synopsis of the research findings is presented below. Eleven resiliency factors are presented in detail.

RESILIENCY FACTORS

Personality related

- Self-efficacy
- Realistic appraisal of the environment
- Social problem-solving skills
- Sense of direction or mission
- Empathy
- Humor
- Adaptive distancing
- Androgynous sex role behavior

Interpersonally related

- Positive, caring relationships
- Positive family or other intimate environment
- "High enough" expectations

Personality Factors

SELF-EFFICACY

The single most important personality characteristic found to be associated with resilient outcome is a sense of self-efficacy. Self-efficacy involves a solid feeling of self-worth, a positive perception of one's ability to perform required life tasks, and confidence that one can deal with whatever comes one's way (Bandura 1977; Rutter 1984). It also includes the sense of security that comes with the belief that one's external and internal world are predictable and hopeful, that life makes sense, and that one has some control over one's self, the current environment, and one's future destiny (Kumpfer 1993; Werner 1985). Self-efficacy includes two essential aspects: a sense of self-worth or self-esteem, and a sense of mastery over one's self and the external environment (sometimes called an "internal locus of control").

Many studies have demonstrated the association between self-efficacy and resiliency. A comparison of resilient and non-resilient participants in a thirty-year longitudinal study (which included the entire cohort of all people born in 1955 on the island of Kauai, Hawaii) indicated that the more resilient Hawaiians were those who believed in their ability to control their environment in a positive way (Werner and Smith 1982, 1992). A study of high-risk children by Michael Rutter (1984), and one of the offspring of mentally ill parents by Norman Garmezy (1985), both discovered that the more resilient felt a greater degree of personal control over their lives and held the belief that effort pays off. A series of studies in Rochester, New York, found greater self-esteem and a greater sense of competence in stress-resistant participants when compared to stress-vulnerable participants (Cowan et al. 1990). The most resilient of the institutionalized females in Rutter's 1984 study were those who attempted some type of mastery over their circumstances and took active steps toward changing their environment (Rutter 1984). The successful street children in Colombia, studied by Felsman (1989), repeatedly reinforced their sense of self-efficacy and control through effective daily behaviors aimed at securing a livelihood on the streets. A high sense of self-worth, mastery, and an internal locus of control marked the resilient participants in a number of other studies (Ellickson 1990; Schwartz et al. 1989, 1993; Wyman et al. 1993).

Self-efficacy is actually the opposite of what Seligman (1975) dubbed "learned helplessness." The latter concept implies a view of the external environment as random and immutable and totally outside of one's personal influence and control (Kumpfer 1993; Luthar and Ziegler 1991). Self-efficacy implies a sense of self-esteem, of confidence, and a belief in one's ability to influence one's fate. It is bolstered by two other resiliency factors: the ability to appraise the environment realistically, and an arsenal of social problem-solving skills that reinforce and sustain a sense of mastery.

REALISTIC APPRAISAL OF THE ENVIRONMENT

This resiliency factor is poetically contained in the well known Alcoholics Anonymous motto about knowing what one can and cannot do, and what one can and cannot change. Research seems to suggest that resilient individuals have the ability to differentiate between the possible and the impossible and are able to appraise the consequences of their actions realistically. In their study of cancer survivors, civil rights workers, and children of parents with affective disorders, Beardslee and Podorefsky (1988) found resiliency to be associated with this characteristic. Better adapted individuals had the ability to more accurately assess the stress that they had to deal with, and to realistically appraise their capacity to act and affect the situation. Cowen and his colleagues (1990), Garmezy and Masten (1986), and Werner (1986) also found resilient persons to have more realistic control perceptions.

SOCIAL PROBLEM-SOLVING SKILLS

Possessing an arsenal of social problem-solving skills reinforces one's sense of self-esteem, sense of competency, and sense of mastery. Several studies have demonstrated the association of resiliency and social problem-solving skills, including the Kauai longitudinal effort of Werner and Smith (1982, 1992), Rutter's study of British children from dysfunctional families (Rutter 1979), and the Project Competence studies by Masten, Best, and Garmezy (1990) at the University of Minnesota. A number of drug abuse prevention programs have recognized the importance of social problem-solving skills and have included them in their participant training (Botvin et al. 1984; Ellickson 1984; Pentz et al. 1989).

SENSE OF DIRECTION OR MISSION

Many of the children in Moskowitz's sample of concentration camp survivors had been given the responsibility by their parents to look after their younger siblings. Most indicated that this task helped them survive, through their focused attention on the survival of their siblings (Moskowitz 1983). Similarly, civil rights workers in the South found personal strength in saving others (Beardslee 1989). Werner and Smith (1982, 1992) discovered that their resilient Hawaiian study participants had a strong sense of responsibility toward others. In all these studies acts of "required helpfulness" added meaning to the lives of the helpers (Garmezy 1985). A special talent, passion, faith, or strong interest can also spark this sense of meaning or purpose, and strengthen resiliency (Cameron-Bandler 1986; Danziger and Farber 1990; Richardson et al. 1990).

EMPATHY

The capacity to understand and respond to another's feelings, usually thought of as empathy, has been identified as a resiliency trait in many studies. Empathy is often considered a traditional feminine characteristic, but resilient Hawaiian study subjects of both sexes were more appreciative, gentle, nurturing and socially perceptive, reflecting a caring and responsible attitude toward others (Werner 1985, 1987). Resilient persons with diabetes were found to have greater interpersonal sensitivity and responsiveness (Schwartz et al. 1989), and resilient youngsters studied by Cowan and his fellow researchers (1990) were found to have greater empathy than their non-resilient fellows.

HUMOR

Research with young adolescents completed by Masten (1982, 1986) revealed that highly stressed participants with greater competence had a greater ability to use humor, were more readily able to find the comic in the tragic, and used humor to reduce tension and to restore perspective. Other studies from the University of Minnesota clearly show the relationship between humor and resiliency. Garmezy and his colleagues (1984) found that highly stressed but able individuals had higher humor generation scores than their equally stressed but less able counterparts. Humor also helps to maintain social relationships, and may augment resiliency in that way as well (Kumpfer 1993).

ADAPTIVE DISTANCING

The ability to psychologically step back from a dysfunctional environment and to maintain a healthy separateness from the maladaptive patterns of significant others, otherwise known as adaptive distancing, has been shown in many studies to be an important resiliency factor. Faced with mentally ill, alcoholic, or drug addicted significant others, or with family dysfunction in other guises, resilient individuals have shown themselves to be able to keep from becoming enmeshed in, and repeating, harmful patterns. They do not identify with the ill others. They do not see themselves as responsible for the illness or the dysfunctional pattern. They have the ability to think and act separately from the troubled persons in their lives. Others' problems sadden but do not overwhelm them. Their relationship is compassionate but detached (Anthony 1987; Beardslee 1989; Beardslee and Podorefsky 1988; Berlin and Davis 1989; Berlin, Davis, and Orenstein 1988; Chess 1989; Wallerstein 1983).

This resiliency trait differs from "reactive distancing," which is generally marked by flight, fight, and isolation. With adaptive distancing self-understanding and separateness prevail and the individual sees him or herself as distinct from the ill person, neither the cause of the illness nor to blame for it (Kumpfer and DeMarsh 1985). While adaptive distancing may be beneficial, it must be kept in mind that it may pose the danger that the intellectualization and rationalization necessary for this way of being might make it difficult to maintain levels of intimacy and generativity in other relationships (Worland, Weeks, and Janes 1987).

ANDROGYNOUS SEX ROLE BEHAVIOR

Although noted in only one study, the relationship between resiliency and sex role behavior is important to mention. In their thirty-year longitudinal research Werner and Smith (1982) found that both male and female resilient youngsters adopted androgynous sex role behavior. They demonstrated both traditionally masculine and feminine characteristics and acted in a flexible non-sex-typed manner. They were yielding and assertive, expressive and instrumental, able to care about themselves and about relationships with others. Resilient girls were more independent and autonomous, and resilient boys were more emotionally expressive, nurturant, and socially perceptive than their non-resilient counterparts. Significantly, their families encouraged this androgynous behavior.

Interpersonal Factors

No one lives in a vacuum. Our environment — especially the people we interact with — can amplify and help to construct whatever resiliency we are capable of. Most of the research concerning interpersonal protective factors relates to children and their families. However, the positive interpersonal factors noted below promote the resiliency of people of all ages.

POSITIVE, CARING RELATIONSHIPS

The single most important factor promoting resiliency, not only in children and adolescents, but also in adults of all ages, is having a positive, caring relationship with another person (Kumpfer 1993; Rutter 1979; Werner 1987; Werner and Smith 1982, 1992). Wolin and Wolin (1993) suggest that such relationships serve as "alternative mirrors" presenting pleasurable images of ourselves and helping us to reframe our identity in a genuinely positive way. Even short term but intense connections of this kind are deeply sustaining and their memory and impact can last a lifetime (Higgins 1994).

Children from dysfunctional families are often deprived of this caring warmth. The elderly are often deprived of it due to the death of loved ones or to physical isolation. When caring and capable family members are not available, resilient individuals seem to find replacements, or surrogates, to take their place. Resilient persons in Higgins's (1998) study played an active role (both conscious and unconscious) in recruiting surrogates. Children's surrogates often included grandparents, aunts, uncles, cousins, parents of friends, teachers, coaches, and other adults who were able to communicate to them a sense that they were "deeply special and important simply by being who they are" (115). These persons offered a safe harbor promoting autonomy and competence. The resilient older person often finds neighbors, friends, and community workers for that same reinforcement. Even the presence of one such significant surrogate can help an elderly person to cope with the challenges faced at the end of life.

POSITIVE FAMILY OR OTHER INTIMATE ENVIRONMENT

Being a part of a positive family or other intimate environment benefits the resiliency of adults, children, and adolescents. There are several aspects to this protective factor. Having a supportive natural or surrogate family, or other intimate environment, in which talents, competencies, and life choices are praised while mistakes, setbacks, and errors are constructively utilized for growth helps to develop resiliency (Kumpfer and DeMarsh 1985; Walsh 1998). Being part of a patterned and structured environment with clear rules that are consistently enforced through praise and concrete discipline builds a sense of security and sends the message that life is predictable (Hauser et al. 1989; Walsh 1998; Werner and Smith 1982, 1992).

Family activities such as regular dinner times, reliable holiday celebrations, and other family rituals that are "reasonable, humane, reverent, communal, hilarious, touching, kind and safe" (Higgins 1994:287) communicate a feeling of solidarity and continuity, adding to a sense of security and predictability that encourages resiliency (Wolin and Bennet 1984; Wolin and Wolin 1993).

In addition, being closely involved with a social network of extended family members, friends, fellow workers, neighbors, or church members, among others, contributes to a protective sense of safety and support in times of joy as well as in times of trouble (Werner 1979).

"HIGH-ENOUGH" EXPECTATIONS

We have all heard comments about individuals or groups of people suggesting that they are incapable of putting in an adequate performance: statements like "inner-city children are just not capable of good school performance," or "government workers just don't have it in them to work a full thirty-five hour week," or simply "he/she just can't do it." Such statements not only mask ugly prejudice; they also have the potential to reinforce and help produce the very behaviors they refer to. Low expectations, especially those held by significant others, breed low productivity. High but reachable expectations motivate performance and encourage excellence. The person who hears the realistic message "You can do it!" from significant others (parents, teachers, employers, friends) internalizes a self-perception of adequacy and is motivated to reach and stretch to their full capacity. Resilient individuals tend to be those who are, or who have been, surrounded by the just "high-enough" expectations of others (Mills 1991; Rutter 1989; Walsh 1998).

The eleven individual and interpersonal resiliency factors discussed above have been highlighted in the recent research literature. All are positive, strengths-based and, most important, *enhanceable* through good social work practice. It seems self-evident that guiding one's practice toward the development of one or more resiliency factors in every client is a concrete way to operationalize the strengths perspective. The two seem to form a natural partnership. Social workers have been recognizing resiliency in their clients and have been attempting to further develop it for some time now. This volume describes recent attempts by experienced social workers to "accentuate the positive" and put the strengths perspective to work with clients through the enhancement of their resiliency.

Part 1 of this book includes three chapters. All three present resiliency factors in specific populations that have often been unrecognized or under-appreciated. In chapter 2 Eunice Matthews discusses care-taking and self-efficacy among African American women. African American women are very often characterized as being self-sacrificing, steadfast, independent, hardworking, and nurturing. They are seen as the backbone of their families and communities. This image is often perceived as blocking African American women in their efforts at self-care. Dr. Matthews's research suggests that this is not so, and that these women receive a source of strength and a sense of their own ability to make things happen from being seen, and seeing themselves, as taking care of others.

In chapter 3 Sandra Turner advocates recognizing and enhancing natural resiliency in boys and girls. Dr. Turner suggests that sex- role-related cultural expectations often undermine the natural resiliency of boys and girls. She discusses some of these inhibiting expectations and offers ways in which social workers, teachers, and parents can modify them to increase youngsters' resiliency.

Chapter 4 by Drs. Irene Gutheil and Elaine Congress looks at adaptive capacities and successful aging. Despite the losses associated with aging, many elders demonstrate remarkable adaptive capacities. The authors review and analyze the current literature to identify factors that are associated with resiliency in old age. They discuss cultural differences and strategies for enhancing resiliency in older people.

Part 2 contains material that specifically addresses enhancing resiliency through social work practice with individuals, couples, groups, and families. In chapter 5, Dr. Carol Kaplan presents a case study of resiliency enhancement interventions with an African American woman which reinforced the client's strengths and resiliency and helped her to survive despite considerable stress.

In chapter 6, Dr. Sharon McQuaide looks at women's resiliency at midlife: what it is, and how to mobilize it. She provides specific clinical interventions that develop resiliency in midlife women, as well as illustrative clinical vignettes.

Dr. Ray Fox presents several case studies of resiliency enhancement interventions with male suicide survivors in chapter 7. The strengths that enabled them to go on, particularly a sense of purpose and a sense of self-efficacy (which the author terms "will"), are explored. The manner in which the clinician worked to enhance these strengths is highlighted.

Resiliency enhancement within the couple relationship is presented in chapter 8 by Dr. Howard Robinson. The author develops the thesis that protective factors identified for individuals in the resiliency literature can be framed to fit the couple system. Specific intervention techniques enhancing couple strengths and promoting couple resiliency were developed and reorganized from prominent theories of couple treatment. Case examples are included.

Chapter 9 by Drs. Michael Phillips and Carol Cohen discusses mobilizing client capacities through group work. This chapter explores the parallel themes of the resiliency/strengths focus and the Mutual Aid Model of social work practice with groups. Examples are presented of the mobilization of client capacities through resiliency enhancement group processes, including mutual aid groups conducted in school settings with latency aged children of alcoholics and drug addicts.

Dr. Rosa Perez-Koenig addresses the development of resiliency in Hispanic youngsters through surrogate family creation, in chapter 10. The author describes the Unitas Extended Family Model that was developed and fielded to promote and enhance resiliency among Hispanic youngsters.

Part 3 includes four chapters that discuss resiliency enhancement in administration, training, and prevention. In chapter 11 Drs. Sharyn Zunz and Rosalind Chernesky see the workplace as a potentially protective environment. They review organizational characteristics that can function as protective factors and can be utilized by managers in that way. Drawing upon both theoretical and empirical literature on organizational behavior, they present strategies that can help build supportive workplace environments that can enable workers to fulfill their potential.

In chapter 12, Dr. Laura Lee discusses the dilemmas faced by African American professionals working in predominantly white organizations, and highlights the resilient manner in which they cope. She provides information on observable behaviors that are often misinterpreted, and a way to further understand the process of coping with the stress of being racially different in an organization.

Chapter 13, written by Dr. Robert Chazin, Shari Kaplan, and Stephen Terio, describes efforts to introduce a resiliency enhancement orientation in two traditional social service agencies. The content and process of the training provided the staffs is described, as is the nature of the staff resistance encountered. The results of a research evaluation of the training and the impact that the training had on organizational change are also discussed.

Chapter 14 presents a resiliency enhancement model based on the strengths perspective that provides social workers with a systematic way to approach the prevention of problems facing young people today, such as AIDS, teen pregnancy, substance abuse, and violence. Written by Dr. Mary Ann Forgey, this final chapter presents ways to design prevention interventions so they enhance identified resiliency factors. Strategies are included for tailoring the interventions to target populations based on race, ethnicity, gender, or geographic setting. Concrete examples of interventions demonstrate the application of the model.

For too long social workers have thought in terms of dysfunction, deficit, and disease. The time has come to shift the emphasis to strengths building and empowerment. The essays in this book paint a vivid picture of how proactive, positive, experienced social work practitioners have done this. An emphasis on factors that encourage competence in the face of adversity offers substantial promise, and illustrates how powerful resiliency enhancement can be.

References

Anthony, E. J. 1987. Children at high risk for psychosis growing up successfully. In E. J. Anthony and B. J. Cohler, eds., *The Invulnerable Child*, 147–184. New York: Guilford Press.

Bandura, A. 1977. *Social Learning Theory*. Englewood Cliffs, N.J.: Prentice Hall.

Beardslee, W. R. 1989. The role of self-understanding in resilient individuals: The development of a perspective. *The American Journal of Orthopsychiatry* 59 (2): 266–278.

Beardslee, W. R. and D. Posorefsky. 1988. Resilient adolescents whose parents have serious affective and other psychiatric disorders: Importance of self-understanding and relationships. *American Journal of Psychiatry* 145:63–69.

Berlin, R. and R. Davis. 1989. Children from alcoholic families: Vulnerability and resilience. In T. Dugan and R. Coles, eds., *The Child in Our Times: Studies in the Development of Resiliency*, 81–105. New York: Brunner/Mazel.

Berlin, R., R. Davis, and A, Orenstein. 1988. Adaptive and reactive distancing among adolescents from alcoholic families. *Adolescence* 23 (91): 577–584.

Botvin, G. J., E. Baker, N. Renick, and A. Filazzola. 1984. A cognitive-behavioral approach to substance abuse prevention. *Addictive Behaviors* 9:137–147.

Cameron-Bandler, L. 1986. Strategies for creating a compelling future. *Focus on Family and Chemical Dependency*, July/August: 6–7.

Chess, S. 1989. Defying the voice of doom. In Dugan and Coles, eds., *The Child in Our Times*, 179–199.

Cowger, C. D. 1994. Assessing client strengths: Clinical assessment for client empowerment. *Social Work* 39 (3): 262–268.

Cowen, E., P. Wyman, W. Work, and G. Parker. 1990. The Rochester Child Resilience Project: Overview and summary of first year findings. *Development and Psychopathology* 2:193–212.

Danziger, S. and N. Farber. 1990. Keeping inner-city youth in school: Critical experiences of young black women. *Social Work Research and Abstracts* 26 (4): 32–39.

Ellickson, P. L. 1984. *Project ALERT: A smoking and drug prevention experiment*. The RAND Corporation, N-2184-CHF: Santa Monica, Calif.

Felsman, J. K. 1989. Risk and resilience in childhood: The lives of street children. In Dugan and Coles, eds., *The Child in Our Times*, 56–79.

Garmezy, N. 1985. Stress-resistant children: The search for protective factors. In J. E. Stevenson, ed., Recent Research in Developmental Psychopathology. *Journal of Child Psychology and Psychiatry (Book Supplement No. 4)*, 213–233. Oxford: Pergamon Press.

Garmezy, N. and A. S. Masten. 1986. Stress, competence and resilience: Common frontiers for therapist and psychopathologist. *Behavior Therapy* 57 (2): 159–174.

Garmezy, N., A. S. Masten, and A. Tellegran. 1984. The study of stress and competence in children: A building block for developmental psychopathology. *Child Development* 55:97–111.

Hauser, S. T., M. A. Vieyrra, A. Jacobson, and D. Wertlieb. 1989. Family aspects of vulnerability and resilience in adolescence: A theoretical perspective. In Dugan and Coles, eds., *The Child in Our Times*, 109–133.

Higgins, G. O. 1994. *Resilient Adults: Overcoming a Cruel Past*. San Francisco: Jossey-Bass.

Jessor, R. 1993. Successful adolescent development among youth in high-risk settings. *American Psychologist* 48 (2): 117–126.

Kumpfer, K. 1993. Resiliency and AOD use prevention in high risk youth. Unpublished manuscript. Available from School of Social Work, University of Utah, Salt Lake City, Utah, 84112.

Kumpfer, K. and J. DeMarsh. 1985. Family environmental and genetic influences on children's future chemical dependency. *Journal of Children in Contemporary Society: Advances in Theory and Applied Research* 18:49–92.

Luthar, S. 1991. Vulnerability and resilience: A study of high risk adolescence. *Child Development* 62 (3): 600–616.

Luthar, S. and E. Zigler. 1991. Vulnerability and competence: A review of research on resilience in childhood. *American Journal of Orthopsychiatry* 61 (1): 7–22.

Masten, A. S. 1982. Humor and creative thinking in stress-resistant children. Doctoral dissertation, University of Minnesota.

Masten, A. S. 1986. Humor and competence in school aged children. *Child Development* 57:461–473.

Masten, A. S., K. M. Best, and N. Garmezy. 1990. Resilience and development: Contributions from the study of children who overcome adversity. *Development and Psychopathology* 2:425–444.

Mills, R. 1991. A new understanding of self: The role of affect, state of mind, self-understanding and intrinsic motivation. *Journal of Experimental Education* 60 (19): 67–81.

Moskowitz, S. 1983. *Love Despite Hate*. New York: Schocken Books.

Pentz, M. A., J. Dwyer, D. MacKinnon, B. R. Flay, et al. 1989. A multicommunity trial for primary prevention of adolescent drug abuse. *Journal of the American Medical Association* 261 (2): 3250–3266.

Rapp, C. A. 1998. *The Strengths Model: Case Management with People Suffering from Severe and Persistent Mental Illness*. New York: Oxford University Press.

Richardson, G., B. Neiger, S. Jensen, and K. Kumpfer. 1990. The resiliency model. *Health Education* 21 (6): 33–39.

Rutter, M. 1979. Protective factors in children's responses to stress and disadvantage. In M. W. Kent and J. Rolf, eds., *Primary Prevention of Psychopathology, Vol. III: Social Competence in Children*, 49–74. Hanover, N.H.: University Press of New England.

Rutter, M. 1984. Resilient children. *Psychology Today* March: 57–65.

Rutter, M. 1987. Psychosocial resilience and protective mechanisms. *American Journal of Orthopsychiatry* 57 (3): 316–331.

Rutter, M. 1989. Psychosocial resilience and protective mechanisms. In Anthony and Cohler, eds., *The Invulnerable Child*, 181–221.

Saleebey, D. 1996. The strengths perspective in social work practice: Extensions and cautions. *Social Work* 41 (3): 296–305.

Saleebey, D. 1997. *The Strengths Perspective in Social Work Practice*. 2d ed. New York: Longman.

Schwartz, J., A. Jacobson, S. Hauser, and B. Dornbush. 1989. Explorations of vulnerability and resilience: Case studies of diabetic adolescents and their families. In Degan and Coles, eds., *The Child in Our Times*, 134–144.

Seligman, M. 1975. *Helplessness: On Depression, Development, and Death*. San Francisco: Freeman.

Wallerstein, J. 1983. Children of divorce: Preliminary report of a ten-year follow-up of older children and adolescents. *Journal of the American Academy of Child Psychiatry* 24:545–553.

Walsh, F. 1998. *Strengthening Family Resilience*. New York: Guilford Press.

Weick, A. 1983. A growth-task model of human development. *Social Casework* 64 (3): 131–137.

Weick, A. 1986. The philosophical context of a health model of social work. *Social Casework* 67 (9): 551–559.

Weick, A., C. A. Rapp, W. P. Sullivan, and W. Kisthart. 1989. A strengths perspective for social work practice. *Social Work* 34:350–354.

Werner, E. E. 1979. The transactional model: Application to the longitudinal study of the high risk child on the Island of Kauai, Hawaii. Paper presented at the Biannual Meeting of the Society for Research on Child Development, San Francisco.

Werner, E. E. 1986. Resilient offspring of alcoholics: A longitudinal study from birth to age 18. *American Journal of Orthopsychiatry* 59:72–81.

Werner, E. E. 1987. Vulnerability and resiliency in children at risk for delinquency: A longitudinal study from birth to young adulthood. In J. Burchard and S. Burchard, eds., *Prevention of Delinquent Behavior*, 16–43. Newbury Park, Cal.: Sage.

Werner, E. E. 1990. High risk children in young adulthood: A longitudinal study from birth to 32 years. *American Journal of Orthopsychiatry* 59 (1): 72–81.

Werner, E. E. and R. S. Smith. 1982. *Vulnerable but Invincible*. New York: McGraw-Hill.

Werner, E. E. and R. S. Smith. 1992. *Overcoming the Odds: High Risk Children from Birth to Adulthood*. Ithaca, N.Y.: Cornell University Press.

Wolin, S. J. and L. Bennet. 1984. Family rituals. *Family Process* 23:401–420.

Wolin, S. J. and S. Wolin. 1993. *The Resilient Self: How Survivors of Troubled Families Rise Above Adversity*. New York: Villard Books.

Worland, J., D. Weeks, and C. Janes. 1987. Predicting mental health in children at risk. In Anthony and Cohler, eds., *The Invulnerable Child*, 185–210.

Part I

Resiliency Enhancement and Specific Populations

2 The Legacy of Caretaking Among African American Women: A Mixed Blessing

Eunice Matthews

I recently completed an intensive qualitative study of college bound African American female adolescents from low-income communities in the New York metropolitan area (Matthews 1994). The young women in the study grew up in single-parent, female-headed, households where economic resources were scarce. These young women all faced a variety of challenges growing up: homelessness, overcrowding, parental addiction, child neglect, and hunger. However, despite these challenges they were all able to beat the odds, to complete high school and go on to college while avoiding early parenting, drugs, and the general lure of the streets.

During the more than two years that I spent with these young women, they shared their life stories, aspirations, and worldviews with me, and I learned more than I had originally expected. These young women gave me a new perspective on an old issue that many African American women, myself included, have struggled with: the issue of the legacy of caretaking that is so much a part of African American female culture. The legacy of caretaking among African American women designates an attitude; a style of approaching relationships in which one feels intensely responsible for the well being of others. Caretakers believe that their primary role in relationships is to be of service to others and that the needs of others take precedence over their own needs.

These college bound women perceived their activities as caretakers as achievements that transformed them into testaments to strength and resilience. While some professionals, including myself, may have seen what seemed to be too much self-sacrifice embedded in these women's role of caretaker, the women themselves saw their activities in that role as supporting their sense of competence and providing them with a source of motivation. As an African American woman and a caretaker, I previously viewed the legacy of caretaking as a destructive force in the lives of African American women. The young women of my study helped me to see it as more of a mixed blessing.

The African American community reveres the image of the caretaker. For centuries it appeared that for African American women our only recognition, our only praise, came as a result of our activities in the role of caretaker. Song, poetry, and literature paid homage to such a person as the ultimate African American woman. It was the standard for womanhood passed down generation after generation from mother to daughter. It has influenced the way African American women are viewed by others and the way they view themselves. The image of the caretaker has played a part in the assignment of which roles African American women are to play in society and the value placed on those roles.

Initially, I was concerned for the future liberation of African American women as I listened to the college bound women and saw the legacy of caretaking in yet another generation. I saw in their lives evidence of both the burden of the legacy and its benefits. It supported them in thinking that their value as human beings was related to their ability to be of service to others. It encouraged them to neglect themselves. And it distracted them from recognizing their own oppressive circumstances as women. However, as I observed these apparent problems associated with the legacy of caretaking I also noticed its functionality and its contribution to their ability to be resilient. It served as a source of motivation, giving them the drive and determination that they needed to overcome their circumstances. It provided them with an arena within which they secured a sense of competence and power, two attributes found to be synonymous with resilient behavior among youth (Norman, Turner, and Zunz 1994). These college bound women illustrated the mixed legacy of caretaking.

The Role of Caretaker

Caretaking as Valuable

For these young women, their roles as caretakers appeared to represent a defining element in their perceptions of themselves. For example, when Carla was asked how she would describe herself, she stated:

I would tell a person that I'm smart intelligent, that I'm easy to get along with, and that if you have a problem I would try to help. I'm not going to say that that's not my issue. I'm going to try to help.

Carla expresses in this statement a sense of confidence, connectedness to others, and a sense of obligation to be of assistance to those with whom she comes in contact. The way Carla chooses to describe herself provides insight into the elements of her self-definition she believes to be important. Her perception of herself as a caretaker is an important part of her self-definition. The other young women who also enrolled in college echoed Carla's self-description.

As caretakers, they expressed strong feelings of responsibility toward a variety of people within their social worlds. Both Charity and Carol shared experiences of taking responsibility for caring for their younger siblings. Charity spoke of feeling responsible for her brother:

I always took care of him. Nothing is wrong with him; it's just that he doesn't have nobody to help him, you know, and it makes me sad, and I want to be there for somebody who doesn't have anybody to help them. I feel responsible for him.

Cori has no siblings with whom to enact her caretaking role. She chooses to focus her caregiving on her friends. Cori explains why she befriended one young lady with whom she appears to have nothing in common. This friend was a victim of sexual abuse, dropped out of high school, and has a bad reputation in the neighborhood. Cori stated:

I mean, what she's going through . . . I had to be her friend, you know what I saying?

Carla related her caretaking role to her relationships with her friends and her community:

I think that every child's dream is to get out of the projects. But, my thing is that when I do decide to leave the projects, I will come back and help my community.

And for Candy, troubled young African American men who were caught up in a life of crime got her attention. She stated:

See, my purpose is to try to get young black males out of that situation.

Their perception of themselves as caretakers was no doubt an important part of their identity. The young women expressed a strong sense of obligation to provide assistance to others. They expressed a sense of commitment to African American people, the members of their communities, their friends, and family members.

During the interviews the significance of their caregiving activities was evident in the amount of detailed discussion that focused on helping others. Their caretaking activities were a major theme in their life stories. Charity brags: "My girlfriend, she calls me all the way at college when she has a problem. She says she doesn't care, when she needs me, she needs me." All the college bound young women spoke proudly of the different people in their lives whom they were able to assist. They mentioned repeatedly that it made them feel good that people called on them when they had problems. Candy states: "I like it when my friends come to me."

The Caretaker's Burden

The Seeds of Self-Neglect

As these college bound women shared their aspirations I could see the seeds of self-neglect being planted, as much by what they did not say as by what they did say. Carla stated:

> I want to get a good job and stuff so that I can make enough money to get my mother out of the project. My mother, she worked hard raising three kids by herself. I want to be able to take care of her.

The other women expressed their goals in similar terms. What they wanted for their future was connected to what they wanted for significant people in their lives. Candy states: "I want to do good so that the young people in the neighborhood could see that it can be done."

On those rare occasions when they did discuss their desires for themselves, they were very modest, as if to say, I don't need much for myself. Carol states "I don't need anything fancy. I just want an apartment not in the projects." There were no discussions of elaborate vacations, fancy cars, or expensive clothes. They weren't looking to make a lot of money; just enough to take care of themselves and be in a position to be of assistance to those they cared about. It was as if their own individual needs were not as important as the needs of others in their lives.

We're Not Oppressed, We're Strong Black Women

The young women did not see gender oppression in their female dominated worlds. They all shared a heightened awareness of the racial oppression that surrounded them and spoke very openly and passionately about it. Yet they denied feeling oppressed as women. They shared the feeling that sexism was a "white women's" issue. According to these college bound women, African American women are the caretakers of their families and communities, and the caretakers are the ones who had the control and the power, not African American men. They saw white society as being their only oppressor. Charity expressed this sentiment:

> I think black women are the strongest people on this earth. I mean it's so much we had to do, so much and we still are surviving. The white man didn't get us. There is just so much stuff they tried to do that, you know, we had to deal with it, and it's like whatever they got for us we'll deal with it.

The existence of sexism appears to be clouded by the image of the caretaker, "the strong black women." Among these women sexism remains unrecognized and unarticulated. Instead, they hold onto their belief in the myth of the African American woman's equality with, if not dominance over, the African American man.

The Benefits of Caretaking

Caretaking as a Source of Competence

Competence is defined as a sense that one has sufficient skills, knowledge, and experience to achieve a certain task. The notion of competence refers to the perception of ability. The competent person is one who has a sense that she can make desirable things happen. An individual's sense of competence speaks to their sense of their own ability. A sense of competence results from the accumulation of experiences of perceived successful outcomes, as defined by the culture (Obgu 1978). For the young women of this study, as with many other African American women, to be of service to others is paramount (Boyd 1993, Collins 1990, James 1993). All the women placed a high value on caretaking, including those who did not perceive themselves as caretakers, such as Nancy and Neda. When asked whom she admired Neda states: "My aunt, everyone comes to her for help. She's the one people go to and she tries to help them out." The young women of this study viewed the actions of individuals in the provision of assistance to others as valuable achievements.

These young women perceived themselves as being competent. Their body language, the way they spoke, and what they said projected their sense of competence. These young women were convinced of their own abilities to make things happen. Charity expressed the sentiments of all the college bound women when she stated:

> You can do whatever you want to. You just have to work for it and plan for it and it's as simple as that, you have to work for what you want. I see the results of just sitting around getting caught up in the life style, you know, drugs and stuff. I'm going to be different. I have dreams.

The college bound women spoke in very definitive terms. They made statements such as "I'm going to college," "I can take care of myself," "I'm not going to end up like that." One could not help but hear the sense of competence that underlined their convictions about what they were going to do.

Through their roles as caretakers they found support for their feelings of competence by framing their caregiving activities in the form of accomplishments. For example, Cori mentioned a 16-year-old friend who was considering having a baby. Cori invited her friend to help her baby sit an infant cousin. During that time, Cori highlighted for her friend the difficulties of caring for a child. Cori wanted to assist her friend in not making what she perceived as a big mistake. After the experience with Cori, her friend seemed to change her mind. Cori felt very good about the experience and named it as one of her important accomplishments. As these young women shared their accomplishments it became apparent that those accomplishments which involved caretaking were perceived as being the most significant. Although they expressed a great deal of pride over completing high school and enrolling in college, their conversations about those accomplishments did not appear to inspire the same level of passion as their accomplishments made in their roles as caretakers.

It appeared that as these young women gave of themselves to others, they received in return confirmation of their own ability to effect change in their own lives and the lives of others. By assisting in solving other people's problems, by changing other people's lives, they appeared to feel more able to change their own lives.

Caretaking as a Source of Support for Perceptions of Control

As caretakers these young women appeared most often to be the initiators in terms of establishing connections and in dictating the nature of those connections. They presented as exerting a great deal of control over their relationships, particularly with their peers. There was a tendency on the part of these young women to take individuals under their wing. The friends with whom they had the most contact and appeared to be closest to were the friends who appeared to be the most needy. They seemed to be attracted to individuals who needed assistance.

Their relationships often appeared hierarchical, with them presiding over others in a maternal way. For example, Charity spoke of a close friend who dropped out of high school to have a baby. Charity mentioned how, over the years, she often encouraged her friend to return to school and enroll in a vocational program to develop a skill. Her friend recently completed a vocational program, found employment, and obtained her own apartment outside of the project where they grew up. In mentioning her friend's accomplishments, Charity spoke of how proud she was of her friend. Charity's body language and the tone of her voice were similar to those of a proud mother. The other young women gave a similar impression as they described their relationships with siblings, friends, and even boyfriends. These young women often used phrases such as "I try to tell them," "I try to show them," "I wish they would listen to me," in their discussions about others.

Their ability to assert themselves in their relationships with others in the context of their roles as caretakers appeared to support their perception that they had a measure of personal control in their lives. Carol stated:

> I feel like, really, that everything I accomplished in my life I accomplished on my own. I'm not saying that nobody gave me any help but if I didn't want to accomplish it, it wouldn't have happened. It was because of me that I am where I am.

These college bound women often used phrases such as "I did it," "It was because of me," "I made it happen," during the interviews. They projected a perception of themselves as being self-directed and in control.

The significance of the caretaker role supporting their sense of control is illustrated by Carol's early experience in foster care. When Carol and her younger siblings entered foster care they were separated for the first time. Carol was deeply worried that she was not there to take care of them and spoke of that period of separation as being very difficult for her. From their birth, Carol viewed herself in relationship to her siblings as being a caretaker. When her mother would leave for days at a time Carol looked after them and made sure their needs were met. Carol expressed how important being a caretaker to her siblings was to her. After about a month, they were all re-united in a new placement with two sisters (foster mothers) who shared a two family home. Carol was relieved and attempted to resume her role as care-taker. However, the foster parents took on the appropriate role as caretakers for Carol and her siblings, providing them with a loving, supportive environ-ment of security and structure. As a result, Carol felt displaced. Carol stated, "I was lost. I no longer had a sense of purpose or focus in my life." She began staying out late, not going to school, and breaking house rules, until she eventually ran away. Carol went on to say, "I was bugging [going crazy], I never did those things when I was with my mother and I could have. I guess I was bugging because I felt they didn't need me anymore." It was not until she was able to recreate her role as caretaker in another relationship that she once again found her sense of direction. The new relationship was with her boyfriend, whom she describes as needing her.

Caretaking as a Source of Motivation

These college bound young women gained a sense of power, the ability to act, from their nurturing relationships. Their actions regarding college en-rollment appeared to be motivated, in large part, by their desire to take care of others. They believed that their enrollment in college and eventually ob-taining a college degree would put them in a better position to take care of others. As the young women talked about their aspirations, there was reluc-tance in their voices to frame such desires in terms of personal needs or ben-efits. To place the emphasis on themselves and to explain their actions in terms of their own needs or personal development would be, according to their definition, selfish. Thus, they framed their actions in terms of being of service to others. In doing so, that seemed to give their actions a higher pur-pose. Their desires to be caretakers seemed to give them an incentive to go that extra mile and to overcome difficult circumstances, to act resiliently. Carla's efforts to complete high school demonstrate this point well. Carla was in danger of not graduating from high school because she could not seem to pass two of the Regents exams required for graduation.

I never told my mother, but I actually thought of dropping out of school when I failed the exams for the second time. But I thought I couldn't do that to her. I wanted her to see me walk across that field because neither my brother nor my sister graduated. I wanted to be able to go to college and get a good job so I could take care of her for once. So I would get up at 6:00 in the morning to study . . . I would go to school before it opened to get tutored. I stuck to my priorities. I went and took both tests and passed.

The other young women had similar stories of successfully overcoming difficulties. They expressed a real sense of determination when it came to their desires to make something of themselves, always keeping the welfare of others in mind.

In the lives of these college bound African American women I could see both the burden and benefits interwoven in the legacy of caretaking that they adopted. My concern regarding the value and significance they placed on caretaking was tempered by the realization that it provided them with an arena within which they could find a sense of power and competence. Although the opportunity structure has recently broadened for African American women, the opportunities are still limited, particularly for low-income African American women, so we must not be too critical of any source of confidence that supports their struggle.

I remain concerned about the seeds of self-neglect that were evident in their discussions since they consistently placed the needs of other before their own needs. But I now believe that the legacy of caretaking is a valuable tool for the African American women in an oppressive society. It fosters strengths, increases self-esteem and a sense of self-efficacy, and enlivens a sense of purpose in the caretakers. We need however to be careful to encourage the caretakers to expand their caretaking to include themselves. We must encourage African American women to see that their value to society extends beyond their ability to serve. They must come to the realization that self-care is not a sin but a necessity. We must help African American women to see that although we respect and admire their dedication to their families, communities, and race, they have an obligation and responsibility to care for themselves.

In addition, those of us who are interested in supporting and increasing the resiliency of African American women must bring to light the reality of the African American women's experience in this society. This study of college bound women helped me to see that the legacy of caretaking is not necessarily a danger to the liberation of African American women. Rather it has proven to be a source of strength and resiliency for us. Perhaps what we must support is the idea that as caretakers we need to take care of not only our families, our communities, and our race, but also ourselves.

References

Boyd, J. A. 1993. *In the Company of My Sisters*. New York: Dutton.

Collins, P. H. 1990. *Black Feminist Thought*. New York: Routledge.

James, S. M. 1993. Mothering: A possible Black feminist link to social transformation? In S. M. James and A. P. A. Busia, eds., *Theorizing Black Feminisms*, 44–54. New York: Routledge.

Matthews, E. 1994. And Still They Rise: College Enrollment of African American Females from Low-income Communities. Unpublished doctoral dissertation, City University of New York.

Norman, E., S. Turner, and S. Zunz. 1994. *Substance Abuse Prevention: A Review of the Literature*. New York State Office of Alcohol and Substance Abuse Services.

Obgu, J. 1978. *Minority Education and Caste*. New York: Academic Press.

3 Recognizing and Enhancing Natural Resiliency in Boys and Girls

Sandra Turner

Adolescence can be a time when resilience is enhanced and protected, or it can be a time of severe stress that leads to vulnerability. One resilience researcher stresses the importance during adolescence of strengthening generative factors, those "unbidden and fortuitous elements of life that dramatically increase learning, resolve, resource acquisition, and hardiness" (Benard 1997:167). What are these unbidden and fortuitous elements of life and how can they be strengthened? Recently researchers have uncovered some surprising findings about events that can affect hardiness and personality development. A recent study of child development found that disease, divorce, accidents, and chance encounters appear to have more of an effect on well-being than the infant bond with the mother (Lewis 1998). Another highly controversial book has found that peers, school, community environment, and financial status have the greatest influence on personality development (Harris 1998). Harris believes that peers and environment, especially socioeconomic status, exert a greater influence on personality development than do parents. She states: "A child is better off living in a troubled family in a good neighborhood than living in a good family in a troubled neighborhood." (Harris 1998:60).

Moving adolescents to good neighborhoods, or fully insulating them from tragedy and accident, is not usually a viable option. However, there are other factors that can be protective and that do enhance naturally occurring resiliency in youngsters. Of the resiliency characteristics listed in the introductory chapter in this book, those that are related particularly to adolescents and are gender specific are discussed in this chapter.

Gender Differences in Identity Development

Feminist scholarship and research as well as some of the most recent literature on resilience addresses gender differences in identity development and exposure to risk (Turner, Norman, and Zunz 1997; Schultz 1991; Gilligan, Rogers, and Tolman 1991; Brown 1992). Girls and boys have different developmental trajectories, different access to sports, different reproductive concerns, different vulnerability to violence and abuse, and different academic and career options (Debold, Wilson, and Malave 1993). Thus it is probable that there are different protective factors for girls and boys as well as differing resiliency traits.

Girls are often more resilient than boys in the first decade of life. As infants and toddlers they tend to be more physically resilient, as well as more adept socially in pre-K and early grammar school (Werner and Smith 1992; Brown 1992). However, they are likely to become more vulnerable starting in the second decade of life. Starting at age eleven or twelve the cultural pressures on girls to be "ladylike" and dependent limits their sense of autonomy and mastery, and results in a loss of self-esteem for many.

Boys, on the other hand, are more vulnerable in the first decade of life and more resilient in the second. They are more susceptible to prenatal stress and are often more physically vulnerable as infants and toddlers (Werner and Smith 1982). It is not uncommon for four- and five-year-old boys to exhibit a combination of shyness and aggressive behavior, which makes it difficult to form positive relationships with teachers or friendships with peers (Hawkins et al. 1992). The cultural esteem for boys, and their greater opportunities for independence and achievement, result in their greater resiliency starting in the second decade of life.

In the United States there has been an emphasis on Erikson's (1968) theories of identity development, which are geared primarily to white boys and men. Although widely accepted, some developmental researchers are questioning the general applicability of Erikson's theories. "Self-direction, autonomy, high activity, differentiation, and self-reliance are valued norms and behavior patterns only with specific cultures, and for men. These beliefs are in direct contrast to the values of group-oriented cultures [such as Japanese, Latino, and Hawaiian] and those that value an unfolding and natural harmony with the universe [e.g. Native American]" (Rotheram-Borus et al. 1997:49).

Self-direction, self-reliance, and individuation are highly valued in the

United States, where boys, but not usually girls, are encouraged to exhibit such behaviors. Girls are socialized to adopt a caretaker identity "in connection" with others, and to maintain a family-oriented rather than a self-oriented focus (Archer 1993; Gilligan 1982). The term "in connection" refers to the strong value that girls and women place on the maintenance of relationships. Even though the previous chapter by Matthews indicated how such an identity can and does increase the resiliency of some females, it is not an identity that is most valued in our culture. Embracing a devalued identity often leads to lowered self-esteem for girls. Can the ability to connect with and care for others be enhanced while at the same time teaching girls to keep their sense of self? Can boys be taught to more highly value the ability to connect with others?

Self-Esteem

A sense of high self-esteem or self-efficacy is an important resiliency trait. Girls, who at age eight or nine were very sure of themselves and able to speak clearly about what they thought and felt, begin to lose their self-confidence and self-esteem at age eleven or twelve. They almost literally "lose their voices" at that time (Gilligan, Rogers, and Tolman 1991; American Association of University Women (AAUW) Report 1992). There are variations in the loss of self-esteem for girls belonging to different ethnic groups. One study found that when self-esteem is conceptualized as both core self-esteem (conceptions of self-efficacy and self-confidence) and public self-esteem (perceived ability to perform in institutional contexts), differences in core self-esteem scores are more effected by gender than by ethnicity. For public self-esteem differences are greater for ethnicity than for gender. The study found that girls, with the exception of black girls, had the lowest core self-esteem. In descending order, the scoring on core self-esteem was: white boys, black and Hispanic boys, black girls, Asian boys, Native American boys, white girls, Hispanic girls, Native American girls, and Asian girls. For public self-esteem, white boys had the highest scores, followed by black girls, Asian boys, white girls, black, Hispanic, and Native American boys, then Asian, Hispanic, and Native American girls. Black girls scored higher than any other girls on both core and public self-esteem (Dukes and Martinez 1994). Another study also found black girls to have high self-esteem in high school, but they reported less positive feelings about their teachers and about schoolwork than elementary school black girls (Phillips 1998).

What may account for the self-esteem of black girls? Perhaps black girls live in more oppressive situations and may develop greater survival or resilience strategies early. Living in oppressive situations may also account for their less positive feelings about their teachers and school. As noted in the previous chapter, it is possible that African American women are more esteemed within their own culture than Hispanic women are within theirs. Hispanic girls have the greatest drop in self-esteem from elementary to high school. In high school they "expressed less confidence about their talent, abilities, physical appearance, and family relationships than their counterparts in elementary school" (AAUW Report 1992).

Another study found that students who have a strong ethnic identity have higher self-esteem (Rotheram-Borus et al. 1997). Perhaps black girls have a stronger ethnic identity than do other adolescent girls. One researcher has proposed a model of ethnic identity for all minorities that calls for recognition and integration of one's ethnic identity in everyday settings (Uba 1994).

The few studies that look at the interplay of race, class, and gender as it effects self-esteem of boys and girls are finding that self-esteem is a multidimensional concept. To consider it from a point of view of gender or race alone is not accurate and does not capture the importance of the nuances in the ways that ethnically diverse groups of boys and girls construct their self-esteem (Phillips 1998). However, the findings about the connection between having a strong ethnic identity and higher self-esteem are noteworthy.

School Curriculum and Climate

More is known about what accounts for the drop in self-esteem in white, Hispanic, Asian, and Native American girls than why the self-esteem of black girls remains relatively higher. Some researchers believe that the social climate in American schools contributes to the fall in pre-teen female self-esteem. Starting in about sixth grade, teachers do not call on girls as often as they call on boys, perhaps because girls are usually less assertive about asking for recognition. Even when boys do not raise their hands, teachers are more likely to call upon them than upon girls (AAUW Report 1992).

One teacher trainer notes that "Students sit in classes that, day in and day out, deliver the message that women's lives count for less than men's" (AAUW Report 1992: 67), and that women have done less that is worth noting or studying. These messages are heard at a time when girls are entering adolescence and becoming more aware of traditional societal standards for feminine behavior (don't be too assertive nor too smart) and for body type (be very thin and not androgynous). A girl would have to have powerful mentors and role models not to lose or at least lower her voice.

If girls do not succeed academically, they and their teachers tend to attribute this to lack of ability, but boys' academic failures are attributed to their not trying hard enough. Not trying hard enough can be changed, whereas lack of ability is harder to rectify (Dweck et al. 1980). Girls tend to internalize this and think that if they did not do well on a test it was because they are stupid. Boys tend to externalize failure and say that the test was too hard, or the teacher was unfair.

Social and Connection Skills

Boys and girls with good social and connection skills tend to be more resilient. These skills can be taught and some school and community prevention programs are instituting training in these areas.

Before they are given negative messages by their schools and their culture, young girls have a higher sense of self-esteem, perhaps because in toddler-age and early grammar school age children, good socialization ability and desire for relational connection is valued, and girls tend to possess these traits more than boys (Gilligan 1982; Brown 1992).

Young boys aged five to eight who are having difficulty forming friendships and bonds with teachers could benefit from being taught social and connection skills by their teachers, mentors, guidance counselors and those working in school prevention programs. This might enhance their resiliency.

When girls enter middle school at age eleven or twelve, they often need help to form independent judgments of themselves and to learn not to be so concerned about the opinions of others (Rogers 1990). Eleven- to thirteen-year-old girls begin to live under the tyranny of the image of "the perfect girl" who is always kind and nice, dependent rather than assertive. This is the time when girls face what Gilligan calls a "crisis of connection." They are learning the socially defined limiting gender roles for women in our society while at the same time they are attempting to hold onto their own contradictory experiences and perceptions (Gilligan, Brown, and Rogers 1989).

Although some suggest that young women of color may face the most difficult time of all in this regard (Fine and Zane 1988), their strong ethnic identity, and perhaps the fact that they do not relate to our culture's image of the "perfect girl" who is white, may protect them somewhat from this "crisis of connection." Programs working with Hispanic, Asian, and Native American girls could develop strategies to support independence and assertiveness as well as to confirm ethnic identity.

Strengthening girls' resistance to conventional feminine norms may enhance their resilience, while strengthening boys' desires to bond and connect with others may enhance theirs (Turner, Norman, and Zunz 1995).

Sports

Our culture has long known about the value of sports for boys. Adolescent boys' easier access and encouragement to play sports may be their single most important resilience enhancing factor, other than their maleness, especially if they are white.

There are several studies indicating that sports are of equal value to girls (Ms. Foundation 1994; Colton and Gore 1991). One study found that 50 percent of girls who were involved in some kind of sports activity had higher self-esteem than those who were not. Sports have a positive effect for white girls and minority girls, as well as rural and urban girls (Women's Sports Foundation 1989).

High school and college sports programs for girls have found that they help girls get past learned resistance to science, math, and technological learning (Schultz 1991). The President's Council on Physical Fitness and Sports (1997) described studies that showed sports enhance the physical and mental health of girls, strengthening their immune systems and decreasing the likelihood of symptoms of depression and stress. Another study found that high school girls who played sports were 40 percent less likely to drop out of school than those who did not play sports; 33 percent less likely to become teen mothers; and less likely to smoke cigarettes (Zill, Nord, and Loomis 1995).

The number of girls who participate in sports is rising, but it is still behind the number of boys who participate. Even fewer non-white girls engage in sports. And the percentage of girls who exercise regularly declines in high school. Sixty-two percent of girls in ninth grade exercise (compared with 80 percent of boys) and in twelfth grade only 42 percent of girls exercise, compared with 67 percent of boys (Phillips 1998).

Many still consider it "not feminine" for girls to become good athletes or even to engage in sports. Some girls fear being labeled as lesbian if they are too active in sports (Feminist Majority Foundation 1995). There are fewer female role models as coaches and sports program directors. And there are simply not the same kind of sports facilities available to girls or, if they do exist, they may be in neighborhoods or areas that are unsafe for girls (President's Council on Physical Fitness and Sports 1997).

The negative message given to girls in the media about sports participation may be changing. The Women's National Basketball Association, the 1999 Women's Soccer World Cup competition, and the 1998 Winter Olympic United States women's hockey team received extensive media coverage and enthusiastic support from both males and females (Phillips 1998).

Body Image

Playing sports enhances self-esteem, sense of belonging, and sense of mastery, and it can have a positive effect on body image. A white middle-age college professor recalled the value of sports in her teen years: "I always thought I was too fat, but it was more important for me to be able to count on my body to be strong so I could play basketball, so I didn't worry about my weight. Years later I realized I was never fat at all!" (personal communication 1999).

A positive body image is an important element of self-esteem. Girls and young women account for 90 percent of all cases of eating disorders. There is a strong association between eating disorders and depression, anxiety, and substance abuse (National Institute of Mental Health 1993). Boys rarely suffer from anorexia or bulimia, but late maturing boys often feel a sense of inadequacy about their bodies for a time. Also some studies are finding that smaller numbers of boys do have a problem with eating disorders. A 1997 survey found that seven percent of high school boys compared to eighteen percent of high school girls binged and purged, and four percent of boys compared to eight percent of girls did so once a day or a few times a week. (The Commonwealth Fund 1997). Twenty-four percent of high school boys (compared to sixty percent of girls) reported that they were trying to lose weight (Kann et al. 1996).

Boys are probably most likely to retain positive body images because our society does not place the same demands for thinness as a criteria for attractiveness on boys and men as it does on girls and women.

It is white and Hispanic girls who most often develop anorexia and bulimia. Black girls have more positive body images (National Institute of Mental Health 1993). Perhaps this is due to the fact that most of the media's messages about body image are delivered by white women and men primarily to white women, and black girls do not relate to them. They may be practicing the resiliency trait of adaptive distancing (Werner and Smith 1982).

Positive Relationships

Possessing androgynous traits has been shown to be a resiliency factor for both sexes. Girls of all ethnic groups who are encouraged by the adults in their lives to be more assertive, active, and androgynous as well as respected for their ability to connect and "stay in relationship" have been shown to be stronger and more resilient. Boys who are encouraged to stay active, independent, and assertive but also to value their more feminine traits of expression and "connection" with others have also been shown to be stronger and more resilient (Werner and Smith 1982).

Programs such as Girls Incorporated, as well as Big Brothers and Big Sisters, in addition to teachers, coaches, mentors, older peer tutors, parents, friends, prevention workers, and school social workers can provide caring and supportive relationships that encourage such androgynous behaviors.

Girls and boys who value their androgynous characteristics have greater self-esteem and a greater sense of mastery (Werner and Smith 1982; Bem 1993). Androgynous adolescents are able to act in a more flexible, non-sex-typed, manner. They are able to be both assertive and instrumental (generally considered to be masculine traits) and expressive and yielding (generally considered to be feminine traits) depending on what is called for in the situation or environment. Parents and schools might encourage children to engage in activities that are not narrowly sex-typed, for example, encouraging girls to learn fencing or karate, and boys to learn dance and gymnastics (Turner, Norman, and Zunz 1995).

Suggestions for Resiliency Enhancing Interventions

More encouragement of and support for sports for girls is essential to protecting and enhancing their resilience. Girls do not have to excel in team sports to benefit: playing or engaging in activities such as cheerleading where they have a sense of belonging and mastery is what is important. A girl on a seventh grade basketball team that has yet to win a game was recently heard to exclaim with joy: "We lost, but we scored 10 points. Isn't that great!" (personal communication 1999).

In fact, any talent or skill that can be supported and nurtured will protect the resiliency of both boys and girls. A passion and talent for singing, pottery, knitting, or any other hobby or interest gives a sense of mastery and purpose.

Given the findings that adolescents who have a strong ethnic identity have higher self-esteem than those who consider themselves "bicultural" or "mainstream," fostering and supporting a strong ethnic identity for adolescents in their everyday lives can have a protective effect on self-esteem and therefore resiliency (Rotheram-Borus et al. 1997).

Parents who encourage both independence and responsibility in their children foster resiliency. In our culture, independence is more encouraged in boys and responsibility, such as taking care of younger siblings or doing household chores, is more encouraged in girls. If that were modified, and boys were asked to be more responsible for younger siblings and if girls were not overprotected and were encouraged to take risks in a positive sense, the resiliency of both boys and girls could be enhanced.

References

American Association of University Women Report. 1992. *How Schools Short-change Girls*. Washington, D.C.: AAUW Educational Foundation.

Archer, S. 1993. Identity in relational contexts: A methodological proposal. In J. Kroeger, ed., *Discussion on Ego Identity*, 75–100. Hillsdale, N.J.: Lawrence Erlbaum Associates.

Bem, S. 1993. *The Lenses of Gender*. New Haven: Yale University Press.

Benard, B. 1997. Fostering resiliency in children and youth: Promoting protective factors in the school. In D. Saleebey, ed., *The Strengths Perspective in Social Work Practice*, 167–182. New York: Longman.

Brown, L. M. 1992. A Problem of Vision: The Development of Knowledge in Girls Ages 7–16. Unpublished manuscript.

Colton, M. E. and S. Core. 1991. *Gender Differences in Stress and Coping Behaviors Among Late Adolescents*. Washington, D.C.: National Institute for Mental Health.

Commonwealth Fund. 1997. *The Commonwealth Fund Survey of the Health of Adolescent Girls*. Conducted by Louis Harris and Associates. New York: Commonwealth Fund.

Deold, E., M. Wilson, and I. Malave. 1993. *Mother Daughter Revolution*. New York: Bantam.

Dukes, R. and J. R. Martinez. 1994. The impact of ethgender on self-esteem among adolescents. *Adolescence* 29 (113): 105–115.

Dweck, C.S., T. E. Goetz, and N. L. Struss. 1980. Sex differences in learned helplessness, part IV: An experimental and naturalistic study of failure generalization and its mediators. *Journal of Personality and Social Psychology* 38:441–452.

Erikson, E. 1968. *Identity, Youth and Crisis.* New York: Norton.

Feminist Majority Foundation Task Force on Women and Girls in Sports 1995. *Empowering Women in Sports.* Arlington, Va.: Feminist Majority Foundation.

Fine, M. and N. Zane. 1988. Being wrapped too tight: When low-income women drop out of high-school. In L. Weis, E. Farrar, and H. Petriek, eds., *Dropout From School,* 23–53. Albany: State University of New York Press.

Gilligan, C. 1982. *In a Different Voice: Psychological Theory and Women's Development.* Cambridge, Mass.: Harvard University Press.

Gilligan, C., L. Brown, and A. Rogers. 1990. *Psyche Embedded: A Place for Body, Relationships, and Culture in Personality Theory.* New York: Springer.

Gilligan, C., A. Rogers, and D. Tolman. 1991. *Women, Girls, and Psychotherapy: Reframing Resistance.* New York: Haworth Press.

Harris, J. 1998. *The Nurture Assumption: Why Children Turn Out the Way They Do.* New York: Free Press.

Hawkins, J. D., R. F. Catalano, and J. Y. Miller. 1992. Risk and protective factors for alcohol and other drug problems in adolescence and early adulthood: Implications for substance abuse prevention. *Psychological Bulletin* 112 (1): 64–105.

Kann, L., C. W. Warren, W. A. Harris, J. L. Collins, R. I. Williams, J. G. Ross, and L. J. Kolbe. 1996. *Youth Risk Behavior Surveillance: United States, 1995.* In Centers for Disease Control Surveillance Summaries MMR 45: SS-4.

Lewis, M. 1998. Reevaluating significance of baby's bond with mother. *The New York Times,* Aug. 4: F1.

Ms. Foundation for Women. 1994. *Body Politic: Transforming Adolescent Girls' Health.* New York: Ms. Foundation.

National Institute of Mental Health. 1993. *Eating Disorders.* NIH Publication No. 93-3477. Washington, D.C.: U.S. Department of Health and Human Services.

Phillips, L. 1998. *The Girls Report.* New York: National Council for Research on Women.

President's Council on Physical Fitness and Sports. 1997. *Physical Activity and Sport in the Lives of Girls: Physical and Mental Health Dimensions From an Interdisciplinary Approach.* Minneapolis, Minn.: The Center for Research on Girls and Women in Sport.

Rogers, A. 1991. A feminist poetics of psychotherapy. In Gilligan, Rogers and Tolman, eds., *Women, Girls, and Psychotherapy,* 33–54.

Rotheram-Borus, M., S. Dopkins, N. Sabate, and M. Lightfoot. 1997. Personal and ethnic identity, values, and self-esteem among Black and Latino adolescent girls. In B. Leadbeater and N. Way, eds., *Urban Girls, Resisting Stereotypes, Creating Identities*, 35–52. New York: New York University Press.

Schultz, J. D. 1991. *Risk, Resiliency, and Resistance: Current Research on Adolescent Girls*. New York: National Council for Research on Women.

Turner, S., E. Norman, and S. Zunz. 1995. Enhancing resiliency in girls and boys: A case for gender specific adolescent prevention programming. *Journal of Primary Prevention* 16 (1): 25–38.

Uba, L. 1994. *Asian Americans: Personality Patterns, Identity, and Mental Health*. New York: Hillsdale Press.

Werner, E., and E. Smith. 1992. *Overcoming the Odds: High Risk Children from Birth to Adulthood*. New York: McGraw-Hill.

Werner, E. and R. S. Smith. 1982. *Vulnerable but Invincible*. New York: McGraw-Hill.

Women's Sports Foundation. 1989. *Minorities in Sports: The Effect of Varsity Sports Participation on the Social, Educational, and Career Mobility of Minority Students*. New York: Women's Sports Foundation.

Zill, N., C. W. Nord, and L. S. Loomis. 1995. *Adolescent Time Use, Risky Behavior, and Outcomes: An Analysis of National Data*. Rockville, Md.: Westat.

4   Resiliency in Older People: A Paradigm for Practice

Irene A. Gutheil and Elaine Congress

This paper considers resiliency in older adults, which is discussed far less frequently than is resiliency in younger people. The existing literature often focuses on resiliency in caregivers of older people (Walsh 1998) rather than in older people themselves.

Although resiliency and the strengths perspective are frequently discussed together, the terms are not interchangeable. The strengths perspective focuses on capabilities, assets, and positive attributes rather than problems and pathologies. The assumption is that clients have within them the qualities and resources necessary to grow and develop. The focus of the strengths perspective is on empowerment, which has been defined as "assisting individuals, groups, families, and communities to discover and expand the resources and tools within them and around them" (Saleebey 1997:8).

Resiliency best describes the application or operationalization of the strengths perspective (Goldstein 1997). Despite the stresses and pain of life's adversities, the resilient individual is able to cope and survive. Rather than a single event, resilience refers to ongoing capabilities that are available to an individual despite the presence of past and present risk factors. Resilience refers to self-righting behavior (Valliant 1993). Resilient individuals are able to draw on internal resources in order to cope with daunting challenges.

There have been numerous attempts to describe interpersonal and social factors that contribute to resiliency, especially among younger people (Kaplan, Turner, Norman, and Stillson 1996). These factors should not be considered in isolation, but rather as part of a dynamic interaction. Success in encountering one stress may lead to renewed confidence in handling another stress. Resilience describes a process which can best be viewed as contextual. Each person has the capacity for resilience. This capacity does not belong only to special people who possess certain qualities (Saleebey 1997). The social worker should recognize each individual's innate potential and work to enhance resiliency by expanding the opportunities for clients to take control of their lives and to participate as much as possible in decision making.

Old Age and Resilience

One does not have to look far to find accounts of older persons who, despite seemingly overwhelming odds, are continuing to live productive lives, providing care to others, and finding meaning in their daily struggles:

> 79-year-old Steven R. has been lovingly caring for his 80-year-old wife in their home since she was diagnosed with Alzheimer's disease 2 years ago
>
> 68-year-old Juan T., having vowed to rebuild his business after it burned to the ground, reopened to great fanfare
>
> 73-year-old Eudora B. has been raising her two teenage grandchildren since their mother died
>
> 87-year-old Rose N. continues to write and publish short stories despite her recent stroke which left her wheelchair-bound and nearly totally blind.

Old age is potentially one of the longest of life's stages. Using the traditional age of 65 as the start of old age, some individuals spend thirty or more years growing old. The changes individuals must deal with over this span of years make serious demands on their ability to cope and adapt. Because these changes frequently include diminishing resources, often the very resources that assist people in adaptation, older persons could be seen as role models for resilience. Koenig and his colleagues note that even in the face of increasing health problems and decreasing social and economic resources, older people tend to have fewer mental disorders and they report a greater satisfaction with life than do younger people (Koenig, George, and Siegler 1988). Yet the prevailing view of older people is not dominated by the concept of resilience or strengths. Instead, older people are more likely to be seen as weak, frail, and needy.

Growing old is a process characterized by challenge. The individual is challenged to adapt and to change, mostly by losses that generally do not

occur sequentially. Rather, they are numerous, interactive, and often ongoing (Kling, Seltzer, and Ryff 1997). Adaptation to the demands of old age in
a way that enables the individual to grow and often flourish despite sometimes overwhelming odds reflects remarkable strength.

Considerable attention has been paid in recent years to the concept of successful aging. Successful aging, as defined by Rowe and Kahn (1998) in their
presentation of the results of the MacArthur Foundation study of aging in the
United States, is "aging well." They identify its three main components as
"avoiding disease and disability, maintaining mental and physical functioning, and continuing engagement with life" (Rowe and Kahn 1998:49). The
third component, continuing engagement with life, is seen as encompassing
both social relationships and productive activity. Prevention and adaptation
play a critical role in the effectiveness of all three components.

The focus on successful aging was, in part, a reaction to the preoccupation with impairment and disability in much of gerontological research
(Berkman et al. 1993). Focusing on impaired older people added to the mis-
perception that old age was defined primarily by physical decline. The work
on successful aging examines the majority of the older population, those who
are free of disability and who are high functioning, and considers factors that
help account for this resilience. However, one risk in equating successful
aging with high functioning is that older people living with disabilities or
deficits may not fit this definition, even though they may be demonstrating
remarkable resilience.

Much of successful aging may be attributed to good genes, good sense,
and good resources. However, for many older people, avoiding disability and
maintaining functioning may become increasingly difficult, if not impossible. This does not mean that they have not aged successfully; it does mean
that their experience of aging involves negotiating very choppy waters. To acknowledge and account for the capacity of these older people to cope with
major stressors, a broader definition of successful aging, which draws on the
resilience literature to provide the paradigm, is necessary.

Resilience is an important factor in helping people, especially those facing
physical, social, or environmental hardships, to successfully navigate aging's
challenges by adapting and continuing on course. Resilience in old age may
be best thought of as the ability to survive and overcome numerous major
stressors, including disease, disability, and a range of other major losses.

Pearlin and Skaff (1995) underscore the importance of understanding the
stressors individuals must deal with and the resources they can marshal when
considering how people age successfully. They discuss three resources older

people use to deal with stress: coping, mastery, and social support. Because many of the stressors faced in late life are not easily controlled, older adults are more likely than younger adults to use coping strategies that manage the meaning of stress rather than those focused on problem solving (Pearlin and Skaff 1995). By redefining the importance of problematic areas, the power of these problems can be diminished.

Noting the intractability of many of the problems of aging, Bower (1996) draws on the work of Jordan (1992) to discuss the importance of relational resilience. "A key idea is that the capacity for resilience has the potential to develop from within a relationship and is dependent on the quality of the connection" (Bower 1996:94). From this perspective, Bower considers the older individual's relationship with the notion of God as a coping resource. Because problem solving opportunities are limited in the face of chronic illness and loss of loved ones, the older person may be able to draw strength and comfort from faith and trust in God (Bower 1996). Mastery, a sense of control, can also help buffer the stresses of aging. Evidence of mastery can be drawn from one's past experience or from manageable areas in one's current life. Evidence of mastery may also be drawn from small successes in negotiating tasks of daily living that have become difficult. To be resilient in old age demands flexibility and acceptance of change. As Pearlin and Skaff note, "the process of adapting to late life may involve staking one's mastery on domains over which one can exert control and yielding it where control is now more difficult" (Pearlin and Skaff 1995:115).

From a different perspective, researchers have drawn on the work of Kobasa (1979) to look at the role of individual hardiness in maintaining health. Hardiness refers to a group of personality characteristics that help individuals resist stress, and is comprised of three components. The first is commitment, a sense of purpose that allows individuals to find meaning in life events. The second is control, belief that one can influence life events, and action based on this belief. The third component, challenge, refers to the perception of stressful events as offering opportunities for stimulation and growth rather than as threats (Drory and Florian 1991; Ross 1991).

Studies have found older individuals high in hardiness to have higher self-perceived health and a greater number of self-care practices (Nicholas 1993); better compliance with a diabetic regimen (Ross 1991); and better long-term psychosocial adjustment to coronary artery disease (Drory and Florian 1991).

Individual hardiness and the concomitant adaptation is related to social support. In their study of women with rheumatoid arthritis (mean average age 57), Lambert and colleagues (1990) found hardiness, a predictor of psychological well being, to be correlated with social support. Reinhardt (1996) found social support to be predictive of better adaptation to vision loss among older people. There is general consensus that social support is one of the factors that fosters resilience in old age.

The literature on aging is replete with references to social support and its importance to well being. Aleman and Paz (1998), in their discussion of the Yaqui elderly of the Southwest, highlight the support this culture provides its people. They suggest that the support fosters a resilience that enables its members to reach old age despite oppression and poverty. The literature makes clear that in general, quality of life is enhanced by good social support. However, while the relationship between social support and physical and mental health is well established, it is not possible to be certain if social support is responsible for better health or if people whose health is better are more involved in social relationships (Quadagno 1999).

For the frail elderly, social support is of particular importance. Most long-term care is provided in the community by families or friends. These informal supports are critical to fostering adaptation to disability. Expanding the conceptualization of resilience in the lives of vulnerable older people, Morris and Sherwood (1984) consider the importance of resiliency in the informal support system. Resiliency enables the system to effectively respond to changing needs. In their study of a diverse sample of 700 vulnerable elders, Morris and Sherwood (1984) found indications of resilient networks which featured flexibility in assuming roles, a wide range of helping behaviors, and good communication about changing needs. Resilience in this context is a family affair. Resilience is fostered by interdependence with others and is grounded in the ability to adapt to changing demands (Walsh 1998). The social world plays an important role in both nurturing hardiness in the individual and in providing support for the individual who is unable to muster the personal resources to deal with overwhelming demands.

Older people, especially those dealing with impairments and infirmities, can be challenged by their physical settings (Golant 1984). Well-being may decline when physical settings are too demanding or are not altered to accommodate impairments. Consequently, modifications of an older person's living space may improve his or her coping and adaption (Hooyman and Kiyak 1996). In fact, a well planned environment can increase one's sense of competence and mastery (Gutheil 1991), factors that are related to resilience. The essential factor is the creation of environments that can be adapted to the individual when necessary, rather than the other way around (Christenson 1990).

Resilience in Practice

Resilience is evident among older persons of different ages with different levels of capabilities and within varied settings. The following practice principles can help social workers identify and foster resiliency in older persons both in the community and in institutional settings.

- Identify indicators of strengths and resilience in the client.
- Involve the client in identifying areas of resilience.
- Help the client to identify what areas he or she can still control.
- Assist the client in letting go of what he or she cannot control.
- Identify and encourage informal and formal supports that foster resiliency.
- Identify new, untapped areas of strength and emerging resiliencies.
- Identify and work to enhance or alter aspects of the physical environment that either support or undermine resilience.
- Reevaluate resiliency based on changing levels of capability.

The following case example focuses on an institutionalized older person with limited mobility and sensory perception, discussed in the context of the practice principles identified above.

Mrs. Dayton is a 94-year-old widow who has been a resident in a nursing home for the last six months. She always prided herself on her independence, first as an actress and then as a tour leader. Since she retired from acting at 65, she had been active in leading senior citizen travel tours, entertained frequently, and maintained a large apartment filed with antiques and mementos.

When failing eyesight and hearing made continuing in this lifestyle increasingly difficult, Mrs. Dayton moved into senior housing, taking with her photographs and a few treasured pieces of furniture. In her new efficiency apartment, she was able to manage with only occasional help from old friends, neighbors, and a daughter who lives in a nearby city. She continued to lead an active social life, performing regularly in the senior housing's theatricals and hosting frequent, large gatherings.

At the age of 90, Mrs. Dayton sustained a fall which resulted in a concussion and skull fracture. She entered the nursing home for rehabilitation, making it clear that she intended to return home within a few months. Despite the concerns of professionals working with her, she was back in her apartment in seven months, this time with a home health aide to assist her. Far from resenting the presence of a stranger, Mrs. Dayton welcomed her caregiver with affection, quickly making her a part of her social circle.

Three years later, Mrs. Dayton again fell at home and returned to the nursing home. Returning to her apartment was impossible, as she was now confined to a wheelchair, almost deaf, with severely limited vision, and unable to care for herself. When the nursing home began a renovation project, she had to change rooms three times, enduring the consequent changes in nursing staff and in the layout of her possessions, which was particularly challenging because of her vision loss.

Despite her diminished mobility and confinement to a nursing home, Mrs. Dayton continues to be very independent. She is able to manage her own finances, chooses her own clothing, and has her hair colored and permed regularly. She entertains groups of her former neighbors in her room, sharing cookies supplied by her daughter. Though unable to leave the room without an escort, she attends a variety of social programs. As always, she takes a small glass of sherry before bed and enjoys an occasional cocktail with her daughter at an area restaurant.

As the first step in working with this client, the social worker identified strengths that had helped Mrs. Dayton cope with stressors throughout her life. Her social skills had always been very strong. Even now with declining motor and sensory abilities, she was able to maintain an active social life with other residents, as well as with former neighbors in her community. Continuing social relationships have been described earlier as an ingredient of successful aging (Rowe and Kahn 1998). Mrs. Dayton is concerned about her physical appearance, has her hair done frequently, and is interested in and able to approve her clothing. These activities, which indicate an ongoing interest in maintaining her appearance, reflect Mrs. Dayton's interest in remaining involved in living.

Like many older people, Mrs. Dayton had to adjust to repeated losses and changes. She managed to thrive despite declining mobility and sensory abilities. In recent years she was able to cope with several moves to more restrictive environments. First, to senior housing, then a nursing home on a temporary basis, and most recently, a permanent move to the nursing home. In addition, within the nursing home, Mrs. Dayton was able to adjust to room changes, even though spatial change is especially difficult for a person with severe vision impairment.

The social worker recognized with Mrs. Dayton her ability to successfully cope with physical losses (mobility, vision, hearing) and social and environmental changes (moving to an institution, room changes). As the losses increased, the social worker supported Mrs. Dayton in her ability to adapt and cope with changes in her world.

At her first admission, Mrs. Dayton had been extremely reluctant to enter a nursing home, even for a limited time. Although there was concern about Mrs. Dayton's health if she returned home, she was supported in making that choice. Now, with declining capability to live independently, Mrs. Dayton had no alternative but to live in an institution. The social worker helped Mrs. Dayton by listening as she mourned her loss of independence and worked to accept the limitations of institutional living.

Social supports can help an older person cope with stress and foster resiliency, and it is apparent that social supports have been a source of strength for Mrs. Dayton, who relishes social contact. Her daughter visits regularly, brings gifts, and takes Mrs. Dayton out. The social worker encourages and fosters these visits. Also, Mrs. Dayton is often visited by other residents as well as by old friends and acquaintances from the community. The social worker tries to facilitate these visits by arranging for refreshments and ensuring that medical visits are not scheduled at these times.

Placement in a nursing home where her basic needs were met provided necessary formal support for this client. The social worker promotes independence in her client as much as possible by encouraging her to make decisions about food, dress, and social activities, and by working with other facility staff to insure that they support Mrs. Dayton in these decisions. In addition, the social worker works with the housekeeping staff to insure that all of Mrs. Dayton's belongings are placed in their appointed spots after the room is cleaned. This enables Mrs. Dayton to function as independently as possible despite her visual impairment.

A final practice principle notes that resilience may have to be continually reevaluated as levels of capability change. At this time Mrs. Dayton demonstrates remarkable resilience in coping with various losses and diminished capabilities. The social worker has worked to foster resilience as much as possible by encouraging her client to act as independently as possible and by working to create an environment that accepts this independence. An emerging problem, however, is Mrs. Dayton's elevated blood sugar level. The physician, concerned that even the small quantity of alcohol that she drank each evening might be deleterious to her health, suggested abstinence. Mrs. Dayton was very depressed about the possibility of giving up alcohol altogether. A dilemma emerged between fostering self-determination in an older client and promoting what was viewed by professionals to be in the client's best interests (Congress and Chernesky 1991). Since Mrs. Dayton has coped with other changes and losses, it is anticipated that she will be resilient in working with the facility staff to find a way to cope with this new challenge.

In Mrs. Dayton's case, her resilience was evident long before she entered the nursing home, and she continued to draw on this resilience in the institutional setting. The second case example concerns an older woman living independently, and also demonstrates an older person's impressive ability to draw on internal resources as well as social support.

Mrs. Roberts, an intelligent and attractive 78-year-old African-American widow, lives alone in an apartment in a major metropolitan area. She receives ongoing treatment at the geriatric practice of a nearby hospital for osteoarthritis and heart disease. Her macular degeneration has resulted in some vision loss. In the past several years Mrs. Roberts sought help from the social worker in the geriatric practice to deal with the loss of her sister and, later, the loss of her granddaughter.

Mrs. Roberts worked as a nursing aide in a large city hospital, where her husband was employed as a maintenance worker. She found her job demanding but rewarding. She and her husband raised three children, the youngest of whom was successfully treated for depression as a teenager. Mrs. Roberts retired at age 65, and was widowed one year later. At age 70, Mrs. Roberts took in and cared for her older sister, who had become demented. Two years later, her sister died, after a serious illness and many difficult medical decisions that Mrs. Roberts was asked to make.

Her sister's death precipitated Mrs. Roberts' first request for treatment. During her meetings with the social worker, Mrs. Roberts struggled with issues related to her retirement, her desire to be productive, her physical aging, and her need to compensate and substitute for lost activities and lost loved ones. Four years later, her beloved granddaughter died of cancer. This painful and untimely loss led Mrs. Roberts to again request help from the social worker.

With the social worker's support, Mrs. Roberts enrolled in poetry classes at both the local Y and community college. She channeled her grief into her writing, using the writing as catharsis and for clarification of her feelings. Some of her poems have been published. Through her work with the social worker and her writing, Mrs. Roberts grieved her losses and has been able to move on. She continues with her classes and her writing.

From the start of their contact, the social worker worked with Mrs. Roberts to identify the many strengths that she has been able to draw on throughout her life. A sensitive and generous woman, she enjoyed caregiving and sought opportunities to help others. In addition, she was realistic about her limitations and able to turn to outside sources of help. When her son became clinically depressed and the consequent demands of caregiving became more than she could handle, Mrs. Roberts sought appropriate help for him. In the face of her son's mental health crisis, Mrs. Roberts' resilience was evident in both her ability to recognize that her family needed help and her willingness to ask for it. She was again able to recognize and respect her own need for help when losses in her life became too great for her to bear. Perhaps her son's earlier successful treatment gave Mrs. Roberts the confidence to seek mental health treatment for herself as well, as she had learned the value of using formal supports to foster coping and adaptation.

Despite serious physical impairments and the loss of three beloved family members, Mrs. Roberts continued to be active and find ways to make life meaningful. The social worker helped her to find a way to do the work of letting go of the loved ones she had lost. After her granddaughter's death, the social worker helped Mrs. Roberts find a new way of working through her grief, using a powerful new tool, poetry. This enabled Mrs. Roberts to heal and to nuture a new strength that emerged as a result of her need to deal with her losses.

Through careful planning and budgeting, Mrs. Roberts had saved a small nest egg which provided Mrs. Roberts a good measure of control over her choices, making it possible to open up new avenues of expression. Her resilience is evident in her willingness to use her money to bring pleasure to herself through the poetry classes.

Mrs. Roberts' resilience is manifested not only in her ability to survive serious losses, both social and physical, but in her growth in the face of these losses. Her poetry writing, a heretofore untapped area of strength, has helped her to deal with her grief. In addition, it has opened a new avenue of self-expression and competence and a new social world of fellow students. As Mrs. Roberts continues to navigate the course of her aging, poetry writing will always be available to her as a means of coping with losses she may face or disability that may challenge her. In addition, because Mrs. Roberts has had positive experiences with the helping professionals she has used primarily as facilitators to help her access resources she carries within herself, it is likely that she will be able to ask for help should she again need it.

It is essential to look beyond the stereotypes that older people are needy and frail or that those who have aged successfully are free of disease or disability. Older people are a diverse group, and resilience can be and is found throughout this diversity. Resiliency can be identified among older adults regardless of the level of their need for care. Instances of resilience exist among nursing home residents as well as among older adults living alone or with their families.

Constantly challenged to adapt to change and loss, most older people are role models for resilience. Generally, they are continuing lifelong patterns of coping and adaptation. Some are developing new, previously unrecognized, areas of resilience in the face of the daunting challenges they must deal with.

Social workers can enhance their practice with older people by recognizing and nurturing the resilience inherent in their clients or in their clients' social worlds. Unfortunately, too much education and training has focused primarily on identifying and addressing physical, psychological, and social problems among older adults. It is essential that helping professionals learn early, as part of their classroom and field work experience, to look for and develop resilience among older persons. Applying the practice principles outlined in this paper can help both the beginner and the advanced practitioner work more effectively with older adults in community and institutional settings. Increased sensitivity to resilience among older people accords with the social work value system, which seeks to maximize the capabilities and opportunities for all persons, regardless of age or limitations.

References

The authors are grateful to Debra Greenberg, MSW, and Paulette Sansone, Ph.D., for contributing case materials for this paper

Aleman, S. and J. Paz. 1998. The Yaqui elderly, cultural oppression, and resilience. *Journal of Aging and Ethnicity* 1:113–127.

Berkman, L. F., T. E. Seeman, M. Albert, D. Blazer, et al. 1993. High, usual, and impaired functioning in community-dwelling older men and women: Findings from the MacArthur Foundation research network on successful aging. *Journal of Clinical Epidemiology* 46:1129–1140.

Bower, G. 1996. Relational resilience: A new perspective for understanding the elderly person's relationship to the notion of God. *Journal of Geriatric Psychiatry* 29:83–104.

Christenson, M. A. 1990. Aging in the designed environment. *Physical and Occupational Therapy in Geriatrics* 8 (3/4): entire issue.

Congress, E. and R. Chernesky. 1993. Representative payee programs for the elderly: Administrative, clinical, and ethical issues. *Journal of Gerontological Social Work* 21 (1/2): 77–93.

Drory, Y. and V. Florian. 1991. Long-term psychosocial adjustment to coronary artery disease. *Archives of Physical Medicine and Rehabilitation* 72:326–331.

Golant, S. M. 1984. *A Place to Grow Old*. New York: Columbia University Press.

Goldstein, H. 1997. Victors or victims. In D. Saleebey, ed., *The Strengths Perspective in Social Work Practice*, 21–35. New York: Longman.

Gutheil, I. A. 1991. The physical environment and quality of life in residential facilities for frail elders. *Adult Residential Care Journal* 5:131–145.

Hooyman, N. and H. A. Kiyak. 1996. *Social Gerontology*. Boston: Allyn and Bacon.

Jordan, J. V. 1992. Relational resilience. *Work in Progress* no. 57. Wellesley: Stone Center Working Paper Series.

Kling, K. C., M. M. Seltzer, and C. D. Ryff. 1997. Distinctive late-life challenges: Implications for coping and well-being. *Psychology and Aging* 12:288–295.

Kobasa, S. C. 1979. Stressful life events, personality, and health: An inquiry into hardiness. *Journal of Personality and Social Psychology* 37:1–11.

Koenig, H. G., L. K. George, and I. C. Siegler. 1988. The use of religion and other emotion-regulating coping strategies among older adults. *The Gerontologist* 28:303–310.

Lambert, V. A., C. E. Lambert, G. L. Klipple, and E. A. Mewshaw. 1990. Relationships among hardiness, social support, severity of illness, and psychological well-being in women with rheumatoid arthritis. *Health Care for Women International* 11:159–173.

Morris, J. N. and S. A. Sherwood. 1984. Informal support resources for vulnerable elderly persons: Can they be counted on? Do they work? *International Journal of Aging and Human Development* 18:81–98.

Nicholas, P. K. 1993. Hardiness, self-care practices, and perceived health status in older adults. *Journal of Advanced Nursing* 18:1085–1094.

Pearlin, L. I. and M. M. Skaff. 1995. Stressors and adaptation in late life. In

M. Gatz, ed., *Emerging Issues in Mental Health and Aging*, 97–123. Washington, D.C.: American Psychological Association.

Quadagno, J. 1999. *Aging and the Life Course*. Boston: McGraw-Hill.

Reinhardt, J. P. 1996. The importance of friendship and family support in adaptation to chronic vision impairment. *The Journals of Gerontology; Psychological Sciences* 51B:268–278.

Ross, M. E. T. 1991. Hardiness and compliance in elderly patients with diabetes. *The Diabetes Educator* 17:372–375.

Rowe, J. W. and R. L. Kahn. 1998. *Successful Aging*. New York: Pantheon.

Saleebey, D. 1997. Introduction. In D. Saleebey, ed., *The Strengths Perspective in Social Work Practice*, 3–19.

Vallant, G. 1993. *The Wisdom of the Ego*. Cambridge, Mass.: Harvard University Press.

Walsh, F. 1998. *Strengthening Family Resilience*. New York: Guilford.

Part II

Resiliency Enhancement and Individual, Family, Couple, and Group Practice

5   A Case Study of Resiliency Enhancement Interventions with an African American Woman

Carol P. Kaplan

This paper describes clinical work with Barbara, an African American woman who entered treatment for severe depression, and will highlight four major themes. First, Barbara showed evidence of vulnerability, in the form of emotional scars from a traumatic childhood which put her at risk. Her early trauma had led her to make certain problematic life choices when she was much younger. Second, in spite of her vulnerabilities and problems Barbara was a highly resilient person who survived devastating childhood experiences and created a life that afforded her significant satisfaction. Third, the treatment not only provided opportunities for revelation and validation of the past trauma, with permission for expression of profound feelings of hurt, disappointment, and anger, but it also focused on Barbara's strengths, reinforced her resiliency, and reframed her story as that of a successful survivor (Wolin and Wolin 1993). This reframing, in turn, enabled her to face the ongoing challenges in her life. Fourth, Barbara's case illustrates that resilience may be best conceptualized not as a finished product but as a lifelong process (Higgins 1994).

Presenting Problem

Barbara, an attractive, well groomed woman in her forties, with a dark complexion, came to the therapist's office dressed tastefully in what appeared to be expensive clothes. She had a gentle, pleasant manner and a beautiful smile, acknowledging some nervousness because she had never consulted a therapist before. She explained that her problem was financial: her husband had experienced a series of reverses in his business over the past few years and they were now facing bankruptcy. Worst of all, they were in imminent danger of losing their house. This made her feel extremely depressed and anxious. She experienced panic attacks at night and was having trouble sleeping. She worried constantly, especially about the loss of their house and the effect it would have on her son, who was attending high school in their predominantly white, middle class neighborhood. He was a good student and was college bound. She felt that her daughter, who was away at college, would not be so directly affected.

Barbara was under the care of a physician for two serious medical conditions, and he had suggested that she try talking to someone because he worried that she was neglecting her health. She suffered from hypertension, yet she was "forgetting" to take her medication, feeling "what's the use, I might as well be dead anyway." She also had stomach ulcers that twice before had begun bleeding, requiring that she be hospitalized. Now she felt that the ulcers were worsening, but again she did not take her medication on schedule, as prescribed.

After a few sessions Barbara admitted that the problem that actually caused her the most suffering was a guilty secret, one she had never discussed before, with anyone. Since the beginning of their marriage, her husband had always worked very long hours and was hardly ever at home. Feeling lonely and unhappy, as a younger woman she had had several affairs. Eventually her husband found out, and she never committed adultery again. Now, however, the thought that her sins had caused her family's present troubles plagued her constantly. She ruminated about the possibility—which increasingly seemed to her a certainty—that their financial problems were God's punishment for her misdeeds. Her guilt, moreover, often made her feel that she was unfit to be among "good" people, and that she would never again be happy. The suffering was so unbearable that she frequently thought death would be preferable. She said that she would never actually commit suicide, but she did sometimes think that death from a stroke or a bleeding ulcer might be better than her present situation.

Barbara was a relatively isolated person who spent long periods of time alone and acknowledged feeling lonely. She attended church every Sunday, as well as weekly prayer meetings, and they provided her some comfort; yet she resisted the attempts of several parishioners to get closer to her. While she did have some friends there was no one person in whom she confided totally because, as she explained, she felt so ashamed of her predicament and guilty about her past "sins." She also did not feel close to her extended family. Her parents had long ago divorced and remarried and she felt that they preferred their new families. She described feeling like a fifth wheel in their presence, a situation that caused her continuing sorrow. To make matters worse, when her husband's financial situation began deteriorating he had borrowed a large sum of money from her father, which he was currently unable to repay. Her father made no secret of his resentment, creating additional tension for her and driving them even further apart.

On the other hand, Barbara described her job as a bookkeeper in the accounting department of a large corporation as "my salvation." This was not on account of either her duties or her extremely modest salary. Rather, she said that at work she was popular and well liked. In the office she could laugh and joke around, enjoying herself as much as others enjoyed her. Colleagues told her she was the most easygoing person they had ever met, little suspecting her inner torment. While on the job she could temporarily forget her troubles: she commented with amazement that only one friend knew even a tiny part of how bad her situation really was. She loved being the life of the party, and was sought out — during work as well as at after work social events — because she was such fun to be with. She could see the humor in even the grimmest situations and make hilarious comments. As she repeated some of her humorous remarks the therapist could not help but laugh also. Barbara lived and worked in a community with a majority of Jewish people, and was attuned to the fact that the therapist was Jewish. She had developed the ability to use Yiddish words in exactly the appropriate context, and her sense of humor included a style both teasing and self-deprecating, similar to that of generations of Jewish comedians. Barbara had assimilated this style and had made it her own.

Barbara's History

Barbara did not recount her history all at once; rather, it emerged gradually, with the most painful aspects told hesitantly over a period of time. She was the only child born to a young African American mother and a father who was an immigrant from the Caribbean. Her parents separated when she was four years old. Barbara had memories of her mother drinking and having sex with a series of men, sometimes while Barbara was in the bed. She believed that her mother was an alcoholic, and had few memories of her father from her early childhood. Evidently he distanced himself and never offered her any emotional support. After the parents separated her mother would frequently leave her alone for what seemed to her to be long periods of time, sometimes without any food. Afraid and often hungry, she would hide in the closet, where she felt safe. The climax of this traumatic period in Barbara's young life occurred when she was six years old. Her mother, who was drunk, sent her out of the apartment one night, telling her to leave and never come back, because she was "too dark."

Barbara remembered leaving with nothing but the clothes on her back and sitting on the steps of her Brooklyn apartment house late at night, feeling frightened, until finally a neighbor appeared and took her to the home of an older, childless relative who lived nearby. Aunt Mary—actually a great aunt, the sister of her grandmother—was to be the one who raised her, with some financial assistance from her father. Over the years he came by weekly, to give money to Mary, but Barbara remembers these occasions as formal ones in which her role was to appear neatly dressed, speak politely to her father, and then make her exit as soon as possible. Her father asked perfunctory questions about her progress in school and her behavior, but never kissed or hugged her, or expressed any affectionate feelings. Her mother soon moved back to North Carolina, and several years passed before Barbara was to see her again.

When Barbara was nine years old her mother sent for her and she went down south for the summer, beginning a yearly ritual that ended only when she became an adolescent. Her mother had given up drinking, had remarried, and had two other children, but the visits were not happy occasions for Barbara. She felt out of place and lonely amidst a collection of relatives who were virtual strangers. Several cousins taunted her because she was from "up north," and her mother, clearly preoccupied with her two younger children, paid little attention to her.

Barbara's father had also remarried and had two children from his second union. He lived nearby and invited Barbara to their home from time to time. However, despite the fact that her stepmother was kind and welcomed her, her father remained distant and showed distinct favoritism towards his children from the second marriage. Thus, she felt that she did not really belong to this family either.

From the age of six, the mainstay of Barbara's life, and the only constant presence in her life, was her Aunt Mary. Barbara said that she regarded her aunt as her real mother. A kind, religious woman, Mary did her best to take care of Barbara's physical and spiritual needs. Barbara was awakened early every Sunday morning in order to attend Sunday school at the church down the block. When she got older she sang in the choir. She recalled that on occasion she seemed to be the only person who was out so early, and that many times she wished she could have stayed in bed. Yet when she walked home from church after the service she felt calm and happy. Church became a safe and peaceful refuge.

Aunt Mary taught the Golden Rule, and she attempted to live by it as well. She emphasized that Barbara must call her "Aunt Mary" because her mother, despite the mistakes she had made, was still "mother." She also insisted that Barbara always look neat and attractive, telling her that even if she had only one outfit it must be washed and ironed every day. She encouraged Barbara to do her best in school and praised her for her accomplishments. As an adult Barbara realized that Aunt Mary was also communicating the unspoken message that she was a lovable and worthwhile person. In addition, from Aunt Mary's example she learned that even in the most difficult circumstances life could be lived with grace and dignity.

Aunt Mary did not have very much money. Her main source of income was public assistance, supplemented by the small allowance provided by Barbara's father. As a result, aunt and niece were forced to live with various members of Mary's extended family in Brooklyn, and they moved several times while Barbara was growing up. In two of these homes, when Barbara was between the ages of nine and 13, older male cousins sexually abused her. They coerced her into silence, but in any event she would have been afraid to tell her aunt because Mary never spoke of sexual matters and the abuse made Barbara feel ashamed and "dirty." She also believed that Aunt Mary would disapprove if she complained, because she often told her niece that they should feel grateful to be given shelter. Thus, despite the knowledge that Aunt Mary truly loved her, Barbara never disclosed her abuse until she told her husband.

Barbara described herself as a rather shy child who began to make friends during her adolescence. She recounted with puzzlement how as a teenager she and her best friend frequented bars and did a lot of drinking. While her friend continued to drink, and eventually became an alcoholic, Barbara one day decided to stop because she disliked the feeling of being drunk, and she never drank again except for an occasional glass of wine during a celebration. She had read about familial susceptibility to alcoholism, and said she had no idea how she had escaped her mother's fate.

Barbara met her husband when she was 17 and he was 25, and they married soon after her eighteenth birthday. When she recalled their courtship she could not say exactly why she decided to marry him, but suspected that his maturity, stability, and kindness appealed to her. Like her father he was an immigrant from the Caribbean. He was steadily employed and displayed a strong work ethic as well as ambition. He made it clear that he was prepared to take care of her. She knew that Aunt Mary approved of him, and also was aware that her aunt was getting old and was planning to move back down to North Carolina. Looking back on that time of her life, Barbara said that she probably felt she needed security and he seemed able to provide it; but neither romance, emotional closeness, nor physical attraction played any real role in her decision. The marriage turned out to be one of mutual regard, but devoid of passion or intimacy. They never communicated their feelings, and their sexual life was always unsatisfying to her; eventually it became nonexistent. Barbara characterized it by saying that rather than marrying, they should have just remained friends. He seemed happiest when working, and worked most of the time. They had little in common, except for devotion to their children, and Barbara, who loved to have fun, found herself bored on those rare occasions when they went out together.

On the other hand, Barbara discovered that she had an aptitude for motherhood. This proved to be another source of amazement to her, since, as she said, she lacked role models for parenting young children. Moreover, she might as well have been a single parent, since her husband was hardly ever at home. She had no idea how it happened, but she found that she not only loved her children, she enjoyed their development and possessed profound empathy for them. Both of her children had grown to be responsible, loving young people who valued education and did not abuse alcohol or drugs. Despite her tendency to minimize her own contribution, Barbara's mothering capacities received further validation when, in the course of her treatment, her daughter gave birth. Barbara commented with wonder on her daughter's excellent attunement to the child, and was eventually able to recognize that she had provided the same for her daughter.

Barbara's Vulnerabilities

Barbara clearly showed the scars of her traumatic childhood in a number of ways (Herman 1992). She suffered from panic attacks, especially at night when she had traumatic dreams, or when a particular situation produced flashbacks of early traumatic experiences. The experiences of neglect, abandonment, and sexual abuse had produced severe depression, characterized by self-destructiveness, excessive shame and guilt, and a pervasive sense of being not just bad, but worse than other human beings. Like many traumatized children, she had internalized the idea that her abuse and neglect were somehow her fault, and she felt stigmatized. In turn, these feelings contributed to her isolation and loneliness, since she shrank from telling others what had happened to her. Few people knew her life story. Even when she told friends that her aunt had raised her, she glossed over the abandonment by her mother and explained it away.

Barbara's low self-esteem was apparent when she expressed surprise that she possessed good qualities and could do things well, or that she had turned out differently than her parents. Her abandonment by her mother was associated in her mind with another aspect of her poor self-concept, namely her appearance, more specifically, her complexion. Barbara had internalized her mother's statement that she deserved rejection because she was "too dark," and actually believed that she was unattractive. She explained her choice of white (specifically Jewish) friends, and the decision to live in a predominantly white neighborhood, as stemming from distrust of black people, due to her history of abuse and maltreatment. While this feeling cannot be denied, Barbara's tendency to distance herself from other people of color can also be viewed as a manifestation of internalized racism.

It eventually emerged that one aspect of her self-torment and guilt over her adulterous affairs took the form of an obsessive doubt about whether her husband was actually her daughter's biological father, since her daughter had a lighter complexion than either parent. She understood intellectually the facts about variations in skin tones among African American people. She also realized that, regardless of biological parentage, her husband and daughter had fully appropriate father-daughter feelings for one another. But only the birth of her grandchild, who clearly resembled her husband, finally put an end to this punishing preoccupation.

Another factor that contributed to Barbara's isolation was a difficulty in allowing others to get too close to her, possibly a reflection of her feeling that she had been rejected and abandoned by both parents. Perhaps this tendency to distrust closeness accounts for the fact that she chose, and then remained in, a marriage lacking in intimacy. Like her father, her husband provided money without emotional support. As she approached middle age, Barbara felt keenly the absence of companionship in her marriage and occasionally contemplated divorce since, in addition to all its other deficits, the marriage was now failing to provide the financial security it had promised. She was about to lose her house, a prospect that filled her with particular fear and dread because it reminded her that as a child she never had a secure home.

Yet she made no attempt to obtain a divorce. In the first place, she felt sincerely sorry for her husband and did not wish to cause him further pain. In the second place, the prospect of still another separation seemed too overwhelming. Another area of vulnerability for Barbara was the fact that, while she saw her parents' weaknesses realistically, she could not finally accept their limitations and approach them with detachment. Instead, each unsatisfying telephone conversation or visit filled her with hurt and disappointment. She could not relinquish the hope that they would change and somehow give her the love she had craved all her life. Instead, she found herself continually astonished that her old feeling of not belonging in their families remained alive, and that her parents never deviated from their individual scripts. Her father became even colder and more distant after the loan of money, making no attempt to hide his preference for his other children. For her part, Barbara's mother constantly attempted to obtain money from her, apparently refusing to believe her daughter's explanation of her financial straits.

Resilience Characteristics and Protective Factors

In their review of the research literature on resilience, Norman, Turner, and Zunz (1994) summarized the individual characteristics and protective factors that have been identified in resilient people. Despite her vulnerabilities, Barbara illustrates many of these. Initially, she possessed an easy temperament and disposition. From childhood she was described as very likable, and her easy going, pleasant manner invariably elicited a positive response in others. Higgins (1994) has written about the capacity of resilient children to "recruit" surrogate caretakers when their own parents are impaired. While one may surmise that Aunt Mary had strong nurturing capacities, Barbara's pleasant nature and likability undoubtedly contributed to strengthening the bond between them.

In adulthood this quality persisted. She was extremely popular among her co-workers. Her physician told the therapist that he regarded Barbara as his favorite patient; so much so that, even after he left her HMO, he continued to treat her without charge, knowing of her financial difficulties. He regularly phoned her to check that she was taking her medications, and when he discovered that she was not he referred her for therapy. Her therapist also found her very likable.

Another genetic or biological factor found in resilient people is intellectual capacity, and Barbara was a highly intelligent woman. She never attended college because it did not seem like an option when she was a teenager. However, she always did well in school, was an astute and well informed person, and encouraged her children in their education. She had at her command all aspects of the bankruptcy proceedings, including certain aspects that her husband did not fully understand.

Barbara also possessed many of the personality characteristics that have been associated with resilient outcomes in people whose life circumstances have put them at risk. She had a sense of self-efficacy, which is related to the quality that Wolin and Wolin (1993) have termed "initiative." According to Norman, Turner, and Zunz (1994), self-efficacy implies self-esteem and self-confidence, as well as a belief in the capacity to influence one's internal and external environment. While Barbara's self-esteem was seriously deficient in certain respects, at the same time, she felt that she could influence, if not control, her environment. She also had confidence in her ability to master life tasks, a quality that first appeared very early in her life, when she forced herself to search her apartment for food after her mother left her alone. In her adult life she successfully parented her two children. She always appeared well groomed and beautifully dressed, even when money was scarce, because she had excellent taste and knew how to shop for the best sales. Eventually she went beyond a mere understanding of the bankruptcy proceedings to an ability to manipulate them, so that a full two years elapsed before the family was forced to vacate their house. At that point, with her husband stunned with grief and unable to take action, Barbara found a suitable apartment in the area, to ensure that her son would be able to graduate from the same high school. With her husband in denial of their straitened circumstances, Barbara took over the task of budgeting and ensuring that the necessary bills got paid.

Related to self-efficacy are three other qualities found in resilient people: realistic appraisal of the environment, social problem-solving skills, and humor (Norman, Turner, and Zunz 1994). Barbara evidenced all of these in good measure. In general she was extremely realistic, recognizing which situations she could, and which she could not, affect. Even with respect to her parents, whose behavior never ceased to hurt her, she knew full well that she could not change them. Her repertoire of social problem-solving skills was extensive. She understood how to negotiate, and how and when to assert herself. She possessed a keen sense of humor, and she frequently used humor to assist with social problem-solving, as well as to relieve her pain. This quality correlates with the concept of creativity described by Wolin and Wolin (1993).

Other personality characteristics seen in resilient people include adaptive distancing, empathy, and a sense of mission (Norman, Turner, and Zunz 1994). Barbara had the capacity to adaptively distance herself from her mother, but it was not absolute, especially at the beginning of her treatment. From early childhood she had perceived clearly that her mother had problems, and also that she was different from her mother. For one thing, she did not become an alcoholic. However, she sometimes believed that she was destined to become sexually promiscuous as her mother had been in her youth.

Empathy can be seen in Barbara's excellent parenting abilities, as well as in her caring and concern for people with serious troubles and the elderly. After moving into the apartment her neighbor was a 90-year-old widow who lived alone. Barbara empathized with this elderly woman's loneliness and isolation, and visited her as often as possible. When her granddaughter was born she took the baby to visit the neighbor, in order to brighten her day. Barbara took care of the baby as often as she could, both to help her daughter and because of her love for the baby. As Higgins (1994) observes about resilient people, through her attunement and connection with others Barbara indirectly nurtured herself.

Connected with Barbara's capacity to empathize was her sense of mission, a quality closely related to the "morality" that the Wolins describe as "the activity of an informed conscience" (Wolin and Wolin 1993:184). The Wolins maintain that morality derives from the resilient person's desire to respond to the suffering of others. And Barbara's morality, or sense of mission, derived additional impetus from her religious convictions. These had been inculcated by Aunt Mary in her childhood, and reinforced her resilience as an adult. While her religious beliefs caused her pain at times (when they translated into guilt and thoughts about punishment for sins), it is also true that faith impelled her to try her best to understand and help others.

Norman, Turner, and Zunz (1994) report on a number of protective factors that have been found in the backgrounds of resilient young people. The factor that seems to be most important is a warm, positive relationship with a caring adult, one who is not necessarily a parent but who may be a caretaker. From the age of six Barbara had a warm positive relationship with Aunt Mary. Her aunt, in turn, provided a number of other protective qualities. She had high expectations of her grandniece in terms of appropriate behavior and positive character traits; she modeled resilience for Barbara because she herself was a resilient person; she built into Barbara's life certain traditions and rituals, such as attending church every Sunday. Finally, her willingness to take the responsibility for raising Barbara exemplifies the extended family support network that is so often found to promote a person's ability to bounce back in the face of adversity.

Treatment

Even when the overriding objective of treatment is to foster resilience, the therapist must begin by establishing an empathic holding environment (Higgins 1994) and helping the client to "name the damage" (Wolin and Wolin 1993). The first stage of Barbara's therapy required the establishment of what Herman (1992) terms a healing relationship and a place of safety, within which it would be possible to bear witness to the trauma that she had experienced in childhood. Barbara began by describing her current situation, including the financial crisis and her own depression. Then, tentatively, and with careful scrutiny of the therapist's reactions, she related the story of her neglect and abandonment by her mother, and her rescue by Aunt Mary. After a few weeks she disclosed the sexual abuse by her cousins, and the earlier recollections of being present when her mother was having sex. The therapist's goal was to establish an atmosphere of openness and trust, in order to help contain her most unbearable memories. Barbara acknowledged that the only other person who knew the full story of her childhood was her husband, and he never felt comfortable discussing it with her.

As it became clear that Barbara had decided to trust the therapist with her most shameful secrets, it seemed important that the issue of racial difference be dealt with in the same spirit of openness, especially since one of the aspects of her low self-esteem was her feeling that she was unattractive and "too dark," as her mother had said. Initially she insisted that she felt quite comfortable with a white therapist and with white people generally; indeed, she maintained that black people had been the ones to hurt her the most in her life. The lifestyle she had chosen — living, working, and raising her children in a predominantly white environment — seemed to bear this out. However, it soon emerged that matters were more complicated. Early in the treatment a fortuitous occurrence led ultimately to the strengthening of the therapeutic alliance. The therapist had inadvertently double booked, and found Barbara in the waiting room along with another client, a child around 10 years old. Barbara agreed to wait until the child's session was over, but she looked sad when she entered the office. When this was explored, she tearfully admitted that she could not help but wonder whether she would have been asked to wait if she were white.

The subject of race was revisited at many points throughout the treatment, strengthening the therapeutic alliance. Barbara's internalized racism was traced to her early abandonment by her mother. In addition, Barbara and the therapist discussed contemporary attitudes about race, such as prevailing images of beauty portrayed in the media. The therapist humorously commented that the "black is beautiful" movement seemed to have passed Barbara by, and she laughingly agreed. Only later did she begin to reveal her deep attachment to her heritage and her community, in terms of food, music, customs, and other aspects of African American culture.

The treatment utilized a variety of traditional techniques: expressive, supportive, reflective, and cognitive. The establishment of a safe place within which Barbara could tell her story provided the foundation for the progress that she made. Gradually, with the therapist's continued empathy and understanding, as well as explanations about the origins of her shame, guilt, anger, and low self-esteem, Barbara was able to empathize with herself as a child and as a young adult (Pine 1985; Mishne 1993). This was a slow process and one with many setbacks along the way. The therapist utilized cognitive techniques to help Barbara understand the impact of trauma on a young person. Barbara and the therapist speculated about the impact of abandonment and abuse on a hypothetical young child. Gradually Barbara was able to comprehend that she was turning her feeling of badness onto herself instead of onto her parents, as children are inclined to do. Her rage had turned inward in the form of excessive guilt (Higgins 1994).

The question of her guilt also required that the religious aspect of her self-destructive ruminations be addressed. Here again the therapist used reflective as well as cognitive techniques, drawing upon Barbara's good intellect. She and Barbara considered the following questions: Is adultery the worst sin? For example, is it worse than murder? Are "bad" people always punished in this life and "good" ones always rewarded? Why would God single Barbara out for special suffering? Does she not have positive qualities, and has she not performed many good and charitable acts, that counterbalance the "sins"? Finally, the therapist asked Barbara to think about how God might judge her if she caused her own death by omitting to care for herself, and caused her family to suffer.

After the first six months of treatment, the focus shifted to the strengths/resiliency perspective (Saleebey 1997). The therapist explained the concept of resilience to Barbara, pointing out how many of the personality characteristics of resilient people she did possess. Her situation was thus reframed (Wolin and Wolin 1993) to highlight her strengths. She was a survivor, not a victim, and she had always demonstrated self-efficacy. In particular, the young married woman who sought love outside her marriage was reframed: rather than being "bad," she had been lonely, and took action (however misguided) on her own behalf. Gradually Barbara began to view herself in a different light.

The therapist also pointed out that Barbara, like many resilient people (Higgins 1994), internalized her pain rather than inflicting it on others. To the contrary, her relationships with her children and grandchild were exemplary; she somehow possessed the "alternative imagination" (Higgins, 1994: 191) to nurture others despite a severe lack of nurturing in her own early life. Similarly, despite the lack of kindness so often shown to her, she never failed to be kind and considerate toward others, especially those in need. She remained a caring wife, notwithstanding the deficiencies in her marriage. Using the paradigm of Wolin and Wolin (1993), the therapist demonstrated to Barbara that her qualities in the areas of relationship, initiative, humor, and morality indicated her resiliency. This was surely the way she had survived and flourished in the face of such adversity, and would continue to do so.

The therapist determined that Barbara's strengths could be drawn upon to shore up those areas in which she was relatively weak. Her realistic appraisal of the environment, along with her ability to connect and form relationships (with her family, her physician, and the therapist), eventually led her to take her anti-hypertensive medication regularly, as well as to follow the physician's advice regarding her ulcer. Similarly, Barbara's capacity for adaptive distancing varied. Not only did she feel at times that she was destined to follow in her mother's footsteps and be promiscuous, she frequently suffered feelings of rejection as a result of both her mother's and her father's behavior towards her. Here again her powerful sense of realism was an invaluable asset. She eventually recognized, on a more consistent basis, that her own life was very different from her mother's, and that she had made entirely different choices. She also became better able to accept that both her parents had severe limitations, none of which were of her making, and to experience their indifference and rejection in a more detached manner.

Higgins (1994) recommends that the therapist who works with a resilient survivor needs to let the person know how much they have accomplished, and suggests that open caring in the treatment situation is not out of place. With Barbara, the therapist essentially adopted this strategy, especially in the latter phases of treatment. The therapist expressed admiration of her resilience and emphasized a fact that she already knew, namely that she might well have turned to alcohol or drugs to alleviate her pain. Instead she kept this pain inside, remained alcohol- and drug-free, and showed care for others. In particular the therapist reinforced the value of Barbara's wonderful sense of humor. Initially she had presented her humor as simply a pretense, "laughing on the outside while crying on the inside," with the emphasis on the negative. The therapist, however, not only appreciated her jokes, but also underlined the value of the ability to experience fun and joy when life was difficult. Rather than portraying her sense of humor as an escape, as Barbara tended to do, the therapist stressed its value as a life affirming attribute that cheered up both herself and others.

Ongoing Issues

Most writers agree that resilience is not synonymous with an absence of pain. Resilient survivors may continue to suffer anxiety or depression, but they are characterized by their "devotion to a humane model" (Higgins 1994: 130). Although they are resilient, they may not be exemplary (Wolin and Wolin 1993). The traumas they have lived through may always cause them discomfort, in the way that healed scars may hurt at times. Despite her capacity for connectedness, Barbara suffered from a deep sense of loneliness in childhood that continued into adulthood. This loneliness may never be totally assuaged. Similarly, although Barbara experienced a dramatic diminution of the symptoms that originally brought her to treatment, in the future she might be vulnerable to reoccurrences of depression or anxiety. In all likelihood, however, the gains made in therapy will help to render these episodes shorter, less severe, or both.

Higgins (1994) reminds us that resilience is not a product, but a continuous process. Barbara will continue to confront challenges in her life which in turn will challenge her resilience. On the other hand, positive developments can occur throughout the life cycle. The treatment experience was one of growth, in which Barbara learned to value herself for her strengths instead of merely focusing on what she regarded as her weaknesses. Her self-esteem did improve, and accordingly she felt less alienated and better able to reach out to others. Increasingly she began to see the "glass is half full" rather than the "glass is half empty," as she internalized both the therapist's regard for her and the inescapable evidence of her resilience.

References

Herman, J. 1992. *Trauma and Recovery.* New York: Basic Books.

Higgins, G. 1994. *Resilient Adults: Overcoming a Cruel Past.* San Francisco: Jossey-Bass.

Mishne, J. 1993. *The Evolution and Application of Clinical Theory: Perspectives from the Four Psychologies*. New York: The Free Press.

Norman, E., S, Turner, and S. Zunz. 1994. *Substance Abuse Prevention: A Review of the Literature*. New York: New York State Office of Alcohol and Substance Abuse Services.

Pine, F. 1985. *Developmental Theory and Clinical Process*. New Haven: Yale University Press.

Saleebey, D. 1997. *The Strengths Perspective in Social Work Practice*. New York: Addison Wesley Longman.

Wolin, S. J. and S. Wolin. 1993. *The Resilient Self: How Survivors of Troubled Families Rise Above Adversity*. New York: Villard.

6   Women's Resilience at Midlife: What Is It? How Do You Mobilize It?

Sharon McQuaide

By midlife, at least for most of us, our resilience has already been put to the test. We have seen ourselves attempt to cope with the challenges and losses of childhood and young adulthood. We have seen ourselves attempt to cope with the imperfections of the world. We have seen ourselves wrestling with the demons within. Our experience with abuse, joy, children, anger, fear, discrimination, money, men, women, love, hate, sorrow, work, food, physical vulnerability, mortality — to name just a few of the phenomena that have made us who we now are — is broad and deep. By midlife, women are experts on survival and resilience.

This paper reviews the factors associated with women's ability to cope successfully and to create a sense of well-being in the face of stress. I will also elaborate a social constructivist model of the process of enhancing resilience, and present a clinical case.

Normative Development, Midlife Experience, and Resilience

The most influential theorists in conceptualizing midlife have been Jung, Jaques (who coined the term "midlife crisis"), Erickson, Vaillant, and Levinson. Their writings suggest that midlife resilience — defined as the ability to meet personal and social challenges and hardships adaptively — is related to having a sense of generativity and giving to future generations (Erikson 1950); to being able to accept one's age, find meaning and purpose, and not yearn for the activities of youth (Jung 1930/1981); to having resolved the fear of death (Jaques 1965); to loosening up and seizing one more chance of rebirth (Vaillant 1977); and to forming a realistic and individuated picture of one's self and the world (Levinson 1978, 1996).

The theoretical and empirical literature focusing specifically on women is much thinner. Heilbrun (1988) contends that meaningful work is critical to a woman's well being as she ages. Apter (1995), one of the few scholars to examine the actual experience of women in midlife, found their greatest challenge to be integrating the images of being female that were formed in adolescence with the experience of being a midlife woman. In addition, she found that a woman's most important insight at midlife was to discover that she could, at last, listen to her own voice. A counterculture of women friends was also found to protect women from the effects of devaluation. Other studies of women in midlife (Greer 1992; Sheehey 1992) focus primarily on menopause, leading to constructions of women's midlife experience that are biologically oriented and that subjugate other aspects of a woman's experience.

The literature on resilience and on coping with stress provides potential insight into other factors that might be associated with successful passage through midlife. Pearlin and Schooler (1978) point to a correlation between coping well and low self-denigration, high self-esteem, and high self-effectance. Self-in-relation theorists (Miller 1976) emphasize the importance to women's identity of having connections with others. O'Connell Higgins (1994) found resilient adults to be proactive, loving, and possessing faith and vision. Other researchers have identified the importance of a friendship network or having a confidante to women's emotional health (Baruch and Brooks-Gunn 1984). Studies of temperament indicate that traits such as an "easy disposition" and an optimistic outlook, which are stable and consistent over the life cycle, are also associated with resilience (Wolin and Wolin 1993). These qualities may also contribute to a woman's midlife satisfaction.

My own research on women at midlife (McQuaide 1998a) found that women who were most resilient and coped well in this stage of life were not isolated from others and did not feel marginal. They were healthy, had good self-esteem, low self-denigration, high feelings of self-effectance, felt they had the right to a life, and did not have a harsh superego.

A Social Constructivist View of the Relationship Between Resilience and Vulnerability

All of the writers cited implicitly share a model in which resilience is defined as characteristics that mitigate the effects of internal and external stress

(Norman, Turner, and Zunz 1994:103). Clinicians working from a strengths perspective would target the identification and development of these resiliency factors in treatment.

Another possible approach, which is based on the related but distinct notions of "multiple selves," of "self-schemas" or "self-narratives," and of "deconstruction," suggests a somewhat more complex approach to resiliency and its enhancement. Such a perspective would take the following form:

1. *The self is not unitary, but multiple.* Each of us consists not of a single self, but of a confederacy of selves (Markus and Nurius 1986; Parry and Doan 1994). The various selves are elicited or triggered in different situations. Some selves are more resilient than others. A person may have a resilient self that dominates when dealing with work challenges and a more vulnerable self that dominates when faced with dealing with a dying parent.

2. *Not all of our selves are equally available, and each of our many selves is itself complex.* One might imagine the self as a set of Russian stacking dolls. Within each doll (self) may be a hierarchy of progressively more deeply buried dolls (selves), containing alternative modes of response to the given situation (or, to use slightly different language, containing a different self-narrative or a different construction of the self in the situation).

3. *Each of these various selves has its own self-narrative.* The different ways a person can story her life (her self-narratives) can be sources of strength and resilience or sources of weakness and vulnerability.

> Most of us have a multiplicity of stories available to us about ourselves, about others, and about our relationships. Some of these stories promote competence and wellness. Others serve to constrain, trivialize, disqualify, or otherwise pathologize ourselves, others, and relationships. Still others can be reassuring, uplifting, liberating, revitalizing, or healing. The particular story that prevails or dominates in giving meaning to the events of our lives determines the nature of our lived experience. When a problem-saturated story predominates, we are repeatedly invited into disappointment and misery.   (White and Epston 1990:x)

The image of the set of Russian dolls helps us recall that any given person is a complex mix of vulnerabilities and resiliencies. At different times and in different situations she may have greater or lesser access to the various selves (or various selves may be elicited or triggered). Yet in any situation, all of the other selves, no matter how deeply buried in the Russian doll, are at least potentially present and have the potential to be elicited if conditions are right.

In the therapeutic relationship we try to create conditions of safety so that the various selves can come forth, so the worker and client can expand the role the preferred selves play in the client's narrative.

4. *These multiple (and differentially accessible) self-narratives are socially constructed.* While they depend on our individual experience, they are controlled by the dominant discourse of one's culture. If one's culture is ageist and sexist, at least some of one's personal narratives cannot but reflect the selves' internalization of that ageism and sexism. Freedman and Combs, drawing from Foucault, write that "we tend to internalize the dominant narratives of our culture, easily believing that they speak the truth of our identities" (1996:39). For oppressed populations, strength- and resilience-centered self-narratives may become "subjugated," while the socially dominant vulnerability-centered narratives may be privileged. For example, a woman's culturally influenced self-narrative might see herself primarily as over the hill, unattractive, osteoporotic, tortured by the empty nest, and likely to be left for a younger partner. Her understandable response would be insecurity, weakness, and vulnerability. An alternative personal midlife narrative would emphasize freedom, competence, the power of knowledge, and feelings of being in the prime of life. This latter narrative may be threatening to those women empowered by the culturally dominant discourse that advantages vulnerability and a sense of helplessness.

5. *The culturally dominant discourse not only helps determine the construction of our self-narratives, but enters into the processes of accessing various selves, as well.* It blinds us to some of our possible self-narratives, makes them less available, while privileging other self-narratives.

> Using terminology from Foucault, people tend to become "docile bodies" under "the internalized gaze" of those who control the discourses of power in our culture. Thus, the dominant narratives tend to blind us to the possibilities that other narratives might offer us.
>
> (Freedman and Combs 1996:39)

Foucault encourages us to look at which groups are diminished by a particular discourse and which are empowered. "What alternative knowledges are disqualified and what persons or groups of persons are likely to be diminished?" (White and Epston 1990:23).

6. *The insidious effects of the dominant culture's language ("over the hill," "has been") and narrative of women in midlife cannot be underestimated or overlooked.* The culture's dominant story is not in the best interests of older

women, and an important resiliency factor is a woman's ability to story her life in a way that privileges alternative knowledge of aging and women. From this perspective, one could see the culturally dominant narrative as a risk factor for any oppressed group — women, racial and ethnic minorities, gays and lesbians, the disabled, the aged, the poor. The ability of a woman (or a person of color, a gay or lesbian person, a disabled person, a poor person) to deconstruct the culture's dominant narrative of who she is and to privilege alternative, "subjugated" narratives then represents a major resilience factor — perhaps the most important. For example, it is hard to imagine that an African American woman could have full self-esteem or lack self-denigration if she accepted the dominant discourse of what it means to be a person of color in this society.

7. *From the perspective of the therapist, to focus exclusively, even with the best intentions, on client vulnerability or pathology (the vulnerable selves) is to participate in a process of subjugation — the subjugation of the resilient selves.* Although the midlife client may not bring up ageism as a specific problem, the problems she does bring up occur in the context of a dominant discourse of ageism and sexism (and, in specific cases, of racism, heterosexism, etc., as well).

> There is always the ubiquity of power pervading all human interaction, such that significant narratives are subjugated to serve the dominant discourse, which comes to define a culture and maintain the status quo. Power operates more like a capillary system that pervades the body than like a sovereign ruling over other people. Its role in families is at least as effective in maintaining the status quo as is the state itself. Power's methods of surveillance and of accumulating information allow it to know all and to see all. As such, it can afford to be benevolent, for it is singularly adept at enlisting the cooperation and even the collaboration of the subjugated in their own subjugation.   (Parry and Doan 1994:17)

Focusing primarily on client vulnerability or pathology is participating in this "benevolent" process, which is actually subjugation. The culture's dominant discourse about women has not empowered women. The mental health field's dominant discourse has privileged pathology over strength, rather than privileging the coexistence of resilience interacting with vulnerability. This would lead clients to story their lives around their experience of vulnerability rather than resilience. In reality, we humans show a complex interaction of vulnerable and resilient selves and traits.

8. *The ability to deconstruct individually and culturally destructive self-nar-*

ratives and construct alternatives can be seen as a "meta-resilience" factor that allows for all of the other resilience factors such as self-esteem, self-effectance, the ability to form authentic intimate connections, the ability to be proactive, and the ability to accept one's age. There are two major components to this meta-resilience. Meta-resiliency involves the ability to perceive that a given presentation of self, a given construction of the world, is only one of many that are possible, that there may be others. It also involves the ability to identify the personally and socially harmful forces embedded in a particular presentation of self or construction of experience. This represents the ability to repudiate harmful selves, to deconstruct self-destructive self-narratives. Second is the ability to believe one has the right to construct alternative narratives, to bring into the foreground subjugated knowledge which represents one's experience in a more authentic way (McQuaide 1998b).

9. *The goal of the therapy, then, is to help the client deconstruct her prevailing narratives, to open the "Russian doll" to uncover the other, stronger selves, to author alternative self stories or privilege previously subjugated knowledge of a woman's midlife experience.*

A Narrative in Progress: Carol's Story

Carol, a 53-year-old woman currently being seen in therapy, felt at a dead end. After living with a deep depression for years, she made the decision to come into treatment when she saw a description for a women's group that described "becoming more empowered" as one of the group's goals. Seeing the word "empowerment" activated a long-buried hopeful self that envisioned a more empowered future for herself. Carol called me to inquire about the group.

White suggests that people come into therapy when the dominant narratives of the culture prevent them from living out their preferred alternative narrative or when

> the person is actively participating in the performance of stories that she finds unhelpful, unsatisfying, and dead-ended, and that these stories do not sufficiently encapsulate the person's lived experience or are very significantly contradicted by important aspects of the person's lived experience.
> (Freedman and Combs 1996:39)

That is, therapy appears as an option when there is an awareness, however dim and fleeting, that an alternative, more authentic, less socially conforming, self-narrative might be possible.

On the telephone, prior to beginning therapy, the conflict between Carol's vulnerable selves and her more resilient selves was played out. She talked about her intense mistrust of people ("Even my best friend, I discovered, was having an affair with my husband"); about the comforting solidarity she had experienced once while working on a group project; about her bad experience with another therapist ("I was so down I was barely surviving and he asked me what was I going to *do* about it . . . He tried to undermine my religion when that was all I had."); and about her recognition that at midlife she needed to learn to trust again and try to fix her problems, or her life would have lacked meaning and purpose. Seeing the announcement for a women's group had awakened a desire for, in her words, "fellowship and bonding with others" that she had known in the past but that she had no longer been able to trust.

I met with Carol to begin to hear her story in person. Her three children were grown and no longer needed her the way they had. Married for 27 years to a man who constantly criticized and belittled her, she had experienced much emotional and physical abuse. She had no friends or confidantes. As a child, she said, her mother would beat her "out of the blue" for no apparent reason. She also remembers being sexually abused by her brother.

A Seventh Day Adventist, Carol described her religion as authoritarian and herself as God-fearing. Believing that it was a betrayal to discuss marital problems, her religion, although a potential protective factor, was actually maintaining her tolerance of abuse. It was a woman's duty, she believed, to obey and serve her husband and children. Carol's husband had had countless affairs, and Carol had contracted sexually transmitted diseases from him during the course of her marriage. A current pressure she was under was feeling guilty for not agreeing to her husband's request to participate in wife swapping arrangements. His temper and loss of physical control kept Carol constantly frightened and submissive to her husband "to protect the children." She described the nausea she felt when she saw her husband and son — now grown and living on his own — fist fighting. Carol storied the problem with her husband as a communication problem. "If we could communicate better the marriage will be fixed and my life can start up again." As if a dam had finally collapsed, the problems she endured gushed out.

In the narrative told by her vulnerable self, I heard internalized sexism ("My husband's word is law"), ageism ("I have to dress seductively so my husband doesn't run off with a younger woman," "I know I'm supposed to have empty nest syndrome now that my kids don't need me"), self-denigration ("I can't do anything right"), and low self-esteem ("I don't even feel like a person; I feel like a living entity"). Her narrative privileged no strength that she would tell me about. She saw herself purely as a victim and could not see ways in which she had fought back or what her survival mechanisms had been or had taught her. Her vulnerability-saturated narrative was her dominant narrative and any alternative knowledge of herself was subjugated.

As Carol told it, this was a story of woe, almost totally unmitigated by any sunshine. Lacking many of the protective factors and sources of resiliency, she seemed at risk of having her midlife years be unhappy ones. But yet a part of her self had a secret story of something different, or she would not have been so intrigued and haunted by the word "power," nor called for and kept our appointment. Inside one of the Russian dolls was some kind of dream of a happier future, mastery over the past, and alteration in her marriage. I hoped that we could enlarge the role that this optimism played in her story.

As a feminist, I wondered how I could work well with her. Would I want my narrative to dominate her narrative about women and midlife? Would I judge her for staying in a relationship that appeared so oppressive and abusive? Where was there resilience to elicit, to enhance? I could sense much anger in her and had already seen signs of the powerless person's passive-aggressive ways of fighting back. I knew I had difficulty with these traits. My countertransference vulnerabilities were being activated and I would need to consult a colleague to keep my own therapeutic resilience.

Our work proceeded along the lines of the narrative therapy outlined by Freedman and Combs (1996). We moved from a phase of joining and listening to a phase of deconstructing problematic narratives. In these early phases of treatment, "facilitating resilience is more a matter of orientation than explicit intervention" (O'Connell Higgins 1994:319). In addition to the basic model of Freedman and Combs I used the Midlife Coping Questionnaire (McQuaide 1998c). It is a scale that I created to give me some information quickly. I use it periodically throughout my work with clients to track changes that we might not have a chance to get to in session.

Joining and Listening

I listened to Carol's problem-saturated, vulnerability-privileging narrative as empathically, nonjudgmentally and nondirectively as possible. Since she had been so controlled by others, I was careful to have her not experience me as being controlling. Carol wanted her story of vulnerability to be heard and understood. Deliberately, I did not, at this stage, rush to remind her of strengths or point out strengths that I was seeing (such as the strength of trying to trust me). This would not have validated the vulnerable self who was, by speaking out at last, allying itself with a stronger, more resilient self. For Carol, paradoxically, giving voice to her vulnerability was itself an act of resilience, the most she was capable of at this early point. She had also let me know, in her criticism of the therapist who had asked her what she was going to do about her problems, that she was not yet ready to take action beyond consulting with a social worker. For now she just wanted her story to be heard.

Joining was hard at times for me since her narrative of herself was so consonant with the culture's dominant discourse about aging women. Within Carol's narrative was much devaluation of older women, acceptance of the appropriateness of compliance with the demands of her husband and her church, and a total lack of assertion of her rights or needs. She was plastic to the will of others and felt that as a mother, wife, and older woman that was the way God wanted it. Getting in touch with areas of my life where I felt more powerless than I actually was helped me to identify with her so that I was able to join with her more empathically.

Deconstructing

Having her story heard and understood, and beginning to feel safe with me, prepared Carol to begin questioning her story. Somewhat freed from having to defend her story, Carol could now entertain alternative stories. Listening to her narrative had shown me both her vulnerable selves and the merest hint of her resilient selves, as well as how the different sides got along with each other. The timing was now right for me to ask questions that could reveal previously buried resilient selves and illuminate subjugated narratives, ones that were less problem-saturated.

The stage of deconstructive questioning begins the process of resiliency enhancement. "Every time we ask a question, we're generating a possible version of life," comments David Epston. For the narrative therapist questions are asked "to generate experience rather than to gather information. When they generate experience of preferred realities, questions can be therapeutic in and of themselves" (Freedman and Combs 1996:113). Hopefully, the preferred realities are resiliency enhancing.

> Deconstruction questions help people unpack their stories or see them from different perspectives, so that how they have been constructed becomes apparent. Many deconstruction questions encourage people to sit-

uate their narratives in larger systems and through time. In bringing forth the history, context, and effects of people's narratives, we are broadening their scope, depicting entire landscapes that support problems.

(Freedman and Combs 1996:120)

Within these broader landscapes more strengths can be brought forth.

Carol's problem was externalized so that she would see the problem as the problem and not herself, as a person, to be a problem (White and Epston 1990). One way I do this is to actually keep unstacked Russian stacking dolls on a table in my office. Depending on the topic being discussed (marital issues, childhood abuse) I ask which size doll best represented her vulnerable self and which her resilient self. Once the dolls have been identified we discuss them and may even talk to them. For example, I might ask after pointing to the doll she has identified as her resilient self, "Today, could we just spend some time talking about this side of you — the side of you that can feel strong when you are facing your husband when he is angry. What is bringing out your resilient self?" (If "resilient" is not a familiar word for the client I use the word "strong.") Other questions might be:

- What does this resilient self feel like?
- Can you get in touch with this self now? What does this self look like?
- When is this self a strength? When a liability?
- What happens to your resilient self when your vulnerability is triggered?
- What would you like to have your resilient self do when your vulnerability is triggered?
- Could you describe for me what life you could imagine if your resilient self was always able to take good care of your vulnerable self?
- Can you tell me what you would like about such a life and what you might not like?
- What is the story of your life (and future) that your vulnerable self tells?
- What is the story of your life (and future) that your resilient self tells?
- If you could talk to this resilient (or vulnerable) self, what would you say?

The questioning has given Carol new perspectives and has opened space for insight to occur, a process Carol has described as being like "connecting the dots. Before it seemed like all these things had happened to me but they were isolated events — individual nightmares that were not connected to each other. Now I see the patterns and connections." She now sees the individual nightmare, the night surrounding the nightmare, the way she tried to wake herself up from the nightmare, and the way the nightmare was altered or not altered. Now we would work on seeing the day, and then on how the day and night flow together.

Reconstruction of Preferred Narrative

This is the stage in which Carol and I are now working. She is authoring her life very differently, privileging her own voice much more than the voice of her husband, the church, or her culture, as she constructs a new individuated narrative. We have discussed some of the resiliency factors that could have a protective effect on her future (self-esteem, a counterculture of women friends, meaningful work) and she is interested in bringing these into her life.

To be made real the new preferred narrative of resilience must be performed. Clients (and therapists) need the reassurance of seeing that the insights they have in session can be translated into action and behavioral change. Right now in our work, much anger has been unleashed. Consequently, feeling less depressed, Carol has been working on finding ways to channel this anger constructively. One channel has been volunteering at the Women's Center, helping women. This is building self-confidence, giving her a sense of purpose and meaning, and providing opportunities to build connections. Aware now that other women, for cultural as well as for personal reasons, have shared her experience of having their power subjugated, she says "Now I want to champion all women."

In the past she felt that her narrative had to be the story of protectiveness and submission. To keep her children safe she had to comply with her husband's demands, and suffer physical abuse. Her children are now grown and do not need her in that way. The empty nest she now experiences not as a crisis but as an opportunity to construct a new story of what her life can be. Previously subjugated ambivalence about her marriage and about her religion are beginning to emerge. She now calls her preferred narrative "the story of getting it together. Of being a whole person. Not just the battered entity that was alive but not living."

Having many different sides to her personality, or many different selves, means that a woman at midlife has a variety of different stories she could tell about who she is. The story she chooses will determine her lived experience to a large extent. Life stories can be organized in ways that predominantly privilege vulnerability or predominantly privilege resilience, or in ways that integrate both the vulnerable and the resilient.

The importance of being able to construct a personal narrative that privileges a woman's unique experience, and not just the culture's dominant discourse regarding aging women, is a major resiliency factor. Currently, Carol is deconstructing both her own personal narrative and the culturally dominant one. Her narratives are expanding to include previously subjugated knowledge. This expansion of new knowledge will, it is hoped, continue to allow for the expression of her inner strengths and for a deeper appreciation of women in general. Since starting her work in therapy her life has blossomed.

I would like to end with a metaphor used by Milton Erikson, a therapist of enormous resilience who struggled for most of his life with polio. Erickson was well known for believing that every individual had, in the unconscious, a vast storehouse of resources, learning, and solutions—everything that would ever be needed to solve the problems encountered in life. In addition he believed that we have internal maps that we follow in life (Lankton and Lankton 1983). On these internal maps are roads that take us to the inner resources that we need to deal with life. However, sometimes our maps lack the roads needed to take us to the resources that are inside of us and that we currently need. Or we use roads that take us repeatedly not to our inner resources but to our vulnerabilities.

Our work with clients involves unblocking and building roads to the resilience that is already inside of them that, for whatever reason, they are not able to access; putting up danger signs and detour signs on the roads that go to places that make clients vulnerable; and keeping the green light on when the client is headed in their preferred direction.

References

Apter, T. 1995. *Secret Paths: Women in the New Midlife*. New York: Norton.

Baruch, G. and J. Brooks-Gunn. 1984. *Women in Midlife*. New York: Plenum.

Erikson, E. H. 1950. *Childhood and Society*. New York: Norton.

Freedman, J. and G. Combs. 1996. *Narrative Therapy: The Social Construction of Preferred Realities*. New York: Norton.

Greer, G. 1992. *The Change: Women, Aging, and the Menopause*. New York: Knopf.

Heilbrun, C. G. 1988. *Writing a Woman's Life*. New York: Ballantine Books.

Jaques, E. 1965. Death and the mid-life crisis. *International Journal of Psychoanalysis* 46:502–514.

Jung, C. G. 1930, reprinted 1983. The stages of life. In A. Storr, ed., *The Essential Jung*. Princeton: Princeton University Press.

Lankton, S. R. and C. H. Lankton. 1983. *The Answer Within: A Clinical Framework of Ericksonian Hypnotherapy*. New York: Brunner Mazel.

Levinson, D. J. 1978. *The Seasons of a Man's Life*. New York: Knopf.

Levinson, D. J. 1996. *The Seasons of a Woman's Life*. New York: Knopf.

Markus, H. and P. Nurius. 1986. Possible selves. *American Psychologist* 41:954–969.

McQuaide, S. 1998a. Women at midlife. *Social Work*, 43 (1): 21–31.

McQuaide, S. 1998b. Opening space for alternative images and narratives of midlife women. *Clinical Social Work Journal* 26 (1): 39–53.

McQuaide, S. 1998c. Discontent at midlife: Issues and consequences in working toward women's wellbeing. *Families in Society* 79 (5): 532–42.

Miller, J. B. 1976. *Toward a New Psychology of Women*. Boston: Beacon Press.

Norman, E., S. Turner, and S. Zunz. 1994. *Substance Abuse Prevention: A Review of the Literature*. New York: New York State Office of Alcohol and Substance Abuse Services.

O'Connell Higgins, G. 1994. *Resilient Adults: Overcoming a Cruel Past*. San Francisco: Jossey Bass.

Parry, A. and R. E. Doan. 1994. *Story Re-visions: Narrative Therapy in the Postmodern World*. New York: Guilford Press.

Pearlin, L. I. and C. Schooler. 1978. The structure of coping. *Journal of Health and Social Behavior* 19:2–21.

Sheehy, G. 1992. *The Silent Passage*. New York: Random House.

Vaillant, G. E. 1977. *Adaptation to Life*. Boston: Little, Brown.

White, M. and D. Epston. 1990. *Narrative Means to Therapeutic Ends*. New York: Norton.

Wolin, S. J. and S. Wolin. 1993. *The Resilient Self: How Survivors of Troubled Families Rise Above Adversity*. New York: Villard Books.

7 Grasping Life: Five Stories of Will-Filled Men

Raymond Fox

Recounted here are the stories of five men seen individually in a clinical practice: Barry, a 26-year-old dancer from America's heartland, who was victimized through incest as a child; Tyle, a 27-year-old African American, alcoholic "cocaine investor" who was raised in dire poverty in the inner city; Innis, a 30-year-old Russian immigrant gay priest who had been brutally abused as a child; Brad, a 26-year-old former Olympic swimmer; and Ramon, a 30-year-old Latino infected with AIDS. Each of these men, resilient in his own way, overcame fierce obstacles, not the least of which were multiple suicide attempts. Their personal and career achievements — indeed, their very survival — were made without the factors considered key in the professional literature for the development of resiliency and empowerment: family, school, peer, and community support.

What accounts for their success? For their resiliency? What factors within the clinical process fostered their recognizing and building upon their strengths and resiliency? While there are no sure answers, various themes, patterns, and clues arising from intensive work with these men may help explain the elusive concept of resiliency and the means for clinicians to locate, nourish, and enhance it. While these men possess varying degrees of intellect, humor, and adaptive distancing, none of these factors — either alone or in combination — satisfactorily explains their success. This paper explores the possible role of a transcending factor, one that the professional literature seldom mentions, and then only to disparage it: Will.

An attempt was made to track down these men to garner their retrospective, post-therapy, reflections on what they believe constitutes their resiliency

and what treatment approaches contributed to their growth. Four of them —
Brad, Ramon, Tyle, Barry — were reached. Each spoke briefly, though
thoughtfully, poignantly, and deeply about his life and his therapy. Their reflections speak to the spirit of human capacity and possibility, courage, and
will.

Resiliency: Theory and Research

Research evidence (Beardslee 1989; Harvey 1996; Moran and Eckenrode
1992; Rutter 1987, 1990) indicates that a sustained perception of one's own
worth, coupled with confidence that one can "successfully cope with life's
challenges" (Rutter 1990:206) result in resilience. Rutter suggests that exposure to risk may have either a devastating or a steeling effect. He argues that
vulnerability and protective factors are, in essence, two sides of the same
coin. Resiliency results from the interaction between risk and protective factors. The key to the development of resiliency is not in avoiding risk, but
rather in accommodating to it successfully. Rutter identifies four primary
processes that operate as mediators or moderators of risk: the reduction of risk
impact, the reduction of negative chain events, the establishment of self-esteem and self-efficacy, and opportunity.

In their recent study of resilience in adults with histories of childhood sexual abuse, Liem, James, O'Toole, and Boudewyn (1997) found that resilient
individuals feel the capacity to bring about desired outcomes, tend less towards chronic self-destructiveness, possess an internal locus of control, and
assume that people and situations are controllable rather than resulting from
inevitable and impersonal external forces.

Although resiliency may change over time (Herrenkohl, Herrenkohl, and
Egolf 1994), it is generally conceived of as a fairly stable set of characteristics
related to managing well in the face of risk factors. It is also defined as the capacity "to prevail, grow, be strong, and even thrive despite hardship" (Wolin
1991:3).

Resiliency is often used interchangeably with "invulnerability." Invulnerability describes the ability of an individual to maintain his or her personal
integrity in the presence of risk, while resiliency refers more inclusively to
the ability to recover from stress or risk and resume the same or higher level
of functioning. Perhaps the most inclusive definition of resiliency come from
Garmezy (1994) who views it as the skills, abilities, knowledge, and insight

that accumulate over time as the individual struggles to surmount adversity and meet challenges. It is an ongoing and ever developing fund of energy and skill that can be mobilized in current situations.

Saleebey, while not directly addressing resiliency, echoes Rutter. He states that "trauma and abuse, illness and struggle may be injurious . . . they may also be sources of challenge and opportunity" (Saleebey 1997:23). He believes that every individual, group, family, and community has strengths. Trauma is not predictive; it may weaken or strengthen the individual. Resilience is not seen by Saleebey as a trait or static dimension. Instead, it

> is the continuing articulation of capacities and knowledge derived through the interplay of risks and protections in the world. The environment continually presents demands, stresses, challenges, and opportunities. These become fateful, given a complexity of other factors — genetic, neurobiological, familial, communal — for the development of strength, of resilience, or of diminution in capacity.   (Saleebey 1996:299)

Individuals are the experts of their own lives and they have continual possibilities for choice, control, commitment, and personal development (Saleebey 1996:298). Mills (1991) proposes that everyone has the innate capacity to function with self-esteem and good judgment. These formulations look strikingly akin to existential constructs.

McQuaide and Ehrenreich (1997), in an extensive review of the literature on strengths, geared to the development of a strengths questionnaire, identify five overlapping and related conceptions of strengths that can be "read" as resiliency: cognitive and appraisal skills ("ability to perceive, analyze, and accurately comprehend a challenging situation"); defense and coping mechanisms ("characteristic mechanisms an individual uses to deal with problematic internal and external sources of stress"); temperamental and dispositions factors ("characteristic ways of seeing and being in the world"); interpersonal skills and supports ("ability to develop and maintain intimate and supportive social networks"); and external factors ("supportive social institutions, financial resources") (McQuaide and Ehrenreich 1997:205).

While the literature and research identify components of resilience, none, alone or in combination, explain resiliency comprehensively. Clearly, resiliency is a complex blend of individual attributes which inextricably intertwine with personality, family, school, peer, and community factors. Most of these factors are descriptive, not explanatory. What explains resiliency when many or most of these factors, identified in theory and research, are absent? Are there yet unspecified factors? "Will" is yet another possible piece of the puzzle of resilience.

The Existential Position

Sartre sees the essence of existential philosophy as the idea that "man is nothing else but what he makes of himself" (Sartre 1960:15). Life, according to Sartre, consists of choices, and the circumstances of one's life are the result of those choices. Briefly stated, man is what he acts to be. He has the power to create himself.

Camus, in a similar vein, comments, "There is just one truly serious philosophical problem, and that is suicide. Judging whether life is or is not worth living amounts to answering the fundamental question of philosophy" (Camus 1969:3). This statement embodies the major tenets of existential thinking since it poses the question of being and non-being, or nothingness. Camus emphasizes choice in embracing life and being, or choosing non-being through suicide. May (1969) defines "being" as the individual's unique pattern of potentialities. Being is the process of self-aware existing. Inherent in this existence is the reality of death, or non-being.

Existential thinkers posit will and self-awareness, coupled with the freedom to make choices and accept responsibility, as the greatest gifts humans possess. Choice is embedded in any situation, and many potential outcomes remain mysterious. Not knowing all the determinants of a situation provides freedom. Yet freedom implies courage; the courage to choose, to act, to choose being, and to accept responsibility for the choices. The greatest responsibility is to choose life. May speaks of this responsibility as "the ability to confront reality directly and to respond to it in a positive manner. . . . To the extent that a person can accept responsibility for his life, he becomes a free moral agent" (May 1969:37). He defines freedom as "the possibility of development, of enhancement of one's life; or the possibility of withdrawing, shutting oneself up, denying and stultifying one's growth" (May 1981:5). This view of responsibility translates to the concept of "will" — accepting responsibility and moving forward toward action, change, and life. He presents self-awareness as not merely a subjective, inner experience, but the basis on which we see the real world in its true perspective.

In addition to responsibility, humans possess the unique capacity for transcendence, "moving past the subject-object (self-world) split" (Bugental

1965:34). This is the ability to overcome the past and the present in order to move toward the future. It implies growth and an ability to reach beyond the concrete, the capacity to transcend the immediate and present situation.

Bugental (1965:15) lists four characteristics of humans and their awareness of the world:

We are limited in our awareness of ourselves and of the world.
We can act in ways that affect our awareness of ourselves and of world.
We have choice about which actions to take and not to take.
While each of us is in one sense alone, in another we are all related.

Yalom avers that the individual has freedom to create his or her own life — to desire, to choose, to act, and to change. He links responsibility to freedom: "one is responsible for one's life, for one's actions, and for one's failures to act" (Yalom 1980:220).

According to Frankl (1992), meanings are found within the individual rather than being a given, and the individual possesses a spirit that is a source of healing and strength because it recognizes the human capacity to aspire to places beyond instinct, exposure, or environment. Frankl asserts that meaning cannot be reached through rational means, but by existential means: meaning can be *willed*, by deciding that there is meaning in the world, rather than meaninglessness. It is possible to find meaning in all of life's events, even when confronted with a fate that cannot be changed or manipulated in any way.

Frankl's own life is testimony to the ability to master the most tragic and traumatic events. He survived almost three years in Nazi death camps, where his pregnant wife, mother, father, and brother perished. Even in a situation where an individual has no external freedom, where there is no choice of action, a person retains the freedom to choose his or her own attitude toward the situation. One does not despair, since this freedom to choose is always with you until your last moment of life. There is a will to meaning. To be human is to strive for something outside oneself, for "self-transcendence," the quality behind the will to meaning, the grasping for something or someone outside of oneself.

Mastering the art of living is critical in finding meaning and purpose in one's life. Frankl (1992) noted that a person's attitude toward his existence, the way one accepts his or her fate and the suffering that accompanies it, can add a deeper meaning to a person's life, and that it is important for a person to see the limit to their provisional existence. The individual must act to secure his or her future, to shape his fate. Striving for a goal or struggling to find meaning sparks tension, conflict, and movement toward a goal. It helps the person transcend the suffering and widen the picture of the world so the meaning is visible.

In summary, there are five central existential themes connected to the construct of will:

1. We are confronted with the unavoidable uncertainty of a world without any fixed meaning and with the certainty of our own eventual non-being, our death.
2. In the face of a given situation, we become aware of our inherent freedom to choose our attitude toward situations and to choose our actions.
3. There are constraints, both biological and environmental, on human freedom, yet within these limits there is always choice.
4. We cannot evade responsibility for choosing for ourselves, for we are constantly creating ourselves by the choices we make or fail to make. It is this awareness of personal freedom and responsibility that leads to anxiety, and how we deal with this anxiety is to a large degree related to our identity.
5. *Not* choosing is in itself a choice, and a source of personal responsibility.

This synthesis encompasses the healthy, aspiring, and positive capacity for choice and growth; the human dilemma of living and struggling to realize oneself; and an exploration into the farthest reaches of the self-mind, body, and spirit. In a word, will. Will is the mental faculty, distinct from knowing and reasoning, responsible for choosing, deciding, and initiating the attainment of certain ends, even in the fact of opposition. Traditionally, it has been associated with "origination," that is, escape from the past and the creation of a new beginning. As with thought and feeling, will is not seen directly, but is discovered from action and behavior. Will incorporates three dimensions — deliberation, determination, and decisiveness — that elude precise definition. Deliberation refers to consciousness, awareness, thoughtfulness, and choice. Determination connotes resolve, perseverance, stamina, energy, courage, and willfulness — the force that propels an individual forward. Decisiveness involves lack of ambivalence, firmness, absence of doubt, and assumption of responsibility. All imply the possibility of exercising a larger degree of control of one's life than one realizes.

The Stories of Five Men

This paper does not trace treatment but presents instead a synopsis of the "stories" of five men. Each story alone could fill a book. The stories of Barry, Tyle, Innis, Brad, and Ramon, have been condensed to provide a background for their reflections on their resiliency. Each man came into therapy at a significant juncture in his life. What makes their stories compelling and instructive is not the choices they faced, but the choices they made in confronting the attraction of suicide. The choice has been faced by people throughout the ages: To be, or not to be. To choose life, or to choose death. Moses put it this way: "I call heaven and earth to witness against you today that I have set before you life and death, blessings and curses. Choose life so that you and your descendants may live." (Deuteronomy 30:15–20).

These men chose life, and continue to choose it, through self-reinvention, overcoming anger, and pushing away the past to spring or crawl towards the future. Through will. Little bitterness stained their characters, and they welcomed, rather than avoided, personal disclosure and discovery. All strongly desired to contact the inner resources they knew lay inside of them. Each man completed at least three years of treatment, some of it irregular and some intermittent.

These men possessed elements of irrational thinking and faulty decision-making as well as elements of drive and determination. Yet their "self appraisal," their "desire to escape" and "to make things different," to rescue and re-form themselves, speak to something more. All risked assuming responsibility for what they did with their lives, both positive and negative, their mistakes as well as their accomplishments. None blamed others. All showed some degree of self-awareness, self-reliance, and goal directedness.

All demonstrated the will to face anxiety and despair. They were undaunted by the recognition of their choice at every turn of deciding how they would live.

All were a bundle of paradoxes: fiercely driven yet gentle, arrogant, timid, and retiring. All had the odds stacked against them but never gave up, never gave in. All thirsted for more. And willed it to happen. And it did.

Barry's Story

Sometimes, as a therapist, I shake my head and wonder how certain people find the will to continue, to proceed. Barry had that effect on me.

Barry, a dancer, came to see me in his early- to mid-twenties. Raised on a farm, Barry looked, with his wheat colored hair, like the proverbial Norman Rockwell kid. Tall and lithe, he was highly suicidal, terribly depressed, and frightened.

Two years before, his sister had taken her life. He was now approaching the age she had been when she committed suicide. He had been rather close to this sister, although she had tortured and sexually abused him when they were younger. In this family of four children, it seemed that every one had been sexually abused and tortured by their father. Most had become abusers themselves. His sister, emotionally devastated and despairing, had shown Barry the razors a few months before she used them.

All the feelings of shame and guilt that he felt in relation to her were coming to the fore as he danced. His dancing, which was his life, was being destroyed. Having his genitals highlighted, as he felt, in tight fitting leotards, was leaving him unable to perform. If he could not dance, he did not want to live. And yet, here he was — in great pain, yes, but looking for a way to get beyond the pain.

His mother may have been mentally ill, possibly bipolar. She was depressed, often unable to get out of bed, overwhelmed, unaware, unresponsive to the children, or alternatively in a state of high drama, screaming and yelling and scaring them all. No one felt that she could be depended on. She was a religious fanatic and imbued in the children a fear of a punishing God who would extract vengeance for their sins.

His father, who Barry likened to sheer brute force, was a threatening, hateful, bestial sadist. He forced Barry to engage in sex with the farm animals, and, if Barry dared refuse, his father would strangle Barry's favorite pets. Just seeing him approach would cause Barry to defecate in his pants. His older brother, a clone of his father, tortured and killed small animals, and abused Barry in bed while throttling him to keep him quiet.

No wonder Barry had trouble breathing when he became anxious.

Barry's talent for gymnastics and acrobatics led him to study dance by junior high school, and dance was his ticket out of the household he loathed. His teacher invited him to live in town with her family and at seventeen he won a scholarship to study in a large city and to dance successfully with a major company.

He was extremely solitary, self-conscious, and introverted. Although he was depressed, and had an obviously sad demeanor, Barry was highly disciplined, never missing a rehearsal or performance. Often he danced despite injuries, but he never ignored his injuries and always sought treatment for them. By some unspoken mutual agreement no one in his family ever saw him dance so his "life" remained uncontaminated. When he returned from his visits with them, he was always miserable, swamped by painful memories, acting out sexually and masochistically.

Therapy was able to break some of this pattern. It validated his experience and showed him that he was not the "bad seed," that he did not deserve the punishment he heaped upon himself. Barry often wondered aloud if sharing and exploring would ever bring relief and yet he was willing to grapple with and confront his demons head on. He understood that he had a choice — to believe in dance and in himself — "and I do."

Tyle's Story

Tyle came to see me ten years ago. He came from dire poverty, never went to college, barely graduated high school. Yet he sought out and was willing to pay a therapist to help him deal with his anxiety as he faced the prospect of going to jail. He thought it better to kill himself than to rot in a prison cell. He wanted me to convince him otherwise. This was the first indication of the level of positive resilience that was Tyle.

One of five boys in a family of ten children, he was the second youngest. Each might be called dysfunctional, alcoholic, or drug addicted. Most could also be called "compulsive." Tyle may have been classifiable as ADD. But where the others might drift, Tyle would drive. The others might drown in their despair, but Tyle was different:he knew what he didn't want and he knew what he did want.

At age 7, he had a paper route. By age 8 he had three routes. Extremes were always part of his make-up, but extremes were necessary, it seemed, to go from the poorest to the richest.

An African American child, living on welfare in the inner city, he felt strongly that anything he wanted he would have to get by himself. His parents could not help themselves, much less him. The children overwhelmed his mother. His father was an artist who believed in his own talent but he died never having sold anything. Was it the confidence that rubbed off on Tyle, or a disgust with his willingness not to be financially successful that drove Tyle?

Nothing came easily to Tyle. He struggled for recognition; he struggled to be accepted and liked. Sexually abused by an older brother, he struggled to escape that fearsome memory while holding on to the family. The struggles manifested themselves in extremes and excesses.

While no great student, he was obviously bright, sharp, and quick. Business and people who were successful in it fascinated him. Working as a teenager in a Wall Street delicatessen, he discovered that the owner played the stock market. Thus began his own career. Tyle picked the owner's brains relentlessly; soon every penny he earned was being invested.

What he had, that many others didn't, was a very simple, one-dimensional goal — to get rich. He was confident that he could always make money and that if he could make money he could escape the poverty he hated. He discovered he could talk anyone into anything. His instincts were superb.

What he could not do was rein in his own compulsiveness. He was alcoholic, cocaine addicted, sexually promiscuous. Any gamble was worth taking and financially it served him well. He make his first million by 23, but he led a double life, one foot in legal business, the other in illegal.

Despite the appearance of being out of control, the will, the deliberate decision to lick the addictions won out. His choice to join a 12-step group, to adhere to its dictates, to be in control of his vices rather than at their mercy, set Tyle apart. Facing the consequences, going to jail, assuming responsibility for past choices, indicated a level of maturity. Coming to me, addressing his fears, determining to survive, bespoke an amazing resiliency.

Innis's Story

Innis came to see me when he was in his mid-thirties. A very handsome and charming man, his outward mien belied the internal anguish with which he struggled.

Innis was both a priest and a musician. He came to me because of the pain caused by being involved in a dangerous homosexual relationship. His vow of celibacy had been compromised and his view of himself as a man shattered.

He was suicidal by the time he came to see me. Yet he "knew," not only in theological terms, that he had to live. He did not understand who he was, and at the same time hated who he was. His desolation and isolation caused enormous grief. His public persona and private one were at odds and the hypocrisy was not lost on his sensitive soul. He complained of being cold and sick to his stomach.

He was raised on a farm in Pennsylvania by parents who were Eastern European immigrants. His mother had been reared in the Orthodox rite. He was sent to Catholic school early on. The youngest of three, his mother had decided while he was very young that he would be a priest. He never knew what choice was his. The nuns who taught him terrified him but the need to please his mother was paramount. He believed that she had all the power.

He remembered her as totally unavailable and distant, unwilling to get off the couch to come to him even as he screamed for her attention as a young child. At the same time, she seemed to smother him and rely on him inordinately.

His revulsion at breasts and thighs made me suspect that she sexually abused him although he was unable or unwilling to explore the possibility. He perceived himself as over-dependent, not a good son, who had let his mother down.

He remembered always feeling "different," always apologizing for it, wanting to scream out loud, "Please understand me." Throughout his life, he felt mocked and ridiculed, while at the same time he was made out to be a hero by his mother and the church, a role he felt totally inadequate to play. Whatever the situation, he believed that "somebody's going to want something from me — something I can't give." If he couldn't provide "the goods," he felt "like a selfish pig." He had received two opposing messages: one was that he couldn't take care of himself, would always have to be taken care of, while the second was that great and wonderful things were expected of him.

At some level, he managed to accomplish both in his priesthood. His musical ability comforted him, distinguished him, and brought another dimension to his worship but a desire to pursue his music seriously, passionately, and non-religiously left him in another double bind.

Brad's Story

When I try to describe Brad, I think of metaphors: he bounces back, he has nine lives, he is self-righting. His ability to survive challenges the commonly held viewpoint that the family influence is paramount; that early trauma is irrevocable, that adversity promotes damage, that children from dysfunctional families are doomed.

Brad was an Olympic athlete and an actor studying at a prestigious drama school. In his late twenties, he had already survived three suicide attempts and years of alcohol and drug abuse.

When I first saw him our mutual goal was to keep him alive. His girlfriend had broken up with him while they were in Asia. He had begun to dissemble, and was in a major depression and suicidal. He could not sleep or eat;thousands of miles from anything familiar, he managed to make his way home. He wanted to die and was determined to live.

Several years previously, he had detoxed and had since attended meetings of AA and NA without fail. Now, however, they offered no relief. His mental health was crashing and yet he believed that "some internal, inexplicable force" had so far kept him alive. After an earlier long-term relationship had failed, he had taken pills and then, when hospitalized, had tried to hang himself. This time he sought help, agreed to an anti-suicide contract, medication, and a mutual attempt to understand the interaction between past and present.

Having grown up in a household where he was continually punished, dismissed, and forced to go to extremes to get recognition, Brad's ongoing emotional anguish and dysfunctional behavior was labeled "nothing but a lack of discipline."

Depression was common in the family. His maternal great-grandmother had received ect; his mother had been on antidepressants since his birth; his paternal grandmother had been hospitalized for depression; her son, Brad's uncle, committed suicide; and Brad's brother was seriously depressed but did not seek treatment because of his political aspirations.

As if that were not enough, medication seemed to interfere with his ability to memorize his lines as an actor. Brad also felt that it bloated and distorted his face and would limit getting the roles he wanted. He worried too that the medication would affect his sexual performance. And yet, while in excruciating psychic agony, attempting to maintain his sobriety, and fighting the medicine's side effects, he plowed on. He got up in the morning, went to work, and came to therapy.

Ramon's Story

By the time I saw Ramon he had already been drug-free for 4 years. Only in his early thirties, he had been diagnosed as HIV positive. While addicted to heroin, he had considered suicide as he battled his dependency. His life, he knew, had been ravaged by drugs and now it was to be further ravaged by the illness that had already taken so many of his friends.

Coming out of the fog of years of drug use, followed by years of getting and staying clean and sober, Ramon adhered rigorously to 12-step programs. Even before his own diagnosis, he had ministered to gay and straight friends with AIDS, nursing several until the moment of their death.

When he himself was diagnosed, he again considered suicide, taking the control into his own hands. He was ashamed, angry with himself, angry that he had wasted his life, angry at all the men in his life that had betrayed him, most especially the father who abandoned him as a child.

A Latino man, Ramon had grown up surrounded mostly by women. His older sister had introduced him, when he was 9, to heroin. Childhood was a dark time. Having a serious speech impediment, he experienced life with great pain and was quick to seek the comfort heroin provided. As bright as he was, and despite a good mother who wanted good things for him, there was no male modeling to encourage anything but the street life.

For most, the street led only to jail or death. Until now, Ramon, however, because of who he was, had somehow escaped both. Something had led him to choose life over death. Something made him determined to make up for those lost years, to make something special of his life. He believed that if he could kick the drug, he could re-create himself anew. And he had.

When he came to see me he was already a highly esteemed mental health professional — a writer, a teacher, a father, a resilient man.

But becoming a success, overcoming all odds, does not protect anyone from new pain, present anguish, past shame. He was the divorced father of a daughter with a serious handicap, and he also had to cope with his own deteriorating health. And he resolved to do so.

Revisitation

Attempts were made to locate these five men to gain their current viewpoints about their strengths and resiliency. Tyle, Innis, Brad, and Ramon were reached. Each man, in reflecting back upon his life and his treatment, spoke mindfully, poignantly, and profoundly. Their own voices, captured here testify to their will to live, of their deliberation, determination, and decisiveness in committing to therapy to live, to examine and improve their lives.

To frame their responses, the questions posed were: What sparked you? How did you go on despite external and internal pressures and stresses? What did you know or discover about yourself? What did you hate? What were or are you doing to yourself? Where do you go from here? What keeps you alive? What keeps you going? What happened in your therapy that helped you along? Why did you stick to it? None answered the questions directly, but "free associated." Here is a distillation of their reflections.

Barry's Reflections

My parents were non-achieving and self-deceptive — losers. They had no power, no choice, no control. I vowed to be different. I always had a keen sense of not failing. Failure to me was unacceptable. I would be a famous dancer. I was determined for as far back as I can remember. The unfairness of the way I was treated and my own determination to not be a victim, the way my parents were, led me on. I had a couple of models in my first ballet teacher and others along the way who encouraged me to be different, to risk, especially as a man. Kind of the way you always did. I wondered what better life there could be. We all lived in the same two-bedroom farmhouse. I had to depend on myself; there was no one else to depend upon. I wanted out. I was always struggling to show that I was not silly, a sissy, stupid, flaky, less than. I remember always feeling insecure and frightened. I wanted to achieve, to be okay. To excel. I knew I could. I sort of took it as a challenge to show them. I pushed myself by saying, "Keep doing it, keep practicing until you get it right." You promoted the idea that I had to take responsibility, even when it went against my grain. But that is what I was doing anyway. Punishment involved not doing what I wanted to do. I had to prove, at least to myself, that I was okay. I was primed by my resolve. Therapy pushed me along further. I learned to trust myself only because your belief in me got me to. You were always there, and you used my own progress as evidence against me when I doubted myself. It was amazing how much you remembered.

Tyle's Reflections

I always had a need to get away from how my parents lived. I hated their lives, I still do. Nobody had faith in me. But I did. I do. And I knew that you did. I knew not because you said so, but because you made me feel safe and pushed me along. You even stuck by me when I went to jail, even when I didn't pay you. I had one very clear goal in mind. That was to make money. To be rich. I wanted more, much more. In ways, I always reached far and, in ways, I believed that I would do it. God put me here, who am I to cheat him. I was always certain of what I didn't want. I wanted to escape. At 13 and again at 16, I took a large piece of oak tag. On it I wrote what I wanted to achieve. I wanted money, friends, and family. I then crossed off things that wouldn't give me the sense of achievement. Despite everything, I have come to like what I do because it gives me what I want. I gave up a lot, but then I have the only thing I always really wanted. Money. I never surrendered. Next step for me is to have more time, to take time. You mentioned the importance of time to me a lot. You also told me to save some energy for my self. I'm doing that. But I don't know if I'll ever stop putting myself out on a limb. I want to be bloody rich. An anecdote: I remember my father had drawings. He laminated them. Nobody bought them. I brought them into school and sold them as book covers to 100 kids. I even took orders for them. Your idea sucked, mine didn't. Then I rented space at a flea market and sold some more. I remember that my father didn't go anywhere. He stood by. I was always focused. Life is a contest. I will win. I never told you how much I appreciated your support when it looked like all else failed and everybody left me. You supported my drive, and it's my strength. I never met anyone more persistent than me. I think you are. And you got me to look at and laugh at myself.

Brad's Reflections

But I always knew it. I never lost a battle. There was something in me, something that was healthy, something that said don't give up. However miserable I was, no matter what way I was hurting myself, I reached out. I got help. I decided to live. I found you, thank God. I guess I learned a lot from my swimming coach. He told me to dive in no matter how scared you are, don't let anything stop you. Inside me was a voice that said stay alive; all will end up the way it should. It's like a matter of attitude. Maybe a mind thing. I was determined to stop the crap and get my dream. I think that you forced me to see how I sabotaged myself, always did. You said that you had confidence in me. I felt your confidence. When I asked you to prove why, you told me why and how. In chapter and verse. How do you remember all the details? I stopped drugging. I stopped drinking. I stopped cutting myself. Yeah, I stopped taking my meds too, but for almost a year now I've been working steadily, not at what I want, but close to it. I think now that I'm talking to you that maybe I'll come back to see you. I want to get over the next hurdle. Put all my training to the test. You showed me how to really rely on myself. You kept showing me that I had choices. And most of the time, when I really thought about it, I came, with your help, to make pretty good ones. I'm a bit scared, but I will do it. You convinced me that I have the potential and raw materials. I will do it. I believe in myself. I will succeed, really, really succeed. I still believe that some internal, inexplicable force of health and place of safety will keep me alive and on course. Somehow you tapped into my stuff, brought the good stuff to the surface. I don't really understand how you did it, but I felt you were 'for' me.

Ramon's Reflections

Ramon began by speaking in metaphors.

Sponge so saturated that I was sinking. I wanted to re-create myself. I cleaned out the closet. Each success, while not fully a surprise, drove me in spite of my physical limitations. I had hope and drive. Ever since I was young, I yearned for life. I've been a fisherman all my life. I check out every angle, trap the bait. I cast. I don't always catch a fish. I cast again. I sometimes do. I know that I'm in a rush to try to get so much in. Revenge played a large part. I was determined to get what I didn't get, what I didn't have in the first place. I wanted my daughter not to suffer the way I did. So I was also determined to give what I didn't get. You helped me recognize that I actually had something to give. You even almost trained me how to do it. I always had a strong urge to prove myself, I will prove myself. I have the utmost confidence that I will beat the odds. I am not resigned; there is a light inside me. I want to be viewed as substantial, reclaiming what my life is about. Over time I came to believe you that my life couldn't be thrown away. Even in the face of my physical deterioration, I can give up like so many and die, or live. Even talking with you now brings relief, support, and gives me motivation. You asked what happened in therapy that helped me. I'll tell you. It's just that you supported me but challenged me, together. You helped me realize that I could design my own life. That's powerful, man. I believe that our fate is ours and ours alone. We have only ourselves to blame or praise for both the good and the bad that happens in our lives. I thank you because you helped me figure out the way to live my life the way I want to live it. Therapy helped me realize that I was a turtle. I could, if I wanted to, close myself up in a shell. I could cut myself off. I could die without seeing what was on the other side. Or I could stick my neck out and go ahead. That's what I've always done, stuck my neck out and move, maybe slowly, but ahead.

Reflections on Reflections

From experience with these men, and from their own reflections on therapy, what elements in therapy can be identified as crystallizing clients' strengths and resiliency? Some are simple — being consistent, available, on time, and returning phone calls. Educating clients about the helping process itself offers clients co-responsibility for the endeavor. Providing practical information and advice appropriate to their specific needs gives them alternative viewpoints to consider in making decisions. Contracting to prioritize targets of attention, agreeing on mutual goals, roles, tasks, and a timetable to work toward solutions, honors their internal capacity. The more significant elements are more complex and elusive.

A strong belief in the process of therapy coupled with a strong belief in the purposefulness of clients' behavior seems to undergird the success of work toward bolstering resiliency. Encouraging clients to be active participants in designing their lives is crucial. When a therapist strives to create a meaningful and reliable relationship, one of mutual exploration and examination, clients come to recognize and appreciate their uniqueness.

Progress is not linear. It frequently comes in inexplicable waves. When they focus on their goals, on what they want for the future, clients are able to edit their scripts, consider and exercise new options, and liberate themselves from crushing past histories (Fox 1993).

The ability of clients to master their lives, their internal conflicts, and external frustration requires meeting their basic needs for security and affirmation. Building a safe house through the dynamic of the relationship provides them the context conducive to their facing the challenge of self-discovery. It also promotes their taking ownership of themselves, their decisions, their mistakes, their triumphs.

Clients are willing to exert great effort and endure considerable hardship when they sense the respect, interest, and motivation of the clinician. Such a stance releases them from suffering, encourages their striving, and builds their efficacy (Fox 1993). It celebrates their refusal to yield.

Moving away from a neutral stance seems instrumental. That is, in addition to an attitude of positive regard, being actively caring and supportive, perhaps even vulnerable. Challenging belief systems, confronting self-destructive choices, constantly providing options and alternative perspectives, makes a difference in how clients contact and ultimately recruit inner strengths and resiliency. It dignifies them. Seek and ye shall find; that is, when looked for, evidence of strength will be found. Breadth of viewpoint, flexibility in response, and collaboration with clients effectively interrupt dysfunctional processes that perpetuate troublesome behavior, feeling, or thinking. It also fosters their recognition that they are their own best key resources.

It is very important to remind clients that their range of choices is greater in the present than it was in the past. It is essential to let them know that their range of choices in the future will be that much greater as they come to terms with themselves and rely on their inner resources, even if these resources are not yet fully recognized (Fox 1993). When the therapist notices and explicitly points out what clients do well, their will, their striving, and their drive is cultivated and activated, thus advancing their sense of competence, of mastery. This assertive exercise of self, for which they assume responsibility, is empowering.

Despite the circumstances, being tempted repeatedly to end their lives, these men willed not to. Why? Their survival seems independent of their differ-

ences in culture, ethnicity, background, and family history. Equally important, each one — Barry, Tyle, Innis, Brad, and Ramon — made his life meaningful where no meaning seemed possible, prospered where no resources
seemed available for such success, forged ahead where neither energy nor
opportunity were at hand. Why? Therapy helped. It helped each man mine
for something within himself that propelled him on. What was it? Factors
identified in the professional literature and research, which are identified as
variables producing resiliency, do not sufficiently explain it. For want of a
fuller and more satisfying explanation, this article proposes will as another
significant element. Does it fully explain how they overcame adversity? How
they came to choose a fulfilling life? No. Not fully. And if will plays some part
in their perseverance, what explains will? Is it innate? Is it learned? Is it temperamental? Constitutional? Learnable? Teachable? These questions direct
all of us interested in human resiliency toward further exploration, further
discovery.

Which ingredients of therapy bolster clients' strengths and resiliency? Although the answer remains intangible, it seems evident from a composite picture of practice experience and client self-report that the following are important components: concentrating on the aspiring and positive aspects of
clients and their capacity for choice; providing a climate conducive to deep
exploration of self; building a relationship that is simultaneously safe and challenging; and continually exercising clients' will — that is, their deliberation,
determination, and decisiveness — augment their strength and resilience.

References

Special thanks to Geraldine Fox, M.S.W., for her invaluable assistance in
preparing the case material for this paper.

Beardslee, W. R. 1989. The role of self-understanding in resilient individuals:
The development of a perspective. *American Journal of Orthopsychiatry*
59:266–278.

Bugental, J. F. T. 1965. *The Search for Authenticity*. New York: Holt Rienhart and
Winston.

Camus, A. 1969. *Lyrical and Critical Essays*. New York: Alfred A. Knopf.

Fox, R. 1993. *The Elements of the Helping Process: A Guide for Clinicians*. Binghamton, N.Y.: Haworth Press.

Frankl, V. E. 1992. *Man's Search for Meaning: An Introduction to Logotherapy*
4th ed. Boston: Beacon Press.

Garmezy, N. 1994. Reflections and commentary on "Risk, Resilience, and Development." In R.J. Haggerty, L. R. Sherrod, N. Garmezy, and M. Rutter, eds., *Stress, Risk, and Resilence in Children and Adolescents: Processes, Mechanisms, and Interventions,* 1–18. Cambridge: Cambridge University Press.

Harvey, M. 1996. An ecological view of psychological trauma and trauma recovery. *Journal Traumatic Stress* 9:3–23.

Herrenkohl, E. C., R. C. Herrenkohl, and B. Egolf. 1994. Resilient early school-age children from maltreating homes: Outcomes in late adolescence. *American Journal of Orthopsychiatry* 64:301–309.

Liem, J., J. James, J. O'Toole, and A. Boudewyn. 1997. Assessing resilience in adults with histories of childhood sexual abuse. *American Journal of Orthopsychiatry* 67 (4): 594–606.

May, R. 1969. *Existential Psychotherapy.* New York: Random House.

May, R. 1981. *Freedom and Destiny.* New York: Norton.

McQuaide, S. and J. Ehrenreich. 1997. Assessing client strengths. *Families in Society: The Journal of Contemporary Human Services* 78 (2): 201–212.

Mills, R. 1991. A new understanding of self: The role of affect, state of mind, self-understanding, and intrinsic motivation. *Journal of Experimental Education* 60 (10): 67–81.

Moran, P. B. and J. Eckenrode. 1992. Protective personality characteristics among adolescent youth. *Child Abuse and Neglect* 16:743–754.

Rutter, M. 1987. Psychosocial resilience and protective mechanisms. *American Journal of Orthopsychiatry* 57:316–331.

Rutter, M. 1990. Psychological resilience and protective mechanisms. In J. Rolf, A. S. Marten, D. Cicchetti, K. H. Neuchterlein, and S. Weintraub. eds., *Risk and Protective Factors in the Development of Psychopathology,* 181–214. New York: Cambridge University Press.

Saleebey, D. 1996. The strengths perspective in social work practice: Extensions and cautions. *Social Work* 4 (3): 296–305.

Saleebey, D. 1997. *The Strengths Perspective in Social Work.* White Plains, N.Y.: Longman.

Sartre, J. P. 1960. *Existentialism and Humanism.* London: Methuen.

Wolin, S. J. 1991. The Challenge Model: How Children Rise Above Adversity. Plenary address at the annual meeting of the American Association of Marriage and Family Therapists, Dallas.

Yalom, I. 1980. *Existential Psychotherapy.* New York: Basic Books.

8   Enhancing Couple Resiliency

Howard Robinson

      This paper explores the concept of resiliency from the perspective of the couple relationship, often seen as the heart of the family system and still acknowledged as one of the most important sources of happiness in adult life (Walsh 1998:9). In order to develop interventions that enhance the couple as a relationship system, this paper offers a framework for thinking about resilience as a relational phenomenon particular to a dyad. Case examples demonstrate how couple categories of resiliency can be enhanced using techniques from a variety of treatment models. This eclectic approach is integrated in the service of resiliency enhancement, and provides a new way to organize known techniques. Because social workers encounter couples every day in their practices, this paper may guide clinicians to help couples cope well and develop stronger, more vital relationships.

     Resiliency has been defined and operationalized in research as an individual construct related to attributes of temperament, personality, and intellect. Protective factors thought to build individual resiliency include specific support from family, school, peers, and community. Having a warm, affirming relationship with an adult, being exposed to high parental expectations, and being shown positive parental modeling, buffer individuals from environmental stress. Other factors — extended family support, opportunities for peer involvement, positive community norms — have been demonstrated to mediate and defuse potential risk factors like parental alcoholism, lack of community role models, and poverty (Turner, Norman, and Zunz 1994). This ecological model of resiliency, which recognizes multiple system influences, retains the individual as its focus (Smith and Carlson 1997). Resiliency is located within the person (Kumpfer 1993), even though environmental factors may contribute to reducing personal vulnerability and bolstering an individual's capacity for sustained competent functioning (Turner, Norman, and Zunz 1994).

More recently the concept of resiliency has been raised to the level of the family system and developed more expansively as a relational process. Walsh (1996), exploring how families are able to weave a supportive fabric of affirming relationships and build cohesive belief systems for their members, attempts to rebalance the negative bias toward families hidden within the clinical literature. Resiliency has often been associated, for example, with an individual's recovery from a dysfunctional or toxic family environment. Families were depicted more as agents of trauma rather than as sources of support for healthy growth. In her study of family processes, Walsh affirms the multiple strengths of family systems and creatively shifts the concept of resiliency to the family as a social unit. By so doing, Walsh expands the definition beyond individual traits and capacities. Walsh demonstrates that a potent source of resiliency exists in the relational dynamics of the family and can be enhanced, as a result, by attending to family transactions that contribute to improved adaptation, communication, collaborative problem-solving, and family cohesion (Walsh 1998).

The shift to a relational definition of resiliency opens new pathways for exploration. This paper uses categories of individual resilience as a point of departure for examining domains of relational resilience in couples. Adult partners, emotionally committed to each other in intimate, loving relationships, comprise a dyadic unit with discrete needs, challenges, and interpersonal dynamics. Couples in life partnerships are viewed here as self-contained relational systems in continuous interaction with each other as partners and with the social environment that circumscribes them as a dyadic unit. An ecosystemic paradigm is used that is consistent with the person-situation model of Kumpfer (1993); the unit of focus, however, is the couple. Categories of individual resiliency are transposed to the dyadic system and explored clinically to help treatment providers identify and enhance strengths of partnership.

Ideally, a well-functioning couple can become its own source for self-repair and regeneration as partners confront challenges together, weather storms, and bounce back from shared adversity. I believe that the couple relationship contains an organic potential to protect and sustain partners as a holding environment (Winnicott 1965) during periods of stress. From this perspective, couple resiliency is, in essence, a gestalt that transcends the single aspects of couple functioning explored analytically in this paper. Interventions discussed here must be understood as ultimately serving a broader effort: to construct stronger and more vital holding environments for partners that renew strength, wellness, and inspiration throughout their life course together.

Adapting Concepts of Individual Resilience to Couple Systems

I have selected six personality characteristics, discussed in the first chapter of this book, and associated with individuals who have adapted well to adverse life circumstances. I have redefined them as relational categories that enhance couple resiliency. The categories — realistic appraisal, efficacy, problem-solving, flexible gender roles, empathy, and mission — represent functions and qualities of relationship that I have found significant in clinical work with couples. In transposing from the individual to the couple, I have emphasized the couple as a team who must learn to cope with external stress and internal tensions, relate well to each other's needs, fears, and capacities, and join in spirit to develop shared goals and a sense of mutual purpose.

These six categories of couple resiliency provide a framework to guide strength-based interventions that draw from a variety of treatment models. An assortment of techniques, culled from problem-solving, task-oriented, cognitive, psychosocial, communications, psychodynamic, narrative, and constructivist models, can be applied to achieve an overarching resiliency-based treatment goal. This approach follows Froma Walsh's directive that what is needed even more than new techniques are strength-oriented conceptual tools that guide intervention (Walsh 1996:275).

Category 1: Couple Appraisal

Realistic appraisal refers to the ability to differentiate between the possible and the impossible and to accurately assess one's own capacity to act and affect the situation (Turner, Norman, and Zunz 1994:111). Studies of resilient individuals indicate that realistic appraisal is associated with managing stress adaptively (Beardslee and Podorefsky 1988) and with experiencing a sense of personal control (Cowen et al. 1990; Garmezy and Masten 1986; Werner 1986). In the case of Dan and Catherine, the couple needed to ap-

Individual Personality Characteristics Associated With Resiliency	Categories of Couple Resiliency Derived From Personality Characteristics
1. **Realistic Appraisal**: the ability to differentiate between what is possible and what is not, through a realistic assessment of situational demands and one's capacity to meet them.	1. **Couple Appraisal**: the ability of the couple, as a problem-solving team, to realistically assess the risk and opportunity inherent in a stressful situation and their joint capacity to change it; the ability of partners to accurately distinguish self from other, to perceive their own relationship dynamics, and to accurately identify areas for self-change that would improve the functioning of the dyad as a whole.
2. **Self-Efficacy**: a positive perception of one's competence, worth, and capacity to influence events.	2. **Couple Efficacy**: the mutually-held perception that the couple performs competently as a unit, that they are capable of meeting stressful life-events effectively and can adapt to or change environmental impingements; the perception that, as a couple, they can master life challenges together.
3. **Social Problem-Solving Skills**: the ability to construct solutions to problems by using social skills to invite ideas and feedback.	3. **Couple Problem-Solving Skills**: a couple's capacity to identify and communicate needs to each other, to negotiate desired goals, to frame workable objectives, to predict likely obstacles and outcomes, to generate potential solutions, and to carry out pragmatic strategies and tasks to meet their needs.
4. **Gender and Sex-Role Behavior**: the capacity, regardless of gender, to be both yielding and assertive, expressive and instrumental, as well as nurturing toward others.	4. **Couple Flexibility in Gender Role Behaviors**: the capacity of partners, regardless of gender, to shift expressive and instrumental role functions, to accept dependency needs as well as the need for autonomy, and to balance self-assertion with receptivity.
5. **Empathy**: the capacity to accurately perceive, understand, and respond to the feelings and needs of another.	5. **Couple Empathy**: the capacity of partners to understand, accept, and respond with care to each other's point of view, emotional fears and vulnerabilities, and unique needs; the ability of partners to accurately imagine each other's felt needs, to hold a sense of a partner's life-experience within oneself as a way to understand a partner's pain, frustration, needs, and joys.
6. **Sense of Direction or Mission**: the ability to construct and maintain a clear sense of role, purpose, or life-task.	6. **Couple Sense of Mission**: the capacity of a couple to construct mutual longterm goals, share common values and ideals, and appeal to them when experiencing stress; the ability of the couple to discover a transcendent meaning and purpose in their relationship.

praise their situation more realistically in order to mobilize healthier coping strategies that preserved their relationship as business executives, marital partners, and parents.

Dan and Catherine: Realistic Appraisal of Illness

PRESENTING SITUATION

Dan and Catherine, married 25 years, managed a corporate business together and parented four children aged 7 through 18. Dan was stricken with a chronic, progressive illness that unpredictably assaulted his functioning, sometimes severely. Although he could no longer perform adequately at work, he refused to acknowledge his disability or delegate any of his assigned responsibilities to his wife. Catherine worried about the business and was afraid to confront the seriousness of her husband's illness. She began to work late hours and ignored the chaos at home, where the children were reacting angrily to the unspoken marital tensions.

ASSESSMENT

The couple minimized the negative course of Dan's illness. They clung to his good days to bolster their misguided belief that he would eventually return to full health. Dan and Catherine, however, were in acute private pain. They argued vehemently at home and at work. Their business began to falter, household tasks were left undone, and the children misbehaved in school. Dan and Catherine needed help to see beyond their sanguine distortions. They not only denied the seriousness of Dan's illness and its effects on the family, but underestimated their own capacity to take greater control of their situation.

TREATMENT

The first goal of treatment was to help Dan and Catherine reappraise Dan's illness more realistically. Because Dan attempted to keep Catherine in the dark about his medical condition, details of his illness and its progression over time were scrupulously reviewed in session. When Dan and Catherine disputed the facts, they were instructed to speak directly to Dan's doctors. A contract between the couple was developed to give Catherine greater access to Dan's medical records and to allow her to investigate his condition more directly.

The second treatment goal focused on clarifying the connection between Dan's illness and their interpersonal and family conflicts. By carefully tracking the sequence of events leading to marital arguments, Dan and Catherine discovered how shifts in Dan's physical, cognitive, and emotional functioning triggered unspoken anxieties in Catherine. Because she experienced Dan's illness as abandonment, Catherine reacted with anger rather than compassion. A cycle of negative transactions developed between them. Their interactive pattern needed to be carefully identified so that Dan and Catherine could catch it in time to circumvent its toxic course.

When difficulties with the children were explored, the full systemic effects of Dan's illness were brought to light. Dan and Catherine's inability to speak candidly with each other affected their capacity as parents to manage their children. However, as their self-protective denial was dislodged, particularly through mutual validation of the facts, Dan and Catherine were able to mobilize more adaptive coping strategies. In business, Dan began to delegate tasks to Catherine and accept a limited work role. Catherine enrolled in business courses to develop the new management skills she needed. Dan and Catherine collaborated more closely to meet their children's needs in a timely way and to structure their activities at home. The children calmed as they sensed that their parents were working together to take charge of the family.

Further counseling was needed for Dan and Catherine to confront the change illness brought to their emotional and sexual relationship. Catherine grew emotionally supportive to her husband, because she understood more clearly the effects of illness on Dan's capacity to work, his sense of self-worth, and his need to feel competent. Dan's greater acceptance of his medical condition allowed him to disengage more easily from his work role and join with his wife and children in creating a less stressful living environment.

INTERVENTIONS ENHANCING DAN AND CATHERINE'S
SITUATIONAL APPRAISAL

An array of techniques were used to help Dan and Catherine more realistically appraise the severity of Dan's illness, its impact on their relationship, and the opportunities available for effecting change.

1. *Careful psychosocial review of person-in-situation to encourage client reflections, solicit pertinent details, and identify patterned behaviors.* I used psychosocial techniques of sustainment, description, exploration, and ventilation (Woods and Hollis 1990) to encourage Dan and Catherine to voice the thoughts and feelings they withheld from each other, to normalize their anxiety-based reactions to illness, and to explore and clarify their complex situation by eliciting pertinent details. These techniques also helped to establish the empathic working relationship necessary to probe, confront, and soothe at the same time. As Dan and Catherine told their story, I was able to point out feelings and behaviors that were the-

matic, such as their consistent minimizing of realistic problems (Dan's illness, their work relationship, and their children's behavior). By mirroring to Dan and Catherine the pattern dynamic (Woods and Robinson 1996:575) that emerged from their reflections, I helped them to see their behaviors more clearly. Dan and Catherine were then able to relinquish dysfunctional coping patterns and channel their energy into new and more adaptive solutions.

2. *Structural-strategic problem-solving to modify patterned interactions, triangulation, and executive hierarchy.* Tracking is a family therapy technique to identify interactive sequences and patterns that characterize the structure of transactions among family members (Minuchin and Fishman 1981). The patterned steps in Dan and Catherine's arguments were sensitively explored so that the trigger to conflict could be identified and their subsequent reactions to each other unraveled. Once explicit, Dan and Catherine's patterned interactions could be modified.

Sometimes I took a directive approach and urged the couple to develop structured agreements, for example, to explore Dan's medical condition. These contracts included mutual tasks that rebalanced the couple as executive partners within the family system. Advocating for Catherine's access to medical information and encouraging Dan to delegate his work assignments helped to equalize power between them. Focusing on Dan and Catherine as a couple removed their children as a triangulating factor, and supported their executive role within the family. As a result, Dan and Catherine could function better in their parental tasks and exercise more authority with their children.

3. *Constructing reciprocal and shared tasks to gain active mastery and control.* Task-centered social work uses task strategies to achieve well defined problem-solving goals (Reid 1996). Dan and Catherine were helped by constructing and carrying out shared and reciprocal tasks (Reid 1992:46–8). Shared tasks included speaking to doctors together, meeting with school counselors, and collaborating on family tasks at home. Reciprocal tasks involve a quid pro quo: Dan, for example, agreed to relinquish work assignments to Catherine in exchange for added quality attention during their weekends at home.

4. *Defining what could and could not be changed.* By defining Dan's illness as a reality over which Dan and Catherine had little if any control, the couple could identify more realistic targets for change: improving their collaboration as a couple, restructuring their work roles, strengthening parent-child relationships, and adopting a less stressful lifestyle.

Dan and Catherine felt better about themselves as a couple when they realized that they could modify their reactions to illness, even if no cure exists for the illness itself.

WHEN REALISTIC APPRAISAL IS NOT ENOUGH

In Dan and Catherine's case, as in others involving the recognition and acceptance of loss, removing psychological denial exposes a deeper grief. Dan and Catherine saw the vital partnership they had known for twenty-five years coming to an end. Illness presented a new challenge: to construct a meaningful relationship as one partner faced progressively more limited functioning. What could help Dan and Catherine stay resilient under these conditions?

First, Dan and Catherine shared their grief in each other's presence, an act that was emotionally binding and validated the significance each attributed to their relationship. Dan and Catherine turned more to spiritual values. They reaffirmed their deep loyalty, mutual commitment, and love for one another. I do not believe that Dan and Catherine could overcome their current adversity without embracing the underlying values that held them in their relationship. Paradoxically, becoming more realistic about the dimensions of Dan's illness evoked spiritual values that helped them transcend physical reality. The important role of spirituality in couple resiliency is discussed later in this paper as a component of couple mission.

Category 2: Couple Efficacy

Self-efficacy refers to one's own feeling and perception of competence, worth, and capacity to influence the environment and exert control, even in the face of adversity. The case of Mark and Bruce illustrates how a gay couple, living in a heterosexist society and stigmatized by homophobic family members, increased their sense of worth as a couple, and improved their ability to affirm their relationship with chosen family members and friends.

Mark and Bruce: Coming Out Together

PRESENTING SITUATION

After five years of marriage, Mark, a 40-year-old Caucasian from a working-class Catholic family, revealed his homosexual preferences to his wife. This began a painful and anxiety-ridden period for Mark, who divorced, keeping his homosexual identity a secret from his mother, father, brothers, and extended family. Mark dated a variety of men for the next two years until he fell in love with Bruce, a 30-year-old African American. When Mark proposed to Bruce that they live together in a committed partnership, Bruce abruptly severed the relationship. Devastated by his loss and confused by the circumstances, Mark sought counseling. He was encouraged to invite Bruce into couple treatment. Bruce timidly agreed.

ASSESSMENT

Bruce passed as straight with his parents, his brothers and sisters, and his friends at work. Mark's request to live together would make their coming out as a couple inevitable, and Bruce was panic stricken by it. Mark was afraid too, despite his courageous invitation to Bruce. Mark's parents were unforgiving about his sinful divorce, and they were likely to reject him completely for being homosexual. Mark remembered his oldest brother's threats to beat up all the fags in the neighborhood and even thought he might be attacked if his brother knew.

Coming out, however, involved more than just telling family or friends; it meant developing a loving acceptance of self. Mark and Bruce internalized the contempt and stigma aimed at homosexuals by society in general. They struggled, as individuals and as a couple, to feel good about themselves. Bruce, in particular, was filled with a self-hatred that Mark recognized from his own experience in coming to terms with a heterosexual marriage that did not fit. Unfortunately, Mark still labeled himself a misfit, especially when he identified with the traditional Catholicism in which he was raised. Bruce and Mark needed help to transform the negative images they associated with their homosexual identity into a positive vision. The self-blame they had internalized from the homophobic attitudes of family and community undermined the development of pride in their couple relationship and a sense of empowerment about their lives.

TREATMENT

Mark and Bruce warily agreed that they wanted to be less secretive about their relationship and come out more to family and friends. Beginning treatment focused on uncovering the fears and anxieties that Mark and Bruce harbored about coming out. My presence was needed to structure and sustain a safe place for Mark and Bruce to talk openly with each other. Within this secure holding environment (Scharff and Scharff 1991), Mark and Bruce explored their most private thoughts and fantasies. Sharing their individual concerns about coming out normalized their feelings and provided an opportunity for each to help the other prepare.

Mark and Bruce were encouraged to plan a series of steps, of increasing emotional difficulty, that would move them through a coming out process with friends and family of their choosing. Mark and Bruce made a list of people each wanted to tell and identified who they expected would be most hostile or most receptive. Role playing was used to rehearse meetings, especially with those people who might react negatively. This permitted Mark and Bruce to anticipate reactions, prepare emotionally, and construct non-defensive, self-respecting responses. With some people, Mark and Bruce decided to come out as a couple by inviting them to dinner in the apartment they now shared. Mark and Bruce felt this reinforced their couple identity and gave them a home court advantage where they were in control.

As Mark and Bruce implemented their plans, their pride grew. Although Mark accurately predicted that his mother and father would be rejecting, two brothers and an aunt were surprisingly accepting. His coming out helped establish new and promising family relationships. Mark and Bruce also expanded their social network by participating in activities sponsored by the gay community. This reflected and reinforced their growing self-acceptance.

During the termination stage of treatment, Mark and Bruce were encouraged to create rituals to mark milestones in their relationship. They threw an open house, took a vacation together, and made plans for a commitment ceremony. These rituals helped Mark and Bruce to affirm their new-found self-esteem and to celebrate a valued and satisfying lifestyle within a hostile social environment.

INTERVENTIONS ENHANCING MARK AND BRUCE'S EFFICACY AS A COUPLE

An overall cognitive-behavioral approach was used to bring out Mark and Bruce's beliefs about themselves, their world, and their future — the cognitive triad (Freeman and Reinecke 1995) underlying their internal schemata. I attempted to help Mark and Bruce transform some of their negative and toxic beliefs by combining new behaviors with positive thoughts. Successful actions helped to build more optimistic beliefs about their future together, and hopeful visions of partnership contributed to more proactive behaviors. The couple's cognitive appraisal of their relationship, the heart of couple efficacy, was transformed into a kinder, more accepting, and more self-respecting image.

1. *Constructing tasks that build on success.* Coming out was carefully structured to build the couple's confidence and competence with each

act. Mark and Bruce considered in advance who they would tell and what they would say. They chose to reveal to the most receptive people first, although even the easiest cases required the stressful psychological act of appealing to one's own self for approval. Nonetheless, positive early feedback helped to build self-esteem and a feeling that coming out to others could be a beneficial experience.

2. *Maximizing elements of control.* Treatment interventions were guided by principles of self-determination and choice. Mark and Bruce were encouraged, above all, to exercise their own preferences in deciding who to tell, how to tell, when to tell, and if they might tell. Alternatives were identified whenever possible to maximize options, and opportunities for self-affirmation were created. Mark and Bruce thought through many different ways to present their couplehood to the world and chose from several possibilities: private individual talks, meetings as partners, dinners at their apartment, or celebrations involving many friends. Mark and Bruce were encouraged, wherever possible, to control the conditions of their coming out and to take a proactive stance toward affirming themselves as a couple. In addition, Mark and Bruce were helped to create their own criteria for judging their needs and evaluating their successes.

3. *Preparing for disappointment and rejection.* By anticipating reactions and replaying worst case scenarios, Mark and Bruce prepared for possible rejection by their parents and other significant family members. Although nothing could prevent the psychological blow of an actual rejection, role playing provided some inoculation. Mark and Bruce were helped to script positive self statements (Granvold 1997) that they could use to praise themselves for their efforts. A simple "I did well to face my father directly" or "I am valuable to myself and my partner" was enough to counter some of the entrenched negative beliefs that Mark and Bruce had internalized about themselves. These cognitive-behavioral interventions strengthened the internal statements (Lantz 1996: 103–4) that Mark and Bruce made about themselves. They learned to identify and self-correct the sometimes hidden attitudes and beliefs that negatively colored their self-evaluations.

4. *Constructing celebrations and empowering rituals.* To celebrate is an affirming act. As Mark and Bruce developed more positive views of themselves and their couplehood, they were encouraged to affirm their newly defined identity through private and public celebrations. Couple rituals (Imber-Black 1998) were constructed, including Sunday morning breakfasts together, camping vacations, and attending a monthly

dance at a gay community center. For this couple, cut off from a number of significant relatives, small rituals such as these symbolized their togetherness and helped to build new avenues for validation and self-affirmation.

5. *Building community support.* Because Mark and Bruce had internalized so many negative attitudes about themselves from family members, affiliation with the gay community provided a healing balance (McFadden 1997). Constructing a new sense of family by networking within the gay community and surrounding themselves with those family members and friends who were accepting (Weston 1991) helped Mark and Bruce to bolster positive attitudes about being a self-affirming gay couple in a hostile social environment.

Category 3: Couple Problem-Solving

Raymond and Shawna illustrate how couples who learn problem-solving skills can work together to design goals, improve their relationship, and feel more in control of their lives. The ability to communicate well with one another is a prerequisite for successful problem-solving (Follette and Jacobson 1990).

Raymond and Shawna: Resolving Marital Conflicts

PRESENTING SITUATION

When Shawna married Raymond fourteen years ago, she traded a law career for motherhood and raised three sons, now aged 12, 8, and 6. Raymond earned an MBA and supported the family as a mid-level bank executive. Raymond and Shawna were a prosperous middle-class African American couple with a stable marriage and home life. They sought marital treatment because conflicts arose between them that were rarely, if ever, resolved. Raymond and Shawna were alarmed because even small arguments escalated quickly and were played out in front of the children. Their inability to resolve differences in a more peaceful and mutually satisfying way evoked frustration bordering on despair.

ASSESSMENT

Although Shawna and Raymond were professionally trained problem-solvers (she as a lawyer and he as a businessman), they did not apply their skills with each other at home. Small conflicts became conduits for venting stress and pent-up emotions. Shawna and Raymond needed to learn communication techniques that would permit them to exercise problem-solving skills effectively as marital partners.

TREATMENT

Raymond and Shawna were coached to problem-solve in sessions where I could intervene to restructure communication, keep them on task, encourage them to continue, and praise their success. When dialogue became heated, communication was deliberately slowed down by assigning one partner as speaker and one as listener. Miscommunication could be identified and clarified by simply asking, "What did you just hear your partner saying?" This active listening technique kept their mutual problem-solving from becoming derailed.

We focused on the basic steps of problem-solving: defining and prioritizing problems, generating a range of actions, exploring likely outcomes and anticipating obstacles, creating an action plan, evaluating results, and revising goals and strategies as needed. Raymond and Shawna then analyzed the structure of their conflicts at home and identified three major stumbling blocks. First, when one partner raised a concern, the other would trump it with a different one. The original issue was co-opted, and the partner who raised it felt ignored (and sometimes attacked). Second, Raymond and Shawna argued endlessly despite diminishing returns. Persisting accomplished little other than spurring mutual antagonism. Finally, Raymond and Shawna ended arguments abruptly without planning to revisit them later. They realized how cutting each other off in this way contributed to their lack of problem resolution.

After identifying these three discrete problem areas, Raymond and Shawna set to work finding solutions. They brainstormed strategies and considered which might work best "in the wild," their term for being at home in their natural state of fatigue and stress. Finally, the couple agreed upon clear rules to follow. They decided that whoever initiates a discussion has the right to set the agenda. Each partner had to assume responsibility for pursuing their most important concerns, and no one was allowed to piggy-back one agenda item onto another. Raymond and Shawna created their own idea of "bookmarking," a way to stop a conversation if it threatened to escalate. Either partner could say, "Let's not pursue this now but bookmark it for later" and end the discussion by scheduling a convenient time to talk, after emotions have cooled. Bookmarking helped Raymond and Shawna feel empowered. No longer did arguments control them; they now decided the fate of an argument.

As Raymond and Shawna tested these new strategies at home, they reported a growing confidence that their problem-solving efforts worked. Raymond, expressing his new feeling of empowerment to Shawna, said "I want to build on what we have now found to work and apply it to other areas of our life."

INTERVENTIONS ENHANCING RAYMOND AND SHAWNA'S MUTUAL
PROBLEM-SOLVING

A combination of communication (Gottman et al. 1976) and problem-solving techniques (Turner and Jaco 1996) improved the couple's capacity to work together. Listening attentively, soliciting feedback, reaching for ideas, clarifying statements and meanings, and coming to verbal agreement are communication skills at the core of collaborative problem-solving. Good communication promotes effective problem-solving. Shawna and Raymond already had individual problem-solving skills but needed some coaching to make them a functional team. Practicing in session prepared them to collaborate at home.

Good problem-solving carries its own reward, as this couple discovered; their hard work resulted in tangible success. Raymond and Shawna assimilated the problem-solving method and enjoyed the sense of control this afforded them. Feeling confident, they were eager to apply their newly honed couple skill proactively to other areas of their partnership.

1. *Direct coaching of the couple in collaborative problem-solving and communication.* Because Raymond and Shawna already possessed the intellectual strengths required to problem-solve, I directed them to work together, in front of me, so I could observe and facilitate their process as a coach. Like any coach, my role was to give clear instruction, provide pointers, encourage do-overs, and praise accomplishment. I had to know the method well. Coaching also included structuring and clarifying communication between them. I posed questions when statements were unclear — "Are you saying that waiting so long for a response got you angry?"; I attacked mind-reading expectations — "You need to tell her directly what you want"; I reframed messages to highlight emotional meanings — "She is saying that she held back her advice because she thought you would feel attacked, and she did not want to hurt you"; I taught them to give validation — "Before you make your criticism, tell him first what you understood him to say, so that he can

know you really heard him"; I structured their communication to block arguments — "Be a listener now and concentrate on what your partner is saying; then you can respond." To help the couple process these methods, I took time to solicit their feedback: "What worked for you today and what didn't?" I would then make the communication techniques more explicit so that Raymond and Shawna could reapply these strategies to new situations.

2. *Permitting the couple to create their own solutions.* I encouraged Shawna and Raymond to develop their own problem-solving ideas by asking "How might you go about this differently?" or "What do you think might work better?" I was convinced that, with some emotional support, they could succeed by themselves. Inviting the couple to problem-solve together instilled a sense of ownership, improved their motivation, and spurred creativity. The novel idea of bookmarking emerged from their brainstorming and was accepted easily because they invented it. Their further insight that any problem-solving strategy needed to be tested in the wild nicely reinforced the empirical component of problem-solving. Incorporating the couple's own concepts of bookmarking and testing in the wild into our discussions helped to personalize the method and improve its utility.

Category 4: Flexible Gender Roles

Werner and Smith (1982) revealed that resilient boys and girls blend both masculine and feminine characteristics, being both yielding and assertive, expressive and instrumental (Turner, Norman, and Zunz 1994:115). Although Wendy and Jim structured their relationship on a gender role reversal (he being more feminine and she more masculine), their fixed role behaviors eventually created marital dissatisfaction. Greater flexibility in their gender roles was needed to adapt to an inevitable change in their life-stage.

Wendy and Jim: Risking Change in Established Gender Roles

PRESENTING SITUATION

Wendy and Jim, aged 48 and 55, were unhappy with each other as they entered the empty nest stage of marriage. Their daughter Amy, a talented student of languages, was completing college in Europe and preparing for a career in international banking. Having successfully launched their daughter into the world, Jim and Wendy were reevaluating the state of their marriage.

Jim and Wendy were not a traditional couple: Jim was a freelance writer who assumed the role of primary caretaker of Amy, and Wendy was an advertising executive who was the family's financial breadwinner. This gender role reversal worked well for twenty-five years of marriage, conforming nicely with Jim's nurturant personality and Wendy's ambitious and autonomous nature. With Amy no longer a focus, however, Jim and Wendy's fixed roles were a source of discontent. Wendy felt overburdened with the financial responsibilities, and Jim felt unfulfilled in his domestic work. In their quarrels, Wendy attacked Jim for his lack of ambition, and he counter-attacked, citing her sense of entitlement and ambition at any cost.

ASSESSMENT

Jim and Wendy needed to develop more balance in their spousal roles. Their rigid division of labor within the family system began when Amy was born, seriously ill. Jim chose to stay home as his daughter's nurse while Wendy pursued lucrative career opportunities. An unspoken contract was based upon this early adaptation to their family situation. Jim tacitly agreed to be the nurturer and Wendy the provider.

Their reverse gender roles were anchored in their formative family experiences and identification with their parents. Jim was tied closely to the needs of his mother and younger sisters. His Calvinist upbringing stressed work and the welfare of the family over personal needs. His choice to be his daughter's devoted caretaker was both an accommodation to stoic Calvinist ideals and a rebellion against his father, whose work interfered with his having a close relationship with his son. Wendy was an emotionally neglected and abused little girl who was forced to develop a precocious autonomy. Wendy coveted the social recognition she received for her academic achievements and her success in the marketplace. Because she had poor role models for caretaking, Wendy was less confident about her own abilities to nurture or to parent competently. Wendy, like Jim, performed roles that were most developed and least threatening to her.

TREATMENT

A psychoanalytic approach was needed at first to understand the full development of the gender roles Jim and Wendy had established in their relationship. By exploring some of their formative experiences, Jim and Wendy understood their reactivity to one another better. The harshness of Wendy's anger toward Jim was fueled by the hurt of being left to fend for herself as a child. Jim's contempt for Wendy's work was displaced anger about the Calvinist work ethic and his father's emotional distance.

Modifying entrenched role behaviors, however, required more than insight. Jim and Wendy needed to be challenged to risk new behaviors and helped to develop the latent strengths within their personalities. Fear — of re-viewing hurtful images of parents, trying new behaviors that felt awkward and unpracticed, risking feelings of incompetence — inhibited change. To make their relationship more mutually satisfying, Jim and Wendy overcame these anxieties. Jim learned to assert himself more in the relationship without feel-ings of guilt, and Wendy derived satisfaction from becoming more emotion-ally responsive to Jim. They developed more flexible roles that combined nurturance with assertion and connection with autonomy.

INTERVENTIONS ENHANCING JIM AND WENDY'S ROLE FLEXIBILITY

A psychoanalytic approach helped to clarify the deeper psychological forces that held Jim and Wendy's fixed gender roles in place. By exploring formative childhood experiences together, Jim and Wendy developed mu-tual empathy and some immediate relief. Knowing that a spouse's intense re-actions are not all driven by one's own behavior often reduces interpersonal stress. As couples identify those portable feelings they carry into their rela-tionship from their childhood experiences, they can work more indepen-dently at resolving their own issues.

Cultivating flexibility in this couple's gender roles also involved support-ive interventions that promoted further growth of their adult egos (Goldstein 1995). For Jim and Wendy, who had already established competency in their narrowly defined roles, learning new role behaviors was anxiety-provoking. Actively challenging them to change supported their adaptation to a new stage of marriage, scary as it might be.

1. *Challenging couples directly to risk change.* After Jim and Wendy un-derstood that their disappointments with each other would require growth in their role behaviors, they needed to risk behaving differently. Jim was not comfortable asserting his own needs directly with his wife, and Wendy was equally uncomfortable reaching for Jim's feelings and responding to them. I challenged them directly to change in my pres-ence by verbalizing their underlying fears and asking them to test a new reality. To Jim, "Do you think you could risk being seen as selfish and say what you really want to to your wife?" or "I know it's difficult to break ranks with your Calvinist upbringing, but can you see that Wendy needs to understand who you really are inside?" To Wendy, "I know you fear not having your own needs met, especially if you relinquish your self-advocacy, but try seeing what happens if you attend first to Jim," or "Let's see if Jim really does abandon you when you focus on his needs

first, instead of your own." Posed in this way, requests for change often evoked validation from the spouse: "Yes, Wendy, I'm much more likely to be receptive to you if I experience your interest in me," or "Jim, that's right, I sometimes don't know what's right for you because you keep yourself so hidden."

2. *Catching couples being successful.* Problematic behaviors are often the focus when observing couples in action. Another, more strength-based, approach is to catch them being effective. When Jim or Wendy made desired shifts in their behaviors, such as Jim being more forthright or Wendy being more emotionally attuned, I immediately acknowledged the difference and validated their courageous work. This provided a corrective emotional experience for Wendy, whose efforts to please had gone unacknowledged in her childhood.

Category 5: Couple Empathy

The case of Sarah and Paul illustrates how empathy supports the process of reaching intimacy, through disclosure and attentiveness (Wallerstein and Blakeslee 1995:66). Paul and Sarah reacted to sexual behaviors that had a very special context. Without fully understanding the life story framing those behaviors, the couple could not respond to their underlying needs in a sensitive, caring way.

Sarah and Paul: Enhancing Sexual Intimacy

PRESENTING SITUATION

Sarah and Paul had been married five years and had one child. Sarah was angry that Paul avoided sexual relations and was frustrated at having to be the one who initiated sex. Paul admitted feeling uncomfortable with intercourse and having difficulty maintaining erections. He complained that Sarah's demands and critical attitude increased his anxiety.

ASSESSMENT

Sarah and Paul had family histories that make sexual intercourse an overdetermined event for them both. Paul, the youngest of three boys, had a quiet nature very unlike his macho brothers. They teased him cruelly for his shy temperament and humiliated him with sexually demeaning comments. His father was loud and crass, drank heavily, and used graphic dirty language in public and private, making Paul ashamed and self-conscious about his own sexual impulses. Once, he witnessed his father drunkenly rape his mother. Paul associated these humiliating and traumatic memories with sexual intercourse and sometimes equated having sexual relations with Sarah as behaving like his father. Wendy was a middle child with two gorgeous sisters. She was born with a prominent skin discoloration on her face that made her feel ugly and different. Her father was emotionally distant, and Sarah blamed his lack of affection on the way she looked. Sarah struggled for acceptance with peers and felt unpopular through high school. With this history, Sarah interpreted Paul's avoidance of sex as a lack of real love for her, and she again felt ugly and unlovable.

TREATMENT

Sarah and Paul were helped to narrate their personal stories so that each could appreciate the underlying meanings attributed to their sexual relations. Their interpersonal behaviors could then be reframed more empathically. Paul wanted to avoid memories associated with his father and brothers, not avoid Sarah, the wife he cherished. And Sarah needed further demonstration of Paul's loving feelings for her, not necessarily sexual performance. Sarah and Paul were encouraged to develop more intimate communication that did not focus on sex but affirmed their strong, loving feelings for one another. Anxiety reduction techniques such as sensate exercises that do not focus on intercourse were also practiced. Even these exercises required the development of deeper empathy between the couple in order to carry them out. Without enhancing their appreciation of the deep hurt and shame experienced in their lives, Sarah and Paul would be unable to move beyond their mutual anger and blame.

INTERVENTIONS ENHANCING SARAH AND PAUL'S EMPATHY

Happily married partners, Wallerstein and Blakeslee write, not only learn the other person's life story, they keep it in mind at all times (1995:65). Paul and Sarah needed to learn each other's life story. This was the key to unlocking their mutual empathy. Telling their stories, replete with fears, vulnerabilities, disappointments, and wishes, was the first step in establishing the intimate connection they really wanted. Although cognitive techniques were useful to understand the meanings and associations that each partner attributed to specific behaviors (Baucom, Epstein, and Rankin 1995), a more heartfelt empathy emerged from simply sharing their personal narratives.

1. *Encouraging the telling of life stories.* Time was needed to explore the individual life stories of Sarah and Paul. Narrating special memories

and events that compose one's life not only provides a helpful catharsis but gives partners an opportunity to share in each other's intimate personal dramas. Sarah did not know about her husband's sibling relationship or the rape of Paul's mother. Hearing about these created an immediate shift in her attitude toward his sexual inhibitions. And Paul did not appreciate how Sarah's demands for sex were driven by her deep fear that she was unlovable. The theme of unlovability emerged clearly as she described her life with her father, sisters, and peers. The empathy created by hearing what each had suffered improved their patience, sensitivity, and sense of connection with each other.

2. *Mirroring narratives to partners.* When partners react in unsympathetic ways to each other, I will intervene by retelling their stories. For example, I might say to Paul, "Let's remember that Sarah carries a fear with her that she is unwanted and unlovable. Her father was unable to demonstrate his feelings and this left Sarah in doubt about his love. When you stay silent, her fears rise quickly to the surface," or, to Sarah, "Paul was deeply shamed by his father's crass, sexual aggression. He needs your reassurance that being assertive with you in bed feels loving and intimate to you."

3. *Recasting narratives to highlight strengths.* Partner stories provide opportunities for positive reframing. When Paul spoke shamefully about his family and himself, his narrative could be recast as a triumph of survival; Paul remained loyal to his own sense of self under conditions that he had no power to change. Sarah's story could be recast as demonstrating her deep knowledge that she deserved something better and could eventually find it in a partner relationship of her own. Qualities of perseverance, hope, and personal fortitude characterized Paul and Sarah's narratives and were emphasized to help them internalize their own strengths.

Category 6: Sense of Mission

No couple I have worked with has exhibited a more conscious sense of couple mission than Lisa and Steve, who intuitively grasped the importance of constructing common goals to build a relationship. Lisa and Steve, children of bitterly divorced parents, anchored their marriage in planned achievements that affirmed their vision of what a functional couple could accomplish. Their mission to build a rewarding and lasting interpersonal relationship gave transcendent meaning to their struggle to succeed where their own parents had faltered.

Lisa and Steve: Building A Better Life Together

PRESENTING SITUATION

Lisa and Steve, children of abusive, alcoholic parents, married with a clear mission to build something better than what they had experienced. Because their parents had divorced and remarried several times, they were committed to making their own relationship work. Lisa and Steve agreed to create a life that was responsible, caring, and purposeful. Every day felt like a battle, but they attended Adult Children of Alcoholics support group meetings, individual therapy, and worked hard at their jobs. Lisa was a paralegal and Steve owned a construction company. They came to couples treatment for additional support, "just to make sure we do things right."

ASSESSMENT

Lisa and Steve possessed many strengths. They were in recovery, used professional and peer support well, maintained successful jobs, and had a proactive attitude about their lives. Their request for support was a safety net, to make sure they stayed on task and did not slip. They had clear goals and demonstrated strong motivation to create a life they could respect.

TREATMENT

Lisa and Steve would enter treatment at various transition points in their lives: before getting married, before building a new house, and before having children. They wanted a therapist who could help give them a reality check and confront them, if necessary, to keep them honest in their relationship. For the most part this was unnecessary, as they were quite vigilant with each other. Instead, our work focused on helping Lisa and Steve to formulate their couple goals. They knew that they wanted to build a solid life for themselves and needed private time to plan it. This planning gave Lisa and Steve a common purpose: to bring accomplishment and meaning to their life as a couple. Our work ended by celebrating their many accomplishments together. I even received an invitation to their tenth wedding anniversary, where they intended to renew their vows.

INTERVENTIONS ENHANCING LISA AND STEVE'S
MISSION BUILDING

Lisa and Steve were highly motivated to create a stable marriage. Their quest for normalcy added zeal to their task, transforming their vision of marriage into a driving mission. They used each other as allies, challenging themselves to achieve, demanding honesty in their relations, guarding each other against game playing, and keeping each other focused on achieving their common goals.

Lisa and Steve used treatment primarily to plan together, to talk out what they wanted, and how they might get it. They did not yet completely trust their own strengths and felt that they needed me to keep them communicating and problem-solving efficiently. I think that I provided a secure holding environment (a sense of stable home) that they had not experienced in their youth. My presence and encouragement provided an added dimension of personal reassurance they needed to keep growing. My availability to them at transition points in their life provided a supportive sense of stability.

Couples like Lisa and Steve teach us how to intervene. We need to explore the ways they found to survive, to overcome, and to thrive. That means asking them how they did it. Strength-based assessments (Cowger 1997) and solution-focused techniques (de Shazer 1991; Shoham et al. 1995) help in this task. Clients and social workers need to focus more effort on identifying what has worked rather than on what has failed. This is at the center of solution-focused techniques, where past success is used as a model for future action, where exceptions to failure serve as solution-oriented paradigms, and where coping strategies already known to work well are reapplied or amplified. Lisa and Steve intuitively applied solution-focused strategies in remaking themselves and their lives. The techniques below represent some of the heuristics for mission-building I learned from them.

1. *Reviewing the past for clues to a better future.* Lisa and Steve had endured harsh childhood experiences. There was a lot to learn about how they derived strength from adversity. I asked them directly, "How did you do it? How did you manage to survive these experiences and develop such will and optimism?" Lisa, I found out, learned from observing, that her mother's passivity led to victimization, and at the age of 10, she made a vow to never become like her mother. Steve also responded adaptively to his family situation. He felt profoundly ashamed by his father's binge drinking and was driven to achieve as a way to recover the self-respect missing in his life. Lisa and Steve transformed their private pain into a couple mission and used each other's energy to keep their mission alive.

2. *Reviewing accomplishments often.* Survivors like Lisa and Steve need constant reminders of their accomplishments and frequent review of

where they have been and how much they have achieved. It was important that I find ways to communicate my true admiration for their achievements. This personal reassurance appeared helpful in sustaining their motivation. I hoped, therapeutically, that my acknowledgment of their hard work would eventually become internalized as a supportive voice within them.

3. *Encouraging couples to affirm spiritual beliefs.* I learned to integrate spirituality into treatment from Lisa and Steve, who returned to the church as adults and used religious ritual to affirm their couplehood. They married in a full church ceremony, baptized their children, and renewed their wedding vows after ten years. Their affiliation with a religious community helped to normalize their life and became a source of hope for them both. Religious faith helped Lisa and Steve recover from a miscarriage and resurrected their hope in having children in the future. When events occur that couples cannot control, transcendent beliefs and values help to sustain a relationship.

Categories of couple resiliency explored in this paper are not independent of each other but are mutually reinforcing. Mark and Bruce certainly needed to develop mutual empathy, as well as exercise good problem-solving skills, to progress in establishing their relationship in the world; Raymond and Shawna could not successfully problem-solve without accurately appraising workable areas for change in their relationship; Catherine and Dan were forced to confront the meaning of their relationship after Dan's illness was more accurately appraised — involving them in a reassessment of their couple mission; and Lisa and Steve's sense of value and power in the world were integral parts of their mission building. Couple resiliency is greater than the sum of its parts and needs to be understood as an integrated weave of components. From this perspective, social workers can feel both reassured and challenged. Reassured, because strengthening one component of resilience will influence others; small strategic interventions, therefore, may create synergistic effects. This same systemic integration presents a challenge, for we must be prepared to intervene in multiple areas of couple functioning, skillfully assessing and effectively using an eclectic repertoire of intervention techniques.

I have tried to demonstrate the broad range of techniques that may be enlisted in service of promoting resilient functioning among couples. I have also derived certain therapeutic heuristics from these cases that any generalist practitioner might use. As Walsh (1998) and others advocating strength-based approaches emphasize, resiliency enhancement involves more than techniques, new or old; resiliency enhancement is dependent upon our willingness to see strength and capacity in the midst of dysfunction: a parallel struggle, perhaps, to our own clients' efforts to rebound from adversity.

A therapeutic belief framing my perspective on couple resiliency is that, as couples develop and use the skills they need to promote the resiliency categories discussed in this paper, a supracategory of resiliency is created — the couple holding environment, with the capacity to become its own resource for resiliency. Over time, as couples are tested by adversity and learn to cope well, their relationship becomes experienced as a shelter from stress, as a springboard for new ideas, as an embrace that calms, as a container for meaningful memories, and as a symbol of accomplishment and hope. If we, as social workers, can help couples to cope well, then a couple holding environment will ultimately grow.

References

Baucom, D. H., N. Epstein, and L. A. Rankin. 1995. Cognitive aspects of cognitive-behavioral marital therapy. In N. S. Jacobson and A. S. Gurman, eds., *Clinical Handbook of Couple Therapy*, 65–90. New York: Guilford Press.

Beardslee, W. R. and D. Podorefsky. 1988. Resilient adolescents whose parents have serious affective and other psychiatric disorders: Importance of self-understanding and relationships. *American Journal of Psychiatry* 145:63–69.

Cowen, E., P. Wyman, W. Work, and G. Parker. 1990. The Rochester Child Resilience Project: Overview and summary of first year findings. *Development and Psychopathology* 2:193–212.

Cowger, C. 1997. Assessing client strengths: Assessment for client empowerment. In D. Saleebey, ed., *The Strengths Perspective in Social Work Practice* 2d ed., 59–73. New York: Longman.

de Shazer, S. 1991. *Putting Differences to Work*. New York: Norton.

Follette, V. M. and N. S. Jacobson. 1990. Treating communication problems from a behavioral perspective. In R. Chasin, H. Grunebaum, and M. Herzig, eds., *One Couple, Four Realities: Multiple Perspectives on Couple Therapy*, 229–245. New York: Guilford Press.

Freeman, A. and M. A. Reinecke. 1995. Cognitive therapy. In A. S. Gurman and S. B. Messer, eds., *Essential Psychotherapies: Theory and Practice*, 182–225. New York: Guilford Press.

Garmezy, N. and A. S. Masten. 1986. Stress, competence, and resilience: Common frontiers for therapist and psychopathologist. *Behavior Therapy* 57 (2): 159–174.

Goldstein, E. 1995. *Ego Psychology and Social Work Practice* 2d ed. New York: The Free Press.

Gottman, J. M., C. I. Notarius, J. Gonso, and J. J. Markman. 1976. *A Couple's Guide to Communication.* Champaign, Ill.: Research Press.

Granvold, D. K. 1997. Cognitive-behavioral therapy with adults. In J. R. Brandell, ed., *Theory and Practice in Clinical Social Work,* 164–201. New York: The Free Press.

Imber-Black, E. 1988. Normative and therapeutic rituals in couples therapy. In E. Imber-Black, J. Roberts, and R. Whiting, eds., *Rituals in Families and Family Therapy,* 47–83. New York: W. W. Norton.

Kumpfer, K. L. 1993. Resiliency and AOD Use Prevention in High Risk Youth. Unpublished manuscript.

Lantz, J. 1996. Cognitive theory and social work treatment. In F. J. Turner, ed., *Social Work Treatment: Interlocking Theoretical Approaches* 4th ed., 94–115. New York: The Free Press.

McFadden, S. 1997. Redefining the family: The concept of family for lesbians and gay men. In E. P. Congress, ed., *Multicultural Perspectives in Working with Families,* 167–180. New York: Springer.

Minuchin, S. and H. C. Fishman. 1981. *Family Therapy Techniques.* Cambridge, Mass.: Harvard University Press.

Reid, W. J. 1992. *Task Strategies: An Empirical Approach to Clinical Social Work.* New York: Columbia University Press.

Reid, W. J. 1996. Task-centered social work. In F. J. Turner, ed., *Social Work Treatment* 4th ed., 617–640.

Scharff, D. E. and J. S. Scharff. 1991. *Object Relations Couple Therapy.* Northvale, N.J.: Jason Aronson.

Shoham, V., M. Rohrbaugh, and J. Patterson. 1995. Problem- and solution-focused couple therapies: The MRI and Milwaukee models. In N. S. Jacobson and A. S. Gurman, eds., *Clinical Handbook of Couple Therapy,* 65–90. New York: Guilford Press.

Smith, C. and B. E. Carlson. 1997. Stress, coping, and resilience in children and youth. *Social Service Review* (June): 231–256.

Turner, J. and R. M. Jaco. 1996. Problem-solving theory and social work treatment. In F. J. Turner, ed., *Social Work Treatment* 4th ed., 503–522.

Turner, S., E. Norman, and S. Zunz. 1994. Resiliency. In E. Norman, S. Turner, and S. Zunz, eds., *Substance Abuse Prevention: A Review of the Literature,* 100–141. New York State Office of Alcohol and Substance Abuse Services.

Wallerstein, J. S. and S. Blakeslee. 1995. *The Good Marriage: How and Why Love Lasts.* New York: Warner Books.

Walsh, F. 1996. The concept of family resilience: Crisis and challenge. *Family Process* 35 (3): 261–281.

Walsh, F. 1998. *Strengthening Family Resilience.* New York: Guilford Press.

Weston, K. 1991. *Families We Choose: Lesbians, Gays, Kinship.* New York: Columbia University Press.

Werner, E. E. 1986. Resilient offspring of alcoholics: A longitudinal study from birth to age 18. *American Journal of Orthopsychiatry* 59:72–81.

Werner, E. E. and R. S. Smith. 1982. *Vulnerable but Invincible.* New York: McGraw-Hill.

Winnicott, D. W. 1965. *The Maturational Processes and the Facilitating Environment: Studies in the Theory of Emotional Development.* New York: International Universities Press.

Woods, M. E. and F. Hollis. 1990. *Casework: A Psychosocial Therapy* 4th ed. New York: McGraw-Hill.

Woods, M. E. and H. Robinson. 1996. Psychosocial theory and social work treatment. In F. J. Turner, ed., *Social Work Treatment* 4th ed., 555–580.

9 Strength and Resiliency Themes in Social Work Practice with Groups

Michael H. Phillips and Carol S. Cohen

This paper explores the remarkable similarities in the themes of the strengths perspective and social work practice with groups, and the ways in which mutual aid groups support the development of resiliency factors in their members. In addition to a discussion on a theoretical level, we present examples from mutual aid groups for children whose parents abuse drugs or alcohol.

The data are drawn from the process recordings of eight groups conducted in grammar schools and the videotape of one group conducted in a community-based mental health clinic. All group members were children from low-income urban communities. The school-based groups included African American and Hispanic boys and girls ages 8 to 10. Each school group had a single adult leader: six of the leaders were white women, one an African American woman, and one a Hispanic man. The mental health clinic group was composed of 5 African American boys ages 8 to 10, and had two adult co-leaders, an African American woman and a white man.

Common Underpinnings

Practice methods and models are rooted in ideas about the nature of human beings, their environments, and their interaction with people, places, and systems within their world. Social work with groups and the strengths perspective share four major beliefs:

Primary resources for change can be found in the clients themselves;
experience is a source of strength;
every environment has resources; and
strengths can be enhanced.

These beliefs serve as a platform for further elaboration of both the strengths perspective and of the group work method.

PRIMARY RESOURCES FOR CHANGE CAN BE FOUND IN THE CLIENTS THEMSELVES

Social work with groups and the strengths perspective are based on a common belief in the capacity of people to make positive changes in their own lives, in those of others, and in their environments. The strengths perspective (Saleebey 1997) is based on the fundamental idea that everyone has strengths that constitute the primary instruments of change. The reciprocal model of social group work shares this belief (Schwartz 1961) and suggests that a group's power comes from the interaction of its members as they engage in a collective process of growth and change.

> The group is an enterprise in mutual aid, an alliance of individuals who need each other, in varying degrees, to work on certain common problems. The important fact is that this is a helping system in which the clients need each other as well as the worker. This need to use each other, to create not one but many helping relationships, is a vital ingredient of the group process and constitutes a common need over and above the specific tasks for which the group was formed.   (Schwarz 1961:18)

Thus the strengths perspective and mutual aid model agree that each individual has the potential for change, and should be the key actor in the process.

EXPERIENCE IS A SOURCE OF STRENGTH

The strengths perspective proposes that while trauma, abuse, illness, or struggle may be injurious, they may also be sources of challenge and opportunity. Fundamental to social work with groups is the belief that people grow and achieve through honoring life experience and drawing from it to help themselves and others. In both models, all experience is considered valuable. People can make use of experiences that have taken place at any time in their lives. They have the capacity to transform hardship, tragedy, failure, or disappointment into life lessons and to use them as motivation towards change and growth (Walsh 1998).

Social work with groups adds the potential of the group-as-a-whole to create a collective experience to further empower members. Building a reservoir of shared history through participation in the group, and then bringing the outside world into the group's safe environment, creates a new reality and sense of support for the members. Through this process members learn that they can use their difficult experiences as sources for change and growth.

EVERY ENVIRONMENT HAS RESOURCES

A major contribution of the strengths perspective is its directive to look at all environments as having resources and capacities to support clients' growth. Sometimes, in our recognition of the problems within particular communities, we miss the significant support systems that exist, and the resiliency factors that clients can call upon to survive. The search for these resources does not imply that these environments are free of troubles, nor that we should overlook problems and focus exclusively on positive attributes. Rather we need to open our field of vision to incorporate the wide range of experiences, including opportunities and threats, strengths and weaknesses.

Social work with groups shares this broad vision, allowing for a full assessment of clients' social systems. Not only are workers expected to make an assessment of each client and system, but they also view each potential member as a resource to the others in the group and in the community. Through the worker mediating between the group and the social context, the environment may be seen as a resource to the group. By extension, if all environments have strengths and social work focuses on mobilizing strengths, there are virtually no environments in which group work cannot be practiced.

STRENGTHS CAN BE ENHANCED

The final area of intersection of the strengths perspective and social work with groups relates to the fundamental belief that a person's strengths are not static, but can be enhanced through a variety of experiences. Saleebey (1997) directs workers to avoid assumptions about the upper limits of clients' capacity to grow and change, and to take individual, group, and community aspirations seriously. Social work groups similarly "start where the clients are," and do not prescribe a ceiling to growth. Group work's extensive planning phase includes bio-psycho-social assessments of client needs and strengths to help establish a baseline from which clients and workers will recognize progress.

The initial engagement phase of the group is characterized by the struggle to find common ground and common purpose among the members. With these, the group can provide an arena in which members make decisions, experiment with roles, solve problems, and help each other-all processes that contribute to the enhancement of strengths. The group pursues its goals with mutual respect and assistance, both as group process and goal achievement.

Resiliency Factors and Social Work Practice with Groups

Fundamental beliefs provide a foundation for work, but do not provide an actual blueprint for practice. While the strengths perspective provides a context for thinking about the nature of the helping process, it does not provide specific areas in which to intervene. By incorporating knowledge about risk and resiliency factors, we have a framework within which to build upon specific strengths of individual clients and their environments.

Resiliency can be defined as the ability to survive, rebound, or overcome a variety of life experiences, including adversity, stress, and deprivation (Hirayama and Hirayama 1998; Kirby and Fraser 1997; Garmezy 1993). Among the individual factors associated with resiliency are genetic and biological characteristics as well as personality factors such as self-efficacy, empathy, humor, and the ability to realistically appraise one's environment. Family protective factors include positive bonds among members, high parental expectations, and extended family support networks. Peer and school protective factors such as a caring, supportive atmosphere in which students are encouraged to teach each other (Riessman 1990), and community factors such as positive cultural norms, have been seen as contributing to resiliency among children and young adults.

The mutual aid group process of social work supports the development of at least the following resiliency factors: a relationship with a significant adult; the belief or hope that things can be different; a sense of control; self-efficacy; adaptive distancing; connection to a pro-social peer group; release from personal blame; enhanced communication skills; and development of problem solving skills.

Mutual Aid Groups of Children of Substance Abusers

Five primary struggles have been identified as common to children of substance abusers (Black 1979; Deutsch 1982). First is the centrality of substance abuse in the lives of these children: they worry about the dangers the abuser's behavior poses to them, their family, and others. The substance-abusing relative is never far from the child's mind. Children tend to modify their own behavior in a vain attempt to avert problems with the substance abuser.

Second is the area of denial and shame. Substance abusers tend to minimize and deny the significant impact that their behavior is having on others, and the family attempts to deny the problem to the larger world, from embarrassment and shame. The problem is kept a family secret. Even when children identify themselves as having a parent with a drug abuse problem, they often minimize or withdraw that statement by indicating that the abuser has stopped or is stopping.

The third theme found in children of substance abusers is inconsistency, insecurity, and fear: the unpredictability of the substance abuser's behavior causes children to be constantly fearful of what the parent or relative may do, especially in front of their friends. Children also fear that something they do may provide an excuse for the abuse. Further, they may fear that they themselves may become substance abusers.

Anger and hatred are the fourth theme, with children both hating abusing parents and at the same time loving them for the parents they are when not intoxicated. Confusion about why a parent becomes drunk or uses other drugs may also cause children to direct their anger at the other parent, feeling that the non-substance-abusing parent must be doing something to cause the abuser's behavior. The common feature of violence in the family leads to further confusion of feelings.

The final theme, of guilt and blame, is an extension of the simultaneous feelings of love and hate toward the parents, in which children tend to turn anger inward, in the form of guilt. They believe that in some way they are the cause of the problem. They may develop an inordinate need to take care of the substance abuser and feel they are the only one in the family who cares about this relative.

The issues that children of substance abusers must deal with have several implications for social work practice. These children have learned to be indirect and ambiguous in their conversations; they must be helped to break through the norm of silence and learn to be open and direct. They must be helped to reveal their feelings so they can sort them out, label them, and attach their feelings to the true cause of their discomfort. They must recognize that they do not need to feel guilty: the abuser's behavior is not their doing. They need to focus on their own survival. However, it is important that they do not simply get caught up in a constant ventilation of feelings. The children need to find a way to achieve a detachment that being trapped in their feelings would not permit.

Given the fact that about two thirds of the children of substance abusing parents do not become substance abusers, they clearly represent a resilient population. Many efforts have been made to understand how some children raised under these circumstances display characteristics of resiliency, while others seem to be defeated by their experience (Merkengas, Rounsaville, and Prusoff 1992; Werner and Smith 1992).

Groups have been seen as an intervention of choice for children of substance abusers (Phillips and Markowitz 1992; Rhodes 1995). They provide an arena for sharing the family secret in a safe environment. When children are able to be specific about their experiences and discover that there are others with similar problems, they feel less isolated. They can overcome the feeling that there is something wrong with them and face their own fears that they may become substance abusers themselves. The norm that it is dangerous to share this secret can be replaced by a better understanding of where, and with whom, they can share it. As they move to the level of coping with the substance abuse situation they come to see how it has run their lives and they gain some understanding of how they may effectively distance themselves from it.

The groups discussed here were conducted in both school and community settings, using the mutual aid model developed by William Schwartz (1961). Participants were latency age children who had at least one parent who abused alcohol or other drugs. Some participants volunteered for the groups, while others were invited to join after review of case records indicated a parent with a history of substance abuse. Regardless of the approach, all groups followed the same general thematic development.

THEMES IN THE BEGINNING STAGE OF GROUP DEVELOPMENT

The initial stage of the mutual aid group invariably includes the development of an agreement (a contract) regarding what the group will work on. In these groups, the process of contracting began even before the first session, with a discussion with prospective members about the purpose of the group. The worker's initial introduction of purpose at the first session is followed by a variety of approaches to highlight the group members' common experience of having a substance abusing relative, and that this commonality is the reason they are in the group. Once the common purpose of the group is identified, members are able to share experiences and talk about how they are affected by having substance abusing family members. One student, whose alcoholic father was no longer in the home, stated: "I still get an uncomfortable feeling-nervous-when I'm at home. Even though I know he's not there, I get panicky."

Another member indicated that even though she was going to Spain during the summer, she felt that her concerns about her parent's alcoholism would "follow me there." She captured the theme that one is not able to get away from these problems, since the problem is all-consuming. The experience of making the common secret public so early in the group contributes to a sense of being "all in the same boat" (Steinberg 1997), in which members recognize that while unique, much of their situation and shame is shared by others. This enables members to begin the process of bonding with peers, broadening their relationships beyond their own family. Such bonding is a factor in building resiliency. However, to activate resiliency, bonding needs to be connected to the idea of hope, rather than just a commonality of problem. Progress needs to be encouraged. The coupling of the worker's empathic understanding with a "demand for work" (Schwartz 1971) helps members see that the boat they are on is not a sinking ship, but a seaworthy vessel.

The discussion of confidentiality becomes an early opportunity to explore issues of trust and the power differential between members and worker. In one case, a worker summarized the confidentiality contract among the members, but excluded herself from the blanket statement that nothing that happened in the group could be shared outside the group. A group member confronted the worker with: "So even if we don't want you to tell, you could anyway, and we, if we hear something we think is serious, cannot tell our parents!" The effective handling of such confidentiality issues can be a potent experience in understanding the dimensions of self-determination. Members become empowered through their informed consent (Cohen and Phillips 1995). There sense of self-efficacy is enhanced as they experience the worker's respect and acknowledgment that they deserve to know where they stand before engaging with the group.

Norms for participation are developed during the initial phase. Contrary to workers' inclination to accept differential participation, in these groups workers must avoid suggesting that it is acceptable for a member not to speak, since the costs to the reluctant member and the group are great. Otherwise, the other members may think that the reluctant member is not committed to the group, making others hesitant to take the risks necessary for progress. Members must be helped to see that it is in their common interest to actively belong to the group. For example, a child in one group expressed reluctance about being a part of the group and suggested the group "would be better off without me." Such reluctance must be faced head-on by workers (if not taken up by other members), and if resolution is not possible, the member should be allowed to drop out of the group. In such a rare event, the worker bears the responsibility to offer and arrange alternate services to the exiting member.

Members move from "I'm the only one with this problem" to "Only those of us with this problem can understand it" and on to "Can a worker who may not be a child of a substance abuser understand?" This process is part of the movement toward hoping that things can be different. There is a hint in the beginning sessions that to understand members' dilemmas, one has to have experienced the same pain. With this comes the related theme of whether the worker can understand the problems faced by the members. Children first worry that their problem is so unique that only someone who has experienced the problem can be of help. While this rejection of people who have not experienced the problem encourages member-to-member bonds, its latent message may be to distance the members from the workers. Questions about the qualifications of workers continue to surface throughout the group's life, serving a variety of purposes. Most often, their underlying meaning is to ask whether workers can be of help to the members (Shulman 1999). When workers respond that they care about the members and can be of help in ways other than "knowing" the problem firsthand, they open the possibility of engagement with adults who have the members' best interests at heart. Working through this stage in the group's development paves the way for members to develop the resiliency factor of making positive connections with caring adults outside the family network.

THEMES IN THE WORK STAGE OF GROUP DEVELOPMENT

Work phase sessions involve moving through the issues of trust in the group to revelations of members' feelings of despair. One child said, "If I share my problem no one will like me." In discussing the family member with the substance abuse problem, members commonly express the feeling that there might be something wrong with themselves. Members talk about the dangers to both the abuser and other members of the family, and about their inability to control the danger. Dangers to the substance abusers and the dangers of the children's neighborhoods grow as prominent themes at this stage. Stories about shootouts may abound, with the underlying message that "No one cares." These children are indirectly asking whether the worker, too, will become overwhelmed and not care about what happens to them. In a sense, talk of danger and lack of control is an indirect way to talk about what good the group can do. Through this discussion, members pose the essential question to the group: "Can you understand the dangers I face both in the family and in the community?" Members feel alone, and workers must help children bring this concern to the surface. It is important to remember that in sharing these comments the members are expressing the belief that things can be different.

Members' feelings may be too intense and frightening for them. They may try to cut themselves off from these feelings. In one case, in response to a worker's question about what has happens in their neighborhoods, a member answered: "The only thing that happened to me is I went over to my mother's house and I saw this man jump off the roof." Other members then added stories of babies being killed in car accidents, robberies, and beatings of people under the influence of drugs and alcohol. Fears must be acknowledged, yet the discussion about these dangers in the community must also be seen as an attempt to externalize the problem, to avoid facing their felt inability to control the substance abuse in their families.

Stories about neighborhood dangers are also an indirect communication about the dangers members feel in revealing themselves. It is important to recognize that these children do live in a world that is dangerous. In fact, the sound of gunfire interrupted some of these group sessions, and many members mentioned relatives and friends who had been shot, killed, or robbed. Workers must acknowledge members' feelings that the world and their lives are out of control, and help members see the group as a safe environment in which they can exercise control. This process of developing a sense that they can exercise some form of control, and the critical judgment to understand what they can and cannot control is a part of building a sense of self-efficacy (Rutter 1985).

Issues of anger often begin to emerge in the middle phase of groups, as in the case of a child who tells of wanting to get a knife to kill his drunken grandfather. Anger and what to do with this powerful feeling is a latent theme in the members' families, and becomes a manifest part of the work within the group. Anger must be seen in a positive light, since it shows that the child has not given up. Members often reframe the issues of danger and death as "people who use substances are crazy." This is seen as both an explanation, and is connected to the idea that there is something defective in the person who uses drugs or alcohol. Seeing the abuser as crazy effectively distances the group member from the abuser. Here we see the beginning of the development of adaptive distancing, the resiliency quality indicating the ability to separate oneself from overwhelming family problems.

The theme of the worker being "one of the gang" reemerges during this stage, and children frequently revisit the question of whether workers share the problem of family substance abuse in their families. In one meeting, a worker was verbally attacked because she would not share whether she had such a problem in her own family. The message here was "Can you understand what it is we are coping with?" as well as an effort to drive the worker away because of the group members' feelings of being unlovable. In this special population it appears that only after children gain experience accepting other group members' help and feeling concern from peers are they able to move on to using the worker to help them make connections beyond the group. This dynamic further legitimizes social work with groups as a method of choice in working with children of substance abusers.

As the members move further into the group process, they often raise themes of unfairness and injustice. Children describe their parents, brothers and sisters, and police as unfair. They often see all authority figures as unfair, presumably including the worker who is making them look at problems they feel they cannot solve. Workers need to consider these expressions a part of a "normative crisis" (Garland, Jones, and Kolodny 1976) in which the members have become invested in the group but are afraid to fully commit to the hard work ahead of them. Workers need to help group members refocus so they can see that they are talking about their feelings of loss of control, the ultimate unfairness. Workers must help children to express the anger that is blocking them from moving on to further exploration of the problem.

Members often complain about their difficulty in sharing in the group, as in "We don't know each other enough" to talk-blaming others for their own unwillingness to be open. They are answered by other members who share their frustration. "Yeah, but we've been meeting long enough to know each other." This complex struggle to share is a particular characteristic of this population, as one child noted: "Sometimes I feel if I talk about people with drug and alcohol [problems] it feels like I'm in a cocoon, but if I talk about fun things it's like I'm a butterfly."

As members make tentative steps to move beyond their feelings of despair, they begin to struggle with the question of why people drink when they know it will hurt them. Group members initially tend to give pat answers like "It makes them look cool," or "You forget your problems [when you drink]." These comments help them rationalize substance abuse by family members. In moving the group forward, members challenge these rationalizations with questions such as "How come that doesn't happen to everyone?" Others respond by deflecting the issue, suggesting that members should ignore what is going on at home. Others in turn challenge this by asking "Don't I have a responsibility to help my relative stop drinking or taking drugs?" As one member put it, "People say you don't get involved. But suppose you can help? My cousin in Puerto Rico always solves his parents' fights. He gets his brothers away from the table and he tells them to stop fighting."

While children of substance abusers generally feel the need to help family members, the worker's responsibility is to help members come to peace with what they can and cannot change. This quality of recognizing that one is not at fault has been identified by Beardslee and Podorefsky (1988) as a resiliency factor among children coming from troubled backgrounds. Members must be able to accept their own realities, such as "My mother and father fight when they drink; when I get involved, I get hit." Group members should be encouraged to explore the options they do have, including trying to achieve a change in the way they reach out to others for help. It is not sufficient to help children release themselves from responsibility, since without a course of action, their powerlessness is reinforced, rather than challenged. The struggle is to establish appropriate adaptive distancing, coupled with the development of problem-solving and an action orientation. At this stage, children will begin to acknowledge that the feelings they are expressing are signals of their own confusion, and to see how the group has enabled them to take control of their own fate. Within the group, they have been able to clarify and label their feelings, to share with others and discuss together how one can cope and avoid being sucked into their parent's problems. This problem-solving process represents the development of yet another resiliency skill.

The acknowledgment by group members in the middle phase of the group that their own families are not like others is accompanied by feelings of loss. Children talk about their disappointment about their family being different, about not being able to even share their feelings at home, and how uncomfortable they are around the substance abusing parent. These feelings were highlighted by a member who said that when she faced the drinking in her house she felt like she was "trapped and wanted to get out." As the group evolves, members bring up their disappointing experiences seeking help from others outside their families. They point out that often people do not listen to them. The group, as a corrective environment, creates an atmosphere of trust in which these things can be discussed and members will not be disappointed. Breaking through the taboos around communication about the family secret also enables members to discuss other subjects that are troubling them, such as smoking or sexual activity.

While group members begin to see coming to the group as helpful, it is not uncommon for group members to have continuing ambivalence around revealing feelings in the group. Often they will continue to avoid exploring the substance abuse problem in depth by returning to injustices they have faced. Fights and bickering among group members are common, and members may express despair that nothing gets done. Just as with the silent member, the worker must avoid the temptation to exclude disruptive members from the group, since exclusion would be seen as a confirmation of failure.

Only well into the middle phase do group members feel comfortable enough to directly and openly discuss the issue of secrets in the family. Generally group members refer to their feelings of being excluded and of secrets being kept from them. They talk about how their parents' attempt to conceal substance abuse problems from them does not prevent them from worrying. In fact, they express thoughts such as "There are a lot of mysteries in my family." There are undercurrents of the fear of death from substance abuse, and fear that the abusing family member is in an even worse condition than they knew. Members acknowledge how they have tried to ignore what was happening at home, and share the problem of being caught between parents asking them to choose sides. The pressures they feel to control the behavior of the substance-abusing parent and the unfairness they feel at being made to take on adult responsibilities become key themes in the group.

Beginning with the unfairness of everything, as in "There is no one to talk to, I get blamed for everything" and "No matter what I do I am blocked," members move to look critically at their parents and their problems. Questions such as "Are my parents just mean, or is there another problem?" open up the discussion, often bringing a new flood of anxieties as members begin to talk about their "nightmares." When members now challenge their capacity to provide mutual aid with questions like "We can't even solve our own problems, how are we going to solve hers?" one can respond by identifying with the frustration, but sharing a growing hope in the mutual aid group's capacity to help. This sense of hope is common to resilient children.

THEMES IN THE TERMINATION PHASE OF THE GROUP

Mixed feelings seem to be prominent as groups move to a close. Members often act out at this stage, possibly challenging workers to expel them in order to avoid the loss of the group.

Some of the early themes of danger and lack of control reemerge at this stage, perhaps as indirect pleas to the worker to continue the group. Some groups meet the news of imminent ending with demands for a party and avoidance of sharing feelings about the end of the experience. In one example of revisiting earlier themes of trust, a worker pointed out that with only a few weeks left, some members might be feeling, "Why bother changing now?" To this, another member responded, "We *do* have a few weeks left, so maybe things [in the group] can get better in that time."

Most group members express the feeling that the group has been helpful because it gives them a chance to talk: "I like having a place to talk about my problems." However, the same member's comment that "I won't have anyone to talk to about my problems [once the group ends]," suggests the complex process of termination. The expression of disappointment as groups end may be manifested in anger at group members who had prevented more from happening in the group: "With all the fighting that went on we didn't have a lot of time to talk." Another comment, "The group didn't stop my parents from drinking," reflects once again the need that children of substance abusers feel to be able to do something about the family problem. In this instance, other members stepped in to defend the group, responding that solving that problem was not the reason for the group, and that the experience had helped them to understand their parents' drinking. Sadness is often expressed at the end of the group, and members try to be supportive by saying good things about each other and the experience.

In final sessions members indicate that they were "glad to hear that other people have the same problems," stating that in the beginning, "I thought I was the only one." In discussing how they experienced the group, members were able to express a variety of feelings, including how hard it had been to share something that had gone on at home, how difficult it was to deal with the way people behave sometimes, and "If you have a problem you could talk about it and maybe get help." These comments reflect the issues of breaking taboos around the family secret, finding one's own way to cope rather than trying to control the situation, and the power of mutual aid both inside and outside the group. In contrast to their views at the beginning of the group sessions, the members see the value of reaching out to others, and have a greater belief that there are people who will listen to them and acknowledge their struggle.

In mutual aid groups of children of substance users, the belief in the fundamental possibility of change through using the resources within the individual child, the group as a whole, and the community, is a dramatic representation of the strengths perspective. Client resources are demonstrated by the fact that the members of all groups raise themes which become the object of the group's work, that reflect issues connected to resiliency factors.

As members talk about the family secret they move from secrecy to communication and are able to look at how the family problem affects them. Their movement toward gaining some distance enables them to reach out to peers and establish helping relationships. In the act of helping each other in the group they develop feelings of self-efficacy, learn more effective communication methods, and develop skills in problem solving. Members learn to clearly identify their problems and the feelings attached to them, thus setting the stage for exploring alternate courses of action and selecting strategies for action.

Children in these groups move from despair to hope that they can in some way control their fate. They recognize that there are both peers and significant adults who are willing to help. All these aspects of the mutual aid approach to social work with groups reflect efforts to develop the resiliency factors that children need to be able to flourish. Group workers sometimes say that starting a group is an affirmative act-a demonstration of faith in the inherent ability of people to help each other. This idea brings the shared themes of the strengths perspective, the resiliency model, and social work with groups into clear focus, and suggests the imperative to further strengthen their connection, on behalf of clients and communities.

References

Beardslee, W. R. and D. Podorefsky. 1988. Resilient adolescents whose parents have serious affective and other psychiatric disorders: Importance of self-understanding and relationships. *American Journal of Psychiatry* 145:63–69.

Black, C. 1979. Children of alcoholics. *Alcohol Health and Research World* 2:3–27.

Cohen, C. S. and M. H. Phillips. 1995. Talking about "not talking": The paradox of confidentiality in groups. Presentation at XVII Annual Symposium, Association for the Advancement of Social Work with Groups in San Diego, California.

Deutsch, C. 1982. *Broken Bottles, Broken Dreams*. New York: Teachers College Press.

Garland, J. A., H. E. Jones, and R. L. Kolodny. 1976. A model for stages of development in social work groups. In S. Bernstein, ed., *Explorations in Group Work*, 17–71. Boston: Charles River Books.

Garmezy, N. 1993. Children in poverty: Resiliency despite risk. *Psychiatry* 56: 127–36.

Hirayama, H. and K. K. Hirayama. 1998. Fostering resiliency in children through group work: Instilling hope, courage, and life skills. Presentation at XX Annual Symposium, Association for the Advancement of Social Work with Groups in Miami, Florida.

Kirby, L. D. and M. W. Fraser. 1997. Risk and resiliency in childhood. In M. W. Fraser, ed., *Risk and Resiliency in Childhood*, 10–33. Washington, D.C.: National Association of Social Work.

Merkengas, K. R., B. J. Rounsaville, and B. A. Prusoff. 1992. Familial factors in vulnerability to substance abuse. In M. Glantz and R. Pickens, eds., *Vulnerability to Drug Abuse*, 75–98. Washington: American Psychological Association.

Phillips, M. H. and M. A. Markowitz. 1992. *The Mutual Aid Model of Group Services: Experiences of New York Archdiocese Drug Abuse Prevention Program.* New York: Fordham University Graduate School of Social Service.

Riessman, F. 1990. Restructuring help: A human services paradigm for the 1990s. *American Journal of Community Psychology* 18 (2): 221–230.

Rhodes, R. 1995. A group intervention for young children in addictive families. *Social Work with Groups* 18 (2/3): 123–133.

Rutter, M. 1985. Resiliency in face of adversity: Protective factors and resistance to psychiatric disorders. *British Journal of Psychiatry* 147:598–611.

Saleebey, D. 1997. *The Strengths Perspective in Social Work Practice*. 2d ed. White Plains, N.Y.: Longman Press.

Schwartz, W. 1961. The social worker in the group. *The Social Welfare Forum, Proceedings of the 88th National Conference on Social Welfare*, 147–177. New York: Columbia University Press.

Schwartz, W. 1971. Social group work: The interactionist approach. In *Encyclopedia of Social Work*, 1252–1263. New York: National Association of Social Work.

Shulman, L. 1999. *The Skills of Helping Individuals, Families, Groups, and Communities* 4th ed. Itasca, Ill.: F. E. Peacock.

Steinberg, D. M. 1997. *The Mutual-aid Approach to Working with Groups.* Northvale, N.J.: Jason Aronson.

Walsh, F. 1998. *Strengthening Family Resilience*. Boston: Guilford Press.

Werner, E. E. and R. S. Smith. 1992. *Overcoming the Odds: High Risk Children from Birth to Adulthood*. Ithaca, N.Y.: Cornell University Press.

10 The Unitas Extended Family Circle: Developing Resiliency in Hispanic Youngsters

Rosa Perez-Koenig

The Unitas Extended Family Circle (UEFC) is a pioneering clinical method for providing mental health services to Hispanic and Latino children and youth. The UEFC sustains, promotes, and enhances resilience among Hispanic and Latino children and youth through an outreach community mental health program for children, youth, and families in the South Bronx. The UEFC model specifically addresses family and community related resiliency protective factors.

Resiliency, or the ability to overcome, to bounce back from, life challenges, is a valuable construct in understanding and better servicing individuals, families, and communities dealing with trauma and adversity (Walsh 1998, Fraser 1997, Gilbert 1997). The resiliency paradigm is closely related to other perspectives such as the strengths perspective; the empowerment perspective; and the social justice perspective. These perspectives emphasize the bedrock of social work, the importance of the environment, and the interplay between people and their contextual influences. They focus on people's strengths and capacities to grow despite adverse situations. Focus is placed on assessments and interventions that identify, promote, enhance, or sustain protective factors and identify, reduce, or eliminate risk factors (Fraser and Galinsky 1997; Nash and Fraser 1997). The resiliency approach integrates both prevention and intervention and addresses the multiple influences that affect development and adjustment (Durlak 1998). Underlying this orientation is the understanding that individuals have numerous untapped internal and external resources.

UEFC, in keeping with the Unitas organization's mission of developing

healing communities for children and youth, recognizes the devastating effects of urban ghettos on people, particularly children and youth, and firmly
believes in the healing power of all people, in their strengths, capacities, aspirations, and the availability of internal and external resources. The UEFC
method facilitates the development of resiliency in children and youth and
provides an environment that offers multiple protective factors known to foster that resilience and to enhance children's competencies and skills.

Unitas Therapeutic Inc. is a preventive mental health organization that
has been servicing a predominantly Hispanic population of children and
youth in the Longwood and Hunts Point section of the South Bronx since
1977. In the 1980s, this geographical area became a nationwide symbol of
economic and social decay (Rogler 1983).

The social record of the United States has been clouded by steep declines
in the quality of life of poor children during the 1980s and 1990s. Poor young
children are not very visible. They live in isolated neighborhoods and are
rarely noticed until they reach the first grade and "fail," or become adolescents and "get in trouble," or reach adulthood and cannot find jobs. Our
country's lack of attention to the poor has created a serious situation (Aber
1995). During the last twenty-five years poverty rates among children have
increased, as has the rate of poor prenatal care and developmental problems.
The violent death rate of teenagers has increased by ten percent, births to
teens have increased twenty-three percent, and arrests for juvenile violence
have increased sixty-six percent (Fraser 1997). Miringoff's (1995) index of the
social well-being of children reveals long term trends in social non-health related to lack of attention to the results of poverty. Trends in the social well-
being of poor children run counter to standard measures of economic
progress such as the Gross Domestic Product. Due to the psychological, social, and economic burdens of poverty and discrimination, poor minority
children and their families are at tremendous risk, faced with multiple stressors in their daily lives. As Harry Aponte (1994) points out, the suffering of
the poor is a warning of the toxicity of our social environment.

In 1990 the enumerated resident population of Latinos, Latin Americans,
and Hispanics in the United States approached twenty-three million, and it
is predicted that they will be the largest minority group by the early twenty-
first century (Garbarino 1992). Hispanics are an ethnic rather than a racial
group. Race and ethnicity are not identical. Hispanics are people from many
different countries with a common cultural heritage and language. They represent a mix of races. In the United States they are a population at risk. Hispanics fare poorly in prenatal care. The high incidence of teenage pregnancy

among Hispanics makes their newborns additionally vulnerable. As a group they have a high incidence of poverty. While in the early 1990s the unemployment rate of non-Latino whites was 6.1 percent, the rate for Latinos was 11.9 percent, with 14.4 percent among Puerto Ricans. The poverty rate per person among non-Latino whites was 9.6 percent, for all Latinos it was 29.3 percent, and for Puerto Ricans 36.5 percent. The proportion of single female households among non-Latino whites was 12.7 percent. It was 23.3 percent for total Latinos and 40.5 percent for Puerto Ricans (Institute for Puerto Rican Policy 1994). Poverty correlates highly with all existing social problems (Zastrow 1994).

The children and youth of the South Bronx have one of the highest incidences of social problems in New York City and in the nation at large (Vera 1994). Hispanics fare poorly in children's mental health, such as childhood depression, delinquency and conduct disorders, adolescent pregnancy, sexually transmitted infections, childhood disability, childhood abuse and neglect, and school drop outs. Yet studies have indicated evidence of resiliency among Hispanic children and youth (Rogler 1983, Procidano and Glenwick 1985).

Young (1990) points out that cultural minorities find themselves defined from the outside, by a network of dominant meanings they experience as arising from elsewhere, from those with whom they do not identify or who do not identify with them. Professionals and experts seldom give the "marginalized," the "other," the "group seen to have problems," opportunities to define themselves, to identify their capabilities and aspirations, and to describe their own perceptions of strengths, protective and risk factors, and stressors. The meanings of life situations for Hispanics often differ from meanings imposed by "experts" or members of the dominant discourse.

For example, Hispanic people have strengths that emanate from the Hispanic culture's core values of "personalismo" and respect, familism and spirituality. Each individual is respected and valued, regardless of status. Respect emphasizes "being" and "who," rather than competition and "what." There is substantial reverence for life, and for living in the moment. Familism locates the family, rather than the individual, as the most important social system. The family is a source of identity and support. Familism for most Hispanics includes the entire extended family. This extendedness emphasizes strong feelings of identification, loyalty, and solidarity. Extended family refers not only to the traditional kin, related by blood or marriage, such as aunts, uncles, and cousins, but also includes non-blood, non-marriage related persons who are considered family — compadres and comadres (godfathers and godmothers) and hijos de crianza (children who are raised as members of the family). The extended family provides an indispensable source of instrumental and expressive support. The Hispanic and Latino culture fosters a strong commitment to the extended family, and places that collective in a primary position. Latinos can tolerate the paradox and value both individual and collective since they are viewed as complementary rather that as opposites.

Spirituality lies at the core of the Hispanic culture. It has shaped the beliefs and norms of the Latinos. Spirituality as an overarching construct can be defined as "that which connects one to all there is" (Griffith and Griffith 1998). Among Hispanics spirituality often includes folkloric or alternative belief systems such as Spiritismo and Santeria, which are generally excluded from the dominant or mainstream religions. Spiritismo is the belief in the world of spirits, in which those spirits have a powerful influence on the living. Some Latinos will resist external interventions of any kind because such interventions are thought to undermine one's capacity to gain control over intrusive spirits. Spiritismo had its origins in Puerto Rico, while Santeria had its roots in Cuba and is a juxtaposition of African beliefs and Catholicism. Both Spiritismo and Santeria are sources of great strength among the Hispanic population. The Catholic religion also has a very strong influence on Latinos. For example, the value of "marianismo," in which women are held in a position comparable to the Virgin Mary, is a strong part of the culture. Motherhood in itself has a very special significance to Hispanics.

Spirituality has until recently been a neglected domain in mental health. However, there has been a growing understanding of the profound influence of spirituality. Walsh (1998) places belief systems, along with organizational and communication processes, as the most powerful forces in family resilience.

UEFC promotes protective factors that facilitate the resilience of its Hispanic participants (children and youth), while at the same time reinforcing their Hispanic values of respect, personalismo, familism, and spirituality.

The Unitas Therapeutic Program

UEFC is a pioneering preventive clinical method for social work with large groups of children and adolescents, and is the hallmark of the Unitas Therapeutic Program. The agency also provides more traditional individual, family, and small group therapies. A brief history of Unitas Therapeutic Inc. is necessary for a better understanding of the UEFC.

Unitas Therapeutic Inc., under the leadership of its social worker founder and director, Edward Eismann, Ph.D., has been described as a mental health organization (Rogler 1983); a program that is physically grounded in the community, making use of its natural indigenous helpers as the fundamental means of intervention—an alternative to traditional mental health intervention for youth (Procidano and Glenwich 1985); and as a mental health treatment and prevention program for youth in the South Bronx—a healing community (Eismann 1996).

Dr. Eismann, discouraged by the limitations and institutional barriers (Rogler 1983) in the provision of mental health services to minority urban poor children, left his office in a mental health community center at Lincoln Hospital and immersed himself in the community, on the clients' own turf. In 1968 he began to take long walks in the streets of the South Bronx.

As I maintained my daily ritual down Beck Street, around Kelly Street, down Longwood and onto Fox Street, I sat to talk to youngsters. When I talked to one child, he would introduce me to his friends, and these friends to their friends, their brothers and sisters and even to their mothers and fathers—from the relationship established with each member of this natural group of children and within the group as a whole, a fearful and drifting collective of youngsters became a small support community for helping one another. (Eismann 1996:1)

He had three major goals in mind: to have children and youngsters bond with him as a "helping friend;" to use the youngsters' relationship with him as a way of bonding others together in order to build a healing community; and to select and build up a cadre of older boys and girls who would start meeting with him to learn how to take care of children and of one other. This social mobilization of the neighborhood teenagers into a motivated and therapeutically trained cadre of symbolic parents was the gateway through which a neighborhood healing community came into being (Rogler 1983). Eismann's vision to develop a healing community of children whose needs could be met by other children and teenagers collectively acting in the capacities of symbolic mothers, fathers, brothers, and sisters to each other became institutionalized in 1977 with the incorporation of Unitas Therapeutic Inc. The program is based on theories of therapeutic community and social psychology and the synergistic integration of, among others things, theories of networking, family therapy, psychoanalytic and other developmental theories, and social learning theory. Unlike many community based organizations, Unitas does not wait for troubled youth to be remanded there for treatment of mental ills (Rogler 1983). Children come on their own initiative, or are referred by teachers from neighborhood schools, or by children who are participants in Unitas. Both the referred as well as the non-referred children are serviced together without labels and stigma. UEFC has from its beginning integrated both prevention and intervention in an innovative manner.

The Unitas Extended Family Circle

UEFC is a synergistic clinical method that integrates individual, family, small group, and community modalities; integrates prevention and intervention approaches, multiple psychosocial theories and spirituality, and professionals and non-professionals in the delivery of services. It is strongly committed to the belief that all humans have healing capacities, and that marginalized people need to be empowered.

The clinical method is based on two major assumptions: that there is an inherent push for growth and development in all human beings, and that people have the capacity to change throughout their life span. It is guided by respect for client strengths; a focus on client empowerment; the idea that individuals, groups, and communities have the capacity to regenerate and heal; that synergy is powerful — people brought together can create new and often unexpected patterns and resources that exceed the complexity of each individual; and the principle of dialogue and collaboration, that humans can only come into fullness through creative and emergent relationships with the external world (Perez-Koenig 1998).

UEFC invites children and adolescents to become members of make-believe small families and of the large, agencywide, extended family. This community of children and adolescents is usually under the leadership of its eldest member — Dr. Eismann — who takes the role of "parent" or "grandfather." The leadership of the Family Circle has also been assumed at times by other professional social worker members of the clinical staff, or by members of the core group of Unitas caretakers who have completed specialized training. Through corrective make-believe family relationships (in small groups as well as in the larger group or the community) participants develop better adaptive or coping mechanisms. UEFC is the therapeutic mode of the Unitas Therapeutic program that brings together its philosophy, therapeutic techniques, and all the children, teenagers, and staff.

The large family circle is decentralized into small symbolic families, to permit an individual sense of belonging without anonymity. It allows for some degree of flexibility to accommodate the needs of different kinds of children and different parenting styles among the teenagers (Rogler 1983). UEFC meetings reinforce in each participant their identity as a member of this extended family (a make-believe extended kinship network), as well as their membership in their small symbolic families. The use of rituals, stories, group discussions, and clear norms and rules maintain a milieu necessary for healing relationships to be experienced in an emotional climate of mutual trust and peaceful, nonviolent transactions. The relationship component is central. Intimate relationships within the small symbolic families are facilitated within the large group through words of encouragement, support, clarification, and modeling of behaviors. In addition, trained caretakers are encouraged to maintain contact with their "family members" outside the UEFC, particularly at times of crisis, when additional demonstrations of caring and support are needed. Through the experience of love and caring-in-relationship healing (from disconnection and trauma) and growth are facilitated.

The UEFC family meets during the school year every Thursday from 3:30 p.m. to 5:30 p.m. (for latency age children) and from 3:30 p.m. to 7:30 p.m. for the teenagers. These weekly meetings also take place as part of the Summer Program.

The make-believe parents, aunts, and uncles (caretakers) participate in an ongoing weekly training program led by a professional social worker. The goal of these sessions is to enable "helpers of children" to learn interpersonal skills which will encourage children to be effective, happy, and cooperative. In the training program they learn skills to raise children's self-esteem and feelings of competency; skills to communicate effectively with children; skills to help children resolve conflicts and solve problems; skills for effectively leading children in small counseling groups and in the larger therapeutic community. The training includes the development of self-regard; empathic communication; conflict resolution; group dynamics; and therapeutic community (Eismann 1996). The goals and objectives of this method are comparable to many of the protective factors that enhance and develop resiliency in children and adolescents (Walsh 1998, Bruckner and Cain 1998, Fraser 1997).

Each small make-believe family of children and teenagers includes the caretaker "parent(s)" who must conform to specific criteria such as a strong commitment to the work, good school attendance and performance, and freedom from alcohol and drug abuse. The "aunts" and "uncles" — who are working toward meeting the criteria to become a "parent" — are monitored by the leader and parents of their assigned small families. These "parents" and "aunts" and "uncles" must be 13 years of age or older; in the family hierarchy, the older siblings, 9 to 12 years of age, come next, followed by the young children, 6 to 8 years of age. UEFC is highly structured, and its participants quickly learn the family rules and its chain of command. Although there is a fit between the UEFC structure and the family structure in the Hispanic family (predominantly hierarchical and patriarchal) the method also introduces a democratic style. All members of the circle are considered equal links in its chain. Children of all ages have the same right to share their thoughts and feelings as their elders, the "parents," "aunts," "uncles," and "grandparents." This is contrary to the traditional Hispanic family in which children can listen but cannot talk. Today we encounter less traditional Hispanic families, who believe that a more democratic approach is very important for younger children's development of their confidence, self-esteem, and competency.

The method encourages children's participation by calling on them during the large circle, after they have indicated their willingness to participate by raising their hands. However, once in the spotlight young children can become intimidated. But in very supportive and empathic ways, coached primarily by the caretakers and older children in their respective small families, children succeed in participating in ways that are heard and understood by the members of the larger circle. This is in keeping with the development of communication skills, an integral aspect of the method (Eismann 1996). The strategies of support, empathic listening with feedback, and coaching allow the child to succeed. This contributes to the child's sense of competency and self-efficacy, which, in addition to the development of communication skills, are all considered protective factors in the development of resiliency in children. The children in each symbolic family are helped by one another and the caretakers to experience a sense of being nurtured, of self-discipline, of group belonging, and how to handle problems in their everyday lives. These are also characteristic of resiliency development in children.

Clinical and other staff also undertake the parental role. Real parents often visit the UEFC, and some have volunteered as caretakers. The majority of real parents however express their need for respite, safe in the knowledge that their children are well cared for here.

UEFC utilizes four stages that contribute to reinforcing the identity of the Unitas community: the engagement phase; the large group discussion period; play time; and the regrouping of the large group to say goodbye. The first stage is outlined here.

Initial engagement occurs after everyone is seated on the floor in a large circle near the small families to which they belong. The leader welcomes everyone and briefly states the purpose of UEFC: "This is Unitas, a make-believe large family made of small symbolic families to help children to help each other and learn better ways of getting along together. We do this in two ways: through talking together, as we are doing now, and through play." Sometimes the leader may review the family rules, which include talking out rather than acting out feelings, respect for each other by attentive listening, and orderly sharing of thoughts, feelings, and concerns. The leader then encourages each of the members of the small families to greet each other and the neighboring families, as a way of reinforcing the bonding among the participants (Eismann 1996). This initial ritual of bonding and reinforcement of purpose and rules provides children with the stability of predictability, clarity of purpose, and patterns of interaction which are considered essential aspects of family organizational patterns.

A fundamental philosophy underlying this preventive methodology is that family is the chief and natural institution through which children's needs are met. Children's psychosocial need for nurturance, self-regard, discipline, problem solving, communication skills, and a sense of belonging are essential protective factors (Fraser 1998), and are clearly the objectives of the UEFC method. Within the context of the large and small make-believe families key processes in resiliency enhancement are reenacted (Walsh 1998).

The method provides participants the opportunity to recreate corrective family relations based on sound psychosocial knowledge, values, and skills. Through the larger group, the community-at-large, social networking among members is developed and reinforced. Protective factors such as social support, networking, and spirituality are key components of the program.

Social support has been found to be an important buffer to environmental stressors. Streeter and Franklin (1992) have cited four components: esteem and emotional support, social companionship, informational support, and instrumental support. In an informal survey of UEFC teenage caretakers, ninety percent indicated that the social support they experienced there made a difference to them. They have internalized the UEFC method as "a way of life" which has contributed to their successes as well as to their ability to adaptively cope with stressors. Modeling from the professional staff to the caretakers during the UEFC meetings has been of great importance in their socialization. In turn these teenagers have been excellent models for the younger children.

Similarly, spirituality is an essential component of UEFC method. Walsh (1998) points out that as we expand our vision of psychotherapy as both science and a healing art we approach Seligman's belief that the soul is the key to change. Spirituality is included in the UEFC program mainly through discussion of the vast repertoire of stories from the Old and New Testament, from Buddhist and Hindu literature, as well as from Native American oral tradition. Major themes include connectedness among all members of the Earth, the importance of altruism and the golden rule, and the brotherhood and sisterhood of all people.

In summary, UEFC is a pioneer endeavor based on the resiliency paradigm. It provides a context for the development of individual resilience by fostering self-regard, a sense of competence, and problem solving skills. The corrective re-creation of adaptive family interpersonal patterns of behavior also serves to increase participants' resiliency. And the social network provided by the Family Circle offers incalculable sources of personal resources and support which also enhance resiliency. Although this program focuses on the Hispanic population of children and youth, the richness of this model is applicable to others.

References

Abers, L. 1995. Number of poor children under six increased from 5 to 6 million 1987–1992. *News and Issues* 5 (1): 1.

Aponte, H. 1994. *Bread and Spirit: Therapy with the New Poor.* New York: Norton.

Buckner, J. and A. Cain. 1998. Prevention science with children, adolescents, and families: Introduction. *American Journal of Orthopsychiatry* 68 (4): 508–511.

Durlak, J. 1998. Common risks and protective factors in successful prevention programs. *American Journal of Orthopsychiatry* 68 (4): 512–520.

Eismann, E. 1996. *Unitas: Building Healing Communities for Children.* New York: Fordham University Press.

Fraser, M. 1994. The ecology of childhood: A multisystem perspective. In Mark W. Fraser, ed., *Risk and Resilience in Childhood,* 1–9. Washington, D.C.: National Association of Social Work.

Fraser, M. and M. Galinsky. 1997. Toward a resilience-based model of practice. In M. Fraser, ed., *Risk and Resilience in Childhood: An Ecological Perspective,* 265–276. Washington, D.C.: National Association of Social Work Press.

Garbarono, J. 1992. *Children and Families in the Social Environment.* New York: Aldine de Gruyter.

Gilbert, M. 1997. Childhood depression: A risk factor perspective. In Mark W. Fraser, ed., *Risk and Resilience in Childhood*, 220–243.

Griffith, I. and H. Griffith. 1994. *The Body Speaks.* New York: Basic Books.

Institute for Puerto Rican Policy. 1994. *Datanote on the Puerto Rican Community* (no. 16). New York: Institute for Puerto Rican Policy.

Miringoff, M. 1995. Toward a national standard of social health: The need for progress in social indicators. *American Journal of Orthopsychiatry* October: 462–467.

Nash, J. and M. Fraser. 1997. Methods in the analysis of risk and protective factors. In Mark W. Fraser, ed., *Risk and Resilience in Childhood*, 34–39.

Perez-Koenig, R. 1998. Unitas: A strengths perspective. Paper presented at December Conference on the Strengths Perspective, New York, Fordham University Graduate School of Social Work.

Procidano, M. and D. Glenwick. 1985. Unitas: Evaluating a Preventive Program for Hispanic and Black Children (Monograph No.13). New York: Hispanic Research Center, Fordham University.

Rogler, L. 1983. *A Conceptual Framework for Mental Health Research on Hispanic Populations.* New York: Hispanic Research Center, Fordham University.

Smokowski, P. 1998. Prevention and intervention strategies for promoting resilience in disadvantaged children. *Social Service Review* September: 337–363.

Streeter, C. and C. Franklin. 1992. Social support and psychoeducational interventions with middle class drop out youth. *Child and Adolescent Social Work* 9:131–135.

Vera, A. 1994. Executive Report. New York: Unitas Board of Directors.

Walsh, F. 1998. *Strengthening Family Resilience.* New York: Guilford Press.

Young, I. 1990. *Justice and the Politics of Difference.* Princeton: Princeton University Press.

Zastrow, C. and K. Kirsst-Ashman. 1994. *Understanding Human Behavior in the Social Environment.* Chicago: Nelson Hall.

Part III

Resiliency Enhancement in Administration, Training, and Prevention

11   The Workplace as a Protective Environment: Management Strategies

Sharyn J. Zunz and Roslyn H. Chernesky

Resiliency is the ability to bounce back in the face of adversity. It is a term borrowed from the physical sciences that connotes a self-righting process that allows a body to spring back to its original shape and level of functioning after external stressors have been applied. Resiliency is achieved when, after experiencing stress, one returns to functioning. Resiliency is enhanced through the development and use of protective factors (Benard 1992; Kumpfer 1993). Such protective factors, therefore, become the mediators between a person or group and their stressful environment; they are the means, while resiliency is the sought after result.

There has been an expansion of interest in the resiliency paradigm as a shift has occurred from a solely risk based analysis of social problems and psychological concerns to one that combines a need to lower risk factors while enhancing protective factors (Barnard 1994; Norman, Turner, and Zunz 1993). This has been sparked by the desire for a model that stops pathologizing those who face adversity and instead embraces a framework that focuses on the strengths that can be drawn upon in the face of challenges. The potential benefits of such a model can be found in the literature on a wide range of populations (Begun 1999; Brandstadter, Wentura, and Greve 1993; Garmezy 1991; Garwick and Millar 1996; Valentine and Feinauer 1993). Although most of this literature focuses on individuals, resiliency concepts have also been expanded to include an examination of interventions with broader systems such as families and schools (Benard 1996; Henderson and Milstein 1996; Smokowski 1998; Walsh 1998).

We will attempt to extend the focus on protective factors and resiliency to the human service organization. We believe that many of the resiliency-based strategies described in the literature about families, schools, and communities can be applied to human service organizations and provide us with clues for building more resilient work environments. The stressors that place these organizations at risk, including those stressors that most directly affect workers, will be explored, as well as the interface of these stressors with the major protective factors, drawn from the resiliency literature. We also present some strategies that managers can use to enhance the resiliency of their workers, with the ultimate goal of improving both the work environment and services to the constituent groups the agency serves.

Risk and Today's Human Service Organizations

Today's human service organizations can be viewed as high risk and high stress environments. Agencies are faced with changing demands and conditions that bring uncertainty, instability, and risk to the workplace. Organizations must cope with the impact of managed care, reduced governmental support, and increased competition from for-profit providers. Such pressures often result in turbulent and sometimes hostile environments, and may compel agencies to restructure, cut back on personnel and resources, shift program priorities and staffing patterns, and expand into new and unfamiliar service domains in order to survive.

Agencies today are faced with a sustained demand for their services in a world of rising insistence on accountability, increasing fiscal austerity, and heightened competition for scarce resources. Not surprisingly, organizational environments appear to be filled with long-term, if not permanent, risk. "We live in an era in which organizational life is characterized by shifting priorities, changing patterns in the allocation of resources, and competing demands . . . the only constant in management today is change" (Edwards, Austin, and Altpeter 1998:5).

As human service organizations struggle to survive, the impact of this changing environment can be seen not only in the way services are delivered and constituents are served, but also in the way employees experience their workplace (Callan 1993). Budgetary constraints can lead to a freeze on hiring and salaries, the elimination of both middle management and support services, and a decreased commitment to staff development. Such actions can result in a climate of organizational decline affecting all workers, including those who do retain their jobs (Edwards, Lebold, and Yankey 1998). A smaller workforce can lead to larger workloads for those who remain, or to the expectation that the continuing staff will take on tasks which they have neither the inclination, skills, or resources to perform. Sometimes the workforce not only shrinks but is deprofessionalized as tighter personnel budgets increase the pressure to employ lower-paid workers. As organizations downsize or realign their staffing patterns, a stress-filled climate is produced where worker frustration, insecurity, rumors, scapegoating, and low morale can prevail.

Even when organizations are not forced to cut back, their constantly changing environment can contribute to workers' stress. Any time agencies move in new directions, there is both a threat to the status quo and a danger that the new direction may be viewed as incongruent with the organization's previously stated mission and goals. Such changes may cause workers to feel that the agency's mission and their own professional values are being compromised to achieve goals which somehow stress "the product" over the people (Maslach and Leiter 1997).

Fiscal management is certainly one area of concern for today's human service organizations and their managers, who must stay constantly alert to the bottom line. This concern often results in a need to continually identify new sources of funding and can cause various programs or departments that had previously been collegial to compete with each other for these new revenues. In addition, in this search to secure financial resources, tensions are heightened between those viewed as entrepreneurial, or chance-takers, and those who desire a more conservative and maintenance-oriented culture.

Changing funding priorities can also cause worker stress since expansion into new service domains may mean working with unfamiliar client populations and in unfamiliar communities. Exacerbating this anxiety about the new and unknown is the desire by funders to incorporate performance contracts with increased outcome based data collection to ensure compliance and accountability. Such demands can increase workers' stress as they worry that their professional skills may not fit in or measure up to these newly tracked expectations (Green 1998).

Organizational change can also cause stress as established communication patterns shift. During times of change and uncertainty, the flow of information is often restricted as leadership ponders the impact of new directions on the organization. As new priorities emerge, new and unfamiliar communication channels are created as attempts are made to reestablish the equilibrium previously established among differing in-groups and out-groups. Change can also result in the introduction of new communication patterns, including the use of new information technologies, that may gradually replace support staff, alter the way professionals interview and work with clients, and impact the way charts and records are maintained.

Not only are human service organizations under stress but individuals in these organizations are also stressed. The challenges agencies confront create a high risk environment for both workers and agency managers, who may need to reconceptualize their roles and their skill base if organizations are to survive and continue to effectively provide services (Austin 1995; Eadie 1998; Menefee 1997; Schmid 1992).

Our call is for managers to appreciate that although today's pressures and demands on human service organizations can place both managers and workers at risk and ultimately effect the quality of their work and the services provided, it is possible to moderate or reduce the impact of the stressors. Despite the potential of the workplace to be both a high risk environment, protective factors can be developed and employed to help reduce these adverse conditions. A workplace can function to augment strengths and amplify resilience if administrators structure the work and the organization with these goals in mind.

A synthesis of some of the literature on both organizational strategies and resiliency enhancement provides a starting place for managers in their quest to create supportive workplaces that enable workers to withstand the challenges they face in today's human service organizations.

Organizational Literature

The idea that the workplace need not be solely a source of stress and risk but can also function to protect, strengthen, and enhance individual workers' capacities to cope and face new challenges is not new in the organizational literature. Theorists and researchers have focused on the potential positives in the work environment, even though they do not use the term "resiliency." They view the organizational environment as a major influence on worker behavior, capable not only of supporting workers and their performance (Shafritz and Ott 1996), but also of creating stressors. Four different organizational themes from this literature are particularly applicable, and because they provide an historical context, they are summarized here.

Occupational Stress

During the past two decades, great strides have been made in the theoretical and empirical work on the growing problem of organizational stress.

Recent efforts have concentrated on generating conceptual frameworks to identify sources of pressure in jobs and the workplace, and interventions to change and manage organizational and personal stress-related costs like increased mental and physical illnesses, absences, employee turnover, accidents, and decreased productivity (Cooper 1998). For example, the theory of person-environment fit, suggests that a misfit between the person and the environment creates stress (Edwards, Caplan, and Harrison 1998). A misfit can arise when the work environment does not meet a person's needs or when environmental demands exceed a person's abilities. The uncertainty theory of occupational stress, on the other hand, proposes that workers experience stress when they are unable to know whether their work will produce the desired outcomes or when they have no clear way of knowing how to reach them. Role ambiguity and role conflict are examples of such work-related conditions that contribute to this form of stressful uncertainty (Beehr 1998).

Job Burnout

Job burnout, which has long been recognized as an occupational hazard for human service workers (Soderfeldt, Soderfeldt, and Warg 1995), has recently been reexamined, in an organizational rather than personal deficit context, and explained by a multidimensional theory (Maslach 1998). A manifestation of burnout is the emotional exhaustion that can come from work overload and unresolved personnel conflicts, making workers feel drained and used up in the absence of sources of replenishment. Both job demands and lack of resources are key contributors. In response to emotional exhaustion, workers become negative and cynical. They frequently become so detached that their work appears depersonalized. Workers can also come to feel inadequate about their ability to help their clients and to cope with the demands of their job, in some instances even in the face of evidence that their actual level of accomplishment is not diminishing.

Burnout, the result of an accumulation of work-related risk factors, is viewed as the opposite of job engagement, the result experienced in a more positive, resiliency enhancing environment. The burnout-to-engagement continuum highlights how the organizational context of work affects workers' well being. It recognizes that there is a range of relationships that individuals can have with their work. Engagement with one's job "consists of a state of high *energy* (rather than exhaustion), strong *involvement* (rather than cynicism), and a sense of *efficacy* (rather than a reduced sense of accomplishment)" (Maslach 1998:73, italics in original). Extensive research demonstrates that high personal accomplishment is associated with such protective factors as supportive personal relationships, the enhancement of sophisticated skills coupled with an appreciation for such work skills, and active participation in shared decision making and problem solving (Cooper 1998; Cordes and Dougherty 1993; Maslach and Leiter 1997; Zunz 1998).

Job Satisfaction

An extensive body of research has been developed since the 1950s based on the assumption that if workers are satisfied with their working conditions and the work they do, they will be more motivated to carry out their tasks and activities, more willing to perform their jobs well, and more willing to remain at their jobs. Studies conducted with both human service and social workers have consistently demonstrated that the work environment and the work itself impact on overall job satisfaction, which then impacts upon worker behavior and performance. Barber (1986) found that workers with very heavy workloads and uninteresting jobs were at risk for dissatisfaction with their work, but were helped to feel more resilient, even in such jobs, if they could be helped to increase their sense of personal achievement or accomplishment. Poulin (1994) found that the strongest factor associated with job fulfillment was satisfaction with opportunities for professional development. In addition, adequacy of both organizational and supervisory support contributed to job satisfaction. Vinokur-Kaplan and her colleagues (1994) found that perceived opportunities for promotion and job challenge were critical influences on job satisfaction among workers in public and non-profit agencies, and influenced job retention. Similar findings have been cited among agency administrators as well as social workers holding various positions (Jayaratne and Chess 1984; Poulin 1995; Vinokur-Kaplan 1996). Other studies show that workers who have more influence over decisions affecting their job tasks had higher levels of job satisfaction (Glisson and Durick 1988; Poulin and Walter 1992).

Worker Motivation

Motivation in the work setting is based on the principle that a worker's behavior, effort, performance, or productivity can be influenced to achieve an organizational goal if the worker can see its relevance to the satisfaction of his or her own needs. Although there are a number of theories related to worker motivation (Bowditch and Buono 1997; Latting 1991), the work of Herzberg (1968) is especially valuable in the context of the discussion of workplace risk and resiliency. Herzberg identifies essential motivators or satisfiers, and concludes that when they are intrinsic to the work itself, workers will experience work as exciting and challenging and be more energized. Motivator factors include the opportunity for achievement and recognition, the possibility of personal and professional growth and career advancement, and the satisfaction of carrying out the challenging responsibilities of the work itself. If these factors are not present, workers are at risk and can become lethargic and lack interest in doing more or doing well.

Herzberg's early work has formed the basis for an expanded conceptualization of job enrichment and job redesign strategies (Hackman and Oldman 1980). Job enrichment emphasizes building opportunities for growth and achievement into the work itself. It entails job redesign that emphasizes core job characteristics that contribute to workers' feeling more connected to their work and the work outcome. It can increase resiliency by making work more psychologically meaningful. Meaningful work can be enhanced if attention is paid to such core job characteristics as skill variety, task identification and significance, worker autonomy, and regular, constructive feedback on job performance.

Several conclusions can be drawn about work-related resiliency factors from the organizational research and theories. A number of what the resiliency literature now labels as protective factors emerge repeatedly in the organizational literature just reviewed. These factors can be seen to operate in many different ways. Some prevent the onset of stress, others reduce or moderate stress, while still others buffer the effects of the stressful environment on employees. Many of these protective mechanisms promote resilience by virtue of their direct interaction with existing risk factors. Again, these protective factors are generally similar to those that have been identified in some of the earlier writings on resiliency.

Resilience Factors in the Work Environment

Past resiliency research has attempted to identify specific protective factors which can be enhanced in the face of high risk individual, group, or organizational environments (Cowen, Wyman, Work, and Parker 1990; Ouellette 1993; Rak and Patterson 1996; Wolin and Wolin 1993). These protective factors are more useful if viewed as additive pathways within a systems context. Just as a piling on of chronic risk factors can form a constellation of hazards, the interplay of a number of coexisting protective factors over time can have an increasingly positive effect (Doll and Lyons 1998). In the school environment, for example, Henderson and Milstein (1996) developed a "resiliency wheel" to describe the constellation of interacting protective factors that they feel schools must strive to possess. These factors are:

1. Setting and communicating high but realistic expectations
2. Providing an atmosphere of care and support
3. Teaching life skills necessary for survival within the organization and in the external world in which one must function
4. Setting clear and consistent boundaries
5. Increasing opportunities for bonding with the school's and community's norms
6. Providing opportunities for meaningful participation

None of these factors alone are seen as wholly protective, but taken together can lead to an environment that can be resiliency enhancing for students facing adversity.

Similarly, we have selected a number of protective factors which we feel should be a part of an organizational "resiliency wheel," a cohort of protective mechanisms that can play a key role in enhancing the resiliency of workers challenged by human service work environments.

Social Support

Social support as a protective factor is almost universally mentioned in the resiliency literature (Henderson 1996; Werner and Smith 1992; Wolin and Wolin 1993) and is also mentioned in studies on combating professional burnout (Himle, Jayarante, and Thyness 1989; Koeske and Koeske 1989; Rahim 1995; Um and Harrison 1998). Social support implies the interaction of individuals with their environment to form an assistance network that helps one find concrete, emotional, and social information that enhances one's feelings of attachment and self-esteem. Social support may be structural — being a part of a social network consisting of others one likes and respects, or functional — receiving emotional or instrumental support from sources such as co-workers or supervisors.

Managers can encourage the development of both structural and instrumental support networks for their employees by expanding the use of work teams, developing peer support networks, and promoting rituals and ceremonies that reinforce a supportive work environment. Managers can also encourage social support by furthering workers' interaction with their external environment by providing both the time and opportunity to take part in collaborations with community partners and by encouraging networking, through participation in professional organizations or by attending local professional conferences or national annual meetings.

Realistic Locus of Control

Control is the ability to choose one's own actions from among a variety of options. It provides a sense of self-efficacy as reflected in the ability to influence one's surroundings in the face of challenges (Levy and Baumgardner 1991; Rotter 1966). Control in the workplace is also related to the concept of autonomy when individuals are able to affect their own schedules and tasks or participate in decision making that might affect their work directly. Autonomy occurs when workers are permitted to determine how and when to do their work, are able to solve problems, make choices, access needed resources, and have some input into the decisions for which they will be held accountable, while control implies the ability to directly influence existing job stressors. Work environments characterized by rigid policies, tight monitoring, chaotic working conditions, and authoritarian leaders do not give workers control over the work they do nor over the stressors they face.

An organization's promise of control and autonomy is not necessarily the same as a staff member's perception that such control and autonomy actually exists in practice. If workers do not trust or believe that the control they are given is real or that they can access this control to accomplish tasks, stress can occur (Spector 1998). Too much control, on the other hand, when associated with greater responsibility but without the necessary available resources, can also create stress. In organizational life, resiliency is enhanced when one neither feels helpless to influence one's environment nor singly responsible for all aspects of one's work. Instead, it is enhanced when one possesses a realistic locus of control and thus makes an accurate appraisal of what one can do at any given time to influence the work environment (Cowen et al. 1990; Werner and Smith 1992). Like the serenity prayer of 12-step programs, resiliency is enhanced when one accepts the things one cannot currently change in one's work environment, works towards changing those things that can be changed, and has the wisdom to know the difference.

Positive Sense of Community

A sense of community is based on positive connections with others in the workplace and to the organization's goals. It manifests itself in feeling proud to be associated with an organization and in seeing how one's individual roles, responsibilities, and contributions fit into the organization's overall mission. Breakdown in community occurs when interpersonal contacts are minimal, impersonal, or conflictual. Sense of community can also break down if pride, loyalty, and commitment are impeded by a conflict in values over agency goals that are pursued without one's input and support. When this occurs, the protective value of belonging to an organizational community with a shared belief system and common goals is diminished as it does not support nor reinforce one's sense of mission or purpose (Rak and Patterson 1996; Richardson, Neiger, Jensen, and Kumpfer 1990; Rush, Schoel, and Barnard 1995).

A sense of organizational community can be protective when individuals are involved in the development of the rules, expectations, and rewards adopted by the community. It is important for workers to feel that the organization is fair and that rules are equally binding under a system they perceive to be just. The real or perceived presence of fairness (in workload, promotions, or training opportunities) can support a climate of mutual respect and the development of a positive sense of community, which, in turn, can decrease burnout and increase resiliency (Cooper 1998; Maslach and Leiter 1997).

Functional Channels of Communication and Information Pathways

Clear and reliable information is essential to understanding task assignments, the expectations of others, job descriptions and limitations, and the ability to receive clear feedback on job performance. Channels of communication can either facilitate or hinder the flow of information. A hindered communication channel might have too many interceptors that can delay timely receipt of information, or which, like in the children's game of "telephone," can subject information to numerous inaccuracies or revisions. When this occurs, the intent of the initial message can be lost. In addition, staff frequently find too much information overloading a wide variety of newer communication channels (voice mail, e-mail, faxes), making it difficult to determine what is a priority. At the same time as there is this information overload in some areas, organizations may not provide enough direct feedback to staff by perpetuating hierarchic communication channels which share crucial information only with certain individuals.

To foster resiliency, organizational communication must be perceived as consistent, congruent, and manageable. Information should be transmitted that has the potential to enhance the delivery of client services and that encourages the staff's access to other protective factors. For example, a good information system can build one's sense of community, augment one's sense of control over job tasks, and provide a connection to social support networks.

Good Problem Solving Skills

Past research on resiliency points to the importance of having good problem solving or conflict resolution skills since no environment, whether it be a family, school, or workplace, is problem free (Norman, Turner and Zunz 1993; Werner and Smith 1992; Walsh 1998). In the organizational context, this translates to such resiliency enhancing abilities as correctly reading social situations, creative brainstorming, realistically weighing available alternatives, and finding solutions through negotiation and collaboration. Once such skills are developed, they can be used not only to address client-related dilemmas, but also to tackle organizational difficulties. The ability to realistically appraise one's work environment, crucial to the development of the protective factor of realistic locus of control, is an example of the need for protective factors to work together.

Implication for Practice: Resiliency Enhancing Management Strategies

We end with an examination of some management strategies derived from both the organizational and resiliency research that provide the basis for what managers can do for their at-risk organizations and workers. These proposed strategies are neither new nor extraordinary, but when seen as part of a planned managerial system designed to counter risk and stressors, these resiliency enhancement strategies become a valuable and potent managerial tool.

Empowerment

Empowerment is a process by which individuals gain mastery or control over their lives through the positive experiences they have as they participate in their workplace or community. Staff empowerment enables workers to increase their capacity to define and attain their own goals and make decisions that affect their work lives (Cohen and Austin 1997). Empowerment strategies can lead to resiliency enhancing outcomes for employees. Such outcomes are reflected in workers' feeling both more powerful and more hopeful about their effectiveness, as well as in higher levels of workers' commitment, motivation, morale, and sense of mission (Shera and Page 1995). Moreover, and not insignificantly, empowered workers have a greater capacity to empower their clients.

Managers must affirmatively empower their employees while also reducing barriers to empowerment. Organizational empowerment includes enhancing self-efficacy among the organization's members as well as the removal of conditions that foster powerlessness (Shera and Page 1995). Managers can begin by dismantling the more traditional, bureaucratic structures that emphasize vertical levels, centralized authority, standardized procedures, and routinized methods, all of which foster powerlessness (Chernesky 1995).

An alternative model of empowering staff was recently proposed that expands upon earlier models that viewed organizational change initiated by staff at lower levels of the organizational hierarchy as a means of staff empowerment (Cohen and Austin 1997). The new model is based on three principles:

1. Worker participation in organizational improvement and efforts at change should be part of the formal organizational structure and sanctioned by agency leadership.
2. Worker participation should be built into the job and recognized as part of the job, and require workers to be responsible for identifying and solving problems, and finding improved ways to provide service.
3. Opportunities for individual and organizational learning should be continuous and designed into the structure. Helping workers to learn to collect and analyze data as part of their work and then use the information for enhancing services is one example of how to incorporate ongoing learning into agency practice.

Although there are both supports for and barriers to using empowerment strategies in an agency or organizational setting, the motivation and influence of administrators are key factors to facilitating and maintaining an empowerment based approach (Gutierrez, GlenMaye, and DeLois 1995). Managers need to be comfortable with, and advocate for, shared decision making, collaborative team models, and an open communication network.

Staff empowerment can be enhanced through other managerial strategies. For example, advocates of feminist administration see their management philosophy as contributing to worker empowerment. Feminist administration has been defined as

> the exercise of a leadership style based on feminist values and principles that recognize, validate, and incorporate traditional feminine attributes and that use organizational structures that shift responsibility, authority, and control away from hierarchical arrangements and relationships to create workplace environments and service delivery systems that improve women's lives and empower individuals whether they are staff, volunteers, or clients. (Chernesky 1995:74)

In contrast to a more traditional management approach, feminist administrators strive to produce a more resilient, autonomous, self-directed workforce with built-in social supports and a sense of community. This is achieved through a relationship oriented leadership style, collaborative consensus building, worker participation, and non-hierarchical, self-managing structures.

Job Enrichment and Design

A major management strategy for enhancing staff resiliency is to make the work so enjoyable and rewarding that workers' sense of well-being is increased simply by performing their jobs. Job enrichment gives workers a sense of ownership, responsibility, and accountability for their work. A highly enriched job provides an opportunity to enhance one's workplace resiliency by enabling employees to satisfy their needs for self-actualization or self-fulfillment. Managers wishing to employ job enrichment strategies need to

1. improve communication and give direct feedback to workers concerning their work performance;
2. provide for ongoing acquisition of new knowledge and skills;
3. include a variety of different activities in each job to draw on different workers' skills and talents;
4. define jobs around complete and natural work units to assure a sense of closure and accomplishment;
5. allow for specialization based on unique qualities or features in jobs;
6. give staff freedom, discretion and control over key aspects of their job, such as resources or scheduling; and

7. expect and build in personal accountability by workers for their own
   work.   (Herzberg 1968)

Organizational Culture

Since the 1970s the notion of organizational culture has rapidly gained
popularity in the organizational and management literature (Schein 1985).
There is general agreement that an organization's culture — the shared
norms, values, and beliefs of its members — can enhance or decrease individual well-being and resiliency. Cultures are considered the glue that holds
organizations together through a common understanding of appropriate
ways of behaving. Its culture is the organization's "personality," making it possible to predict attitudes and behaviors. Culture can create order from the potential chaos that permeates a high-risk work environment. Custom and continuity anchor organizational members, and enhance feelings of belonging
and commitment that can aid the development of social supports and a sense
of community. For example, a culture that values creativity and innovation
encourages workers to try new ways of doing things. Workers will therefore
be willing to experiment without concern that they will be punished should
their ideas fail.

How an organizational culture meets workers' expectations is generally referred to as its climate. Workers may perceive their organization's climate to
be supportive, warm, rewarding, fair, or hostile. An organizational climate
that fosters respect for workers, integrates workers into the decision making
process, and gives them autonomy in planning and carrying out tasks contributes to a more resilient workforce.

Because agency leaders are the most influential members of an organizational culture, their behavior sets a standard and influences others, even
when that is not their intention. What they do and say is interpreted and
given meaning by members within the cultural context. Thus organizational
cultures can be transformed by managers into environments that hinder or
promote resiliency. Administrators can deliberately attempt to change their
cultures as a strategy to encourage innovation, enhance quality and productivity, revitalize operations, promote good problem solving, and strengthen
functional communication channels.

Advocacy

Finally, we need to remember that managers must also reduce risks to
their organizations. There is increasing evidence that effective managers can

actively manage their organizations' environments, thereby reducing the impact of changes, demands, and pressures that place them at risk. Managers need to engage in advocacy and develop the political savvy to be effective on behalf of their own interests as well as the interests of their constituencies. Failure to undertake such activities may be very shortsighted since it increases the risks faced by agencies from social, economic, and political factors in the environment (Gibelman and Kraft 1996; Heimovics, Herman, and Coughlin 1993). If agency administrators are to lower these environmental risk factors, they need to hone their advocacy skills in order to

1. shape and influence organizational environments as well as deal with environmental pressures and demands (Menefee and Thompson 1994; Schmid 1992);
2. become entrepreneurs, generating new ideas on how to deliver services, and introducing and sustaining innovations (Edwards and Austin 1991);
3. become market-oriented, assessing and repositioning the agency and its programs to be more competitive in the context of supply and demand (Edwards, Cooke, and Reid 1996).

Since resiliency is a protracted, transactional process, human service organizations are in an ideal position to serve as the mediators between worker risk and protection (Doll and Lyon 1998). Yet resilient organizations are neither unique nor mysterious. They possess many of the same qualities that are associated with effectively run organizations. Agencies managed with an eye toward enhancing protective strategies like worker empowerment, functional communication systems, and a positive "corporate" culture with a strong sense of community, develop competencies that will stand them in good stead in the face of any challenging current or future environment.

References

Austin, D. M. 1995. The human service executive. In J. E. Tropman, J. L. Erlich and J. Rothman, eds., *Tactics and Techniques of Community Intervention*, 248–263. Itasca, Ill.: Peacock.

Barber, G. 1986. Correlates of job satisfaction among human service workers. *Administration in Social Work* 10 (1): 25–38.

Barnard, C. 1994. Resiliency: A shift in our perception? *American Journal of Family Therapy* 22 (2): 135–144.

Beehr, T. 1998. An organizational psychology meta-model of occupational stress.

In C. Cooper, ed., *Theories of Organizational Stress*, 6–27. Manchester: Oxford University Press.

Begun, A. 1999. Intimate partner violence: An HSBE perspective. *Journal of Social Work Education* 35 (2): 239–252.

Benard, B. 1992. *Protective Factor Research: What We Can Learn From Resilient Children*. San Francisco: Far West Lab.

Benard, B. 1996. Creating resiliency-enhancing schools. *Resiliency in Action* 1 (2): 5–8.

Bowditch, J. L. and A. F. Buono. 1997. *A Primer on Organizational Behavior*. New York: Wiley.

Brandstadter, J., D. Wentura, and W. Greve. 1993. Adaptive resources of the aging self. *International Journal of Behavioral Development* 16 (2): 323–349.

Callan, V. 1993. Individual and organizational strategies for coping with organizational change. *Work and Stress* 7 (1): 63–75.

Chernesky, R. H. 1995. Feminist administration: Style, structure, purpose. In N. Van Den Bergh, ed., *Feminist Practice in the 21st Century*, 70–88. Washington, D.C.: National Association of Social Work.

Cohen, B. J. and M. J. Austin. 1997. Transforming human service organizations through empowerment of staff. *Journal of Community Practice* 4 (2): 35–50.

Cooper, C. 1998. *Theories of Organizational Stress*. Manchester: Oxford University Press.

Cordes, C. and T. Dougherty. 1993. A review and an integration of research on job burnout. *Academy of Management Review* 18 (4): 621–656.

Cowen, E., P. Wyman, W. Work, and G. Parker. 1990. The Rochester child resilience project: Overview and summary. *Development and Psychopathology* 2 (2): 193–212.

Doll, B. and M. Lyon, issue eds. 1998. Resilience applied: The promise and pitfalls of school-based resilience programs. *School Psychology Review* 27(3): entire issue.

Eadie, D. C. 1998. Planning and managing strategically. In R. L. Edwards, J. A. Yankey, and M. A. Altpeter, eds., *Skills for Effective Management of Nonprofit Organizations*, 453–468. Washington, D.C.: National Association of Social Work.

Edwards, J. R., R. D. Caplan, and R. V. Harrison. 1998. Person-environment fit theory. In C. Cooper, ed., *Theories of Organizational Stress*, 28–67.

Edwards, R. L. and D. M. Austin. 1991. Managing effectively in an environment of competing values. In R. L. Edwards and J. A. Yankey, eds., *Skills for Effective Human Services Management*, 5–22. Washington, D.C.: National Association of Social Work.

Edwards, R. L., P. W. Cooke, and P. N. Reid. 1996. Social work management in an era of diminishing federal responsibility. *Social Work* 41 (5): 468–479.

Edwards, R. L., D. M. Austin, and M. A. Altpeter. 1998. Managing effectively in an environment of competing values. In R. L. Edwards, J. A. Yankey, and M. A. Altpeter, eds., *Skills for Effective Management of Nonprofit Organizations*, 5–22.

Edwards, R. L., D. A. Lebold, and J. A. Yankey. 1998. Managing organizational decline. In R. L. Edwards, J. A. Yankey, and M. A. Altpeter, eds., *Skills for Effective Management of Nonprofit Organizations*, 279–300.

Garmezy, N. 1991. Resiliency and vulnerability to adverse developmental outcomes associated with poverty. *American Behavioral Scientist* 34 (4): 416–430.

Garwick, A. and H. Millar. 1996. *Promoting Resilience in Youth with Chronic Conditions and Their Families*. Minneapolis, Minn.: University of Minnesota Center for Children with Chronic Illness and Disability.

Gibelman, M. and S. Kraft. 1996. Advocacy as a core agency program: Planning considerations for voluntary human service agencies. *Administration in Social Work* 20 (4): 43–59.

Glisson, C. and M. Durick. 1988. Predictors of job satisfaction and organizational commitment in human service organizations. *Administrative Science Quarterly* 33:61–81.

Green, R. K. 1998. Maximizing the use of performance contacts. In R. L. Edwards, J. A. Yankey, and M. A. Altpeter, eds., *Skills for Effective Management of Nonprofit Organizations*, 78–97.

Gutierrez, L., L. GlenMaye, and K. DeLois. 1995. The organizational context of empowerment practice: Implications for social work administration. *Social Work* 40 (2): 249–257.

Hackman, J. R. and G. R. Oldman. 1980. *Work Redesign*. Reading, Mass.: Addison-Wesley.

Heimovics, R. D., R. D. Herman, and C. L. J. Coughlin. 1993. Executive leadership and resource dependence in nonprofit organizations: A frame analysis. *Public Administration Review* 53 (5): 419–427.

Henderson, N., issue ed. 1996. Creating connections for resiliency: Mentoring, support, and peer programs. *Resiliency in Action* 1 (4): entire issue.

Henderson, N. and M. Milstein. 1996. *Resiliency in Schools: Making It Happen for Students and Educators*. Thousand Oaks, Calif.: Corwin Press.

Herzberg, F. W. 1968. One more time: How do you motivate employees? *Harvard Business Review* 46 (1): 53–62.

Himle, D., S. Jayarante, and P. Thyness. 1989. The buffering effects of four types of supervisory support on work stress. *Administration in Social Work* 13 (1): 19–34.

Jayaratne, S. and W. Chess. 1984. Job satisfaction, burnout, and turnover: A national study. *Social Work* 29:448–452.

Koeske, G. and R. Koeske. 1989. Work load and burnout: Can social support and perceived accomplishment help? *Social Work* 34 (3): 243–348.

Kumpfer, K. 1993. Prevention: Current research and trends. *Psychiatric Clinics of North America* 16 (1): 11–20.

Latting, J. 1991. Eight myths on motivating social services workers: theory-based perspectives. *Administration in Social Work* 15 (3): 49–66.

Levy, P. and A. Baumgardner. 1991. Effects of self-esteem and gender on goal choice. *Journal of Organizational Behavior* 12:529–541.

Maslach, C. 1998. A multidimensional theory of burnout. In C. Cooper, ed., *Theories of Organizational Stress*, 68–85.

Maslac   nd M. Leiter. 1997. *The Truth About B⁻ rnout: How Organizations Cause Personal Stress and What to Do About It.* San Francisco: Jossey-Bass.

Menefee, D. 1997. Strategic administration of nonprofit human service organizations: A model for executive success in turbulent times. *Administration in Social Work* 21 (2): 1–19.

Menefee, D. and J. J. Thompson. 1994. Identifying and comparing competencies for social work management: A practice driven approach. *Administration in Social Work* 18 (3): 1–26.

Norman, E., S. Turner, and S. Zunz. 1993. *From Risk to Resiliency: A Literature Review and Annotated Bibliography*. New York: Fordham University Graduate School of Social Service.

Ouellette, S. 1993. Inquiries into hardiness. In L.Goldberger and S. Breznitz, eds., *Handbc   of Stress: Theoretical and Clinical Aspects*, 78–100. New York: Free Press.

Poulin, J. E. 1994. Job task and organizational predictors of social worker job satisfaction change: A panel study. *Administration in Social Work* 18 (1): 21–38.

Poulin, J. E. 1995. Job satisfaction of social work supervisors and administrators. *Administration in Social Work* 19 (4): 35–49.

Poulin, J. and C. Walter. 1992. Retention plans and job satisfaction of gerontological social workers. *Journal of Gerontological Social Work* 19:99–114.

Ra.   .ı, A. 1995. Stress, strain, and their moderators: An empirical comparison of entrepreneurs and managers. *Journal of Small Business Managers* 34 (1): 46–59.

Rak, C. and L. Patterson. 1996. Promoting resilience in at-risk children. *Journal of Counseling and Development* 74:368–373.

Richardson, G., B. Neiger, S. Jensen, and K. Kumpfer. 1990. The resiliency model. *Health Education* 21 (6): 33–39.

Rotter, J. 1966. Generalized expectancies for internal versus external control of reinforcement. *Psychological Monographs* 80 (1): 1–28.

Rush, M., W. Schoel, and S. Barnard. 1995. Psychological resiliency in the public sector: "Hardiness" and pressure for change. *Journal of Vocational Behavior* 46 (1): 17–39.

Schein, E. H. 1985. *Organizational Culture and Leadership*. San Francisco: Cal.: Jossey-Bass.

Schmid, H. 1992. Executive leadership in human service organizations. In Y. Hasenfeld, ed., *Human Services as Complex Organizations*, 98–117. Newbury, Cal.: Sage.

Shafritz, J. M. and J. S. Ott. 1996. *Classics of Organization Theory*. New York: Harcourt Brace.

Shera, W. and J. Page. 1995. Creating more effe⋯ ⋅e human service organizations through strategies of empowerment. *Administration in Social Work* 19 (4): 1–15.

Smokowski, P. 1998. Prevention and intervention strategies for promoting resilience in disadvantaged children. *Social Service Review* 72 (3): 337–364.

Soderfeldt, M., B. Soderfeldt, and L. Warg. 1995. Burnout in social work. *Social Work* 40 (5): 638–646.

Spector, P. E. 1998. A control theory of the job stress process. In C. Cooper, ed., *Theories of Organizational Stress*, 153–169. Manchester: Oxford University Press.

Um, M. and D. Harrison. 1998. Role stressors, burnout, mediators, and job satisfaction. *Social Work Research* 22 (2): 100–116.

Valentine, L. and L. Feinauer. 1993. Resilience factors associated with female survivors of childhood sexual abuse. *American Journal of Family Therapy* 21 (3): 216–224.

Vinokur-Kaplan, D., S. Jayaratne, and W. A. Chess. 1994. Job satisfaction and retention of social workers in public agencies, non-profit agencies, and private practice: The impact of workplace conditions and motivators. *Administration in Social Work* 18 (3): 93–121.

Vinokur-Kaplan, D. 1996. Workplace attitudes, experiences, and job satisfaction of social work administrators in nonprofit and public agencies: 1981 and 1989. *Nonprofit and Voluntary Sector Quarterly* 25 (1): 89–109.

Walsh, F. 1998. *Strengthening Family Resiliency*. New York: Guilford Press.

Werner, E. and R. Smith. 1992. *Overcoming the Odds: High Risk Children from Birth to Adulthood*. Ithaca: Cornell University.

Wolin, S. J. and S. Wolin. 1993. *The Resilient Self: How Survivors of Troubled Families Rise Above Adversity*. New York: Villard.

Zunz, S. 1998. Resiliency and burnout: Protective factors for human service managers. *Administration in Social Work* 22 (3): 39–54.

12 The African American
Professional's Resiliency

Laura J. Lee

This paper describes the challenges and dilemmas faced by African American professionals in predominantly white human service agencies and the ways in which they resiliently cope with them. The focus is on the African American professional's process of resiliency, rather than on a cluster of traits. The trait approach can be misleading because it overlooks the fact that behaviors that are often construed as stable personality traits are, in reality, highly specific and situational (McDaniel and Balgopal 1978).

Any group may be oppressed because of their difference. The difference may be gender, religion, age, sexual preference, or skin color. The two common characteristics shared by African Americans are the color of their skin and the necessity to live in two cultural arenas — one African American and one white (McDaniel and Balgopal 1978; Gutierrez and Lewis 1999). Beyond this, African Americans share the range of life experiences of any other group living in the United States.

Theoretical Framework

See (1998) recommends the use of "theoretical strips" in explaining the African American experience, since traditional theories constructed to understand practice with African Americans lack a "goodness of fit." Theoretical strips involve extracting usable parts from known theories and fusing those parts with culturally sensitive, contextual, and situational material. The

African American professional's workplace reality might best be understood through fusing parts of role theory (Biddle 1979), exchange theory (Blau 1970), and cognitive dissonance (Festinger 1957).

Role Theory

Professional personnel are expected to carry out specific roles and functions in the organization. Role refers to characteristic, expected behavior by people occupying specific social positions within the social structure. It is a patterned sequence of learned actions or deeds performed by a person in an interaction. Individuals occupy many roles in relation to their status in the social structure (Biddle 1979). For example, in addition to a formally assigned position such as supervisor, community liaison, or executive director, the African American professional has the dual role of being an easily identified African American. Within an agency, the African American professional may be an informal adviser to other persons of color, an agency representative on committees which need an African American presence, or serve a highly visible role in spanning community boundaries. Generally, role behavior is structured upon reciprocal expectations. Role theory illuminates the critical issue that the African American professional has some roles that are defined by power-holders other than himself.

Exchange Theory

Blau (1970) posits exchange theory as a guide to understanding the reciprocity between the individual and the organization. Professionals who choose to be employed in organizations anticipate continued career development. They expect their employment to be rewarding. The individual is interested in doing a good job and in reaping benefits from the work, the organization, and association with colleagues. The organization's expectation is that the professional's job performance will help move the organization toward its mission.

Disruption of this exchange process can give rise to power differentials, with either the employer or the employee changing the normalized reciprocity (Blau 1970). Professional social workers do have power and alternatives. They are prepared with knowledge and skills that make it possible to leave the organization and practice social work in a different setting. Gouldner labels such professionals cosmopolitans (Gouldner 1970).

The Theory of Cognitive Dissonance

When individuals are presented with evidence contrary to their worldview or are placed in a situation where they must behave contrary to their worldview, they experience dissonance. The dissonance can be resolved by increasing the number of consistent cognitions or decreasing the number of inconsistent cognitions. Often the dissonance remains unresolved. In the United States, African American and white perceptions of racial reality — while occasionally convergent — are for the most part quite different. There is a nearly universal opinion among African Americans and Hispanics that discrimination remains common today (Joint Center for Political and Economic Studies 1997). However, many white people do not believe racism constitutes a significant problem.

For African Americans, a major cause of tension is having a value system that runs counter to behaviors carried out in organizations. The African American may believe the prevailing ethos that working long and hard results in being compensated for so doing, but observe that people are promoted in the organization who do not meet those criteria, or that people who do meet those criteria are not promoted. In terms of the social structure, the decisions may be political. For the professional, these actions create cognitive dissonance.

This overview of theoretical strips from exchange theory, role theory, and cognitive dissonance provides one perspective for understanding a portion of the issues and dilemmas for the African American professional in human service organizations.

The Issues

Workplace Dilemmas

Social work is an agency-based profession. Most social work professionals are employed in organizations as opposed to being vendors or private contractors. The organization is their context for practice. Personnel are the organization's most valuable resource. Internal and external pressures on the organization affect the staff. Organizational trends are changing the utilization, roles, and responsibilities of the professional. These shifts are being brought about through organizational downsizing, managed care, devolution of social services, and shifts in the definitions of affirmative action. Organizational staff are expected to do more with fewer resources. Productivity is emphasized. Accountability for use of resources has become more stringent and ever more extensive documentation is being required. More sophisticated technology has added elements of efficiency and complexity to what is expected of staff. Methods of working with clients have become more streamlined and refined. In some instances there is the added pressure of fundraising. These demands have changed the nature of organizational work for all staff, and have exacerbated the workplace dilemmas faced by African American professionals.

NEGATIVE MEDIA IMAGES

The media portrayal of social workers tends to be of failed practice with clients, for example in the area of child abuse or neglect. Portrayal of African Americans in general, and African American professionals specifically, fare no better. An overabundance of negative media and social science coverage, research studies, and articles are geared to the deficiencies, criminality, struggles, and problems of African Americans. African Americans are viewed as a homogeneous group, regardless of station in life. The media and the social science literature paint a painfully negative and inaccurate portrait of African American people and neglect to celebrate strengths, assets, and resiliency. This carries over into organizational culture.

ORGANIZATIONAL MYTHS AND RATIONALIZATIONS

The myth of the inadequacy of African Americans persists in human service organizations. The sobering reflection of an African American women speaking of her workplace experience illustrates this point.

> Myths about people like me were the antithesis of everything the firm's culture prized. I was presumed to be of inferior intellectual stock; my breeding was, by definition, not breeding at all; and I carried the taint of the field and the bedroom, both of these locales as far from the boardroom as could be.   (Parker 1997:164)

The myth persists that African Americans understand and can serve other African Americans better than can whites. The assumption is made that if an African American client walks through the door, the best person to provide service is an African American, because of shared race. If the client's behavior is below the standard expectation — aggressive, hostile, or intimidating — the African American professional gets the assignment. Although at times such assignment might be appropriate, it is certainly not so all, or perhaps even most, of the time. Most African Americans experience discomfort in the informal label of being the resident African American expert. Yet it is a fact that the person may know more about, or be better able to assist, African Americans than a white counterpart. Taking honest responsibility for the knowledge or capacity one does or does not have is the key in such situations.

The work place is bombarded with catch words of the day. "Diversity" and "multiculturalism" represent current catch phrases. Organizations spend vast amounts of manpower hours thrashing through how to implement diversity in the workplace, training staff, or developing a policy regarding multiculturalism. Often this proves to be an exercise in futility. After the discussion, it is back to normative agency business, or organizational sabotage negates any advance. For example, most organizations use as a hiring criterion an assessment of the "fit" between the potential employee and the culture of the organization. Once an African American applicant is selected, plans are made for supporting, mentoring, and otherwise helping the person become an integrated member of the organization. But often the person who appears competent, with appropriate credentials, and ready to be a peer, is viewed as a threat and does not gain entrance or remain long. This can be seen as a case of cognitive dissonance. The individual meets the stated criteria for the position but not the unwritten expectations.

TOKENISM

In most white institutions there are few African American professionals on the staff. Tokenism usually involves the absence of social support to facilitate success. Tokens are often either successful in terms of rigid conformity to traditional white male organizational values, which usually means they have dissociated themselves from others in their group; or because of the intense pressures of isolation, they are unsuccessful and are used as justification for not hiring more African Americans (Feagin and Feagin 1978). The token African American may go through all the rituals of the organization such as becoming a member of a committee, producing the necessary level and quality of work, and being invited to agency functions. Without a critical mass of others, the African American can find him- or herself in a fish bowl. Their language, contributions, presence, and presentations are closely scrutinized. If they miss a meeting their absence is noted and commented upon. On the other hand, if their verbal contribution in a meeting goes against the "group think," it is usually ignored.

ISOLATION

Isolation is often a problem for the African American professional. African American professionals may not be invited to social interactions in the workplace, such as group lunches. Valuable opportunities to network and learn via the grapevine are missed. The result is serious isolation. An African American colleague reported she felt she could die in her office and only be discovered when the night cleaning crew arrived.

TRANSPARENCY

A different kind of isolation exists in the workplace, which could be called invisibility or transparency. For example, in the distribution of leadership opportunities, or assignments that might lead to advancement or upward movement in the organization, the African American is often not considered. The name of the person as a viable candidate is not remembered. The individual is invisible (Ellison 1964).

Assumptions are made in workplace-related functions that deny the full reality of the person. A lawyer attending a meeting where she was the only woman and the only African American present noted:

> People rarely spoke to me at functions like this. They stared and talked about me, but did not address me directly. So I was startled when the man beside me spoke. "Are you a lawyer?" the man asked. That was all. He didn't say hello, or introduce himself or even ask if I was enjoying the meeting. There it was, that insanity again. This was after all a meeting of lawyers. I was sitting there in my pinstriped suit with my name tag and my briefcase just like the rest of them.   (Parker 1997:60)

Given these difficulties it is not a surprise that a recent study indicated that a third of new African American workers leave their company within a year. Poor performance, absenteeism, and inability to adapt to the work environment are the most frequent causes of high turnover (Bellison 1990). The concept of a hostile environment is well known to African American employees in white organizations.

Another recent study found that 41 percent of 1,562 women of color reported that they felt racial discrimination affected their efforts to balance work and family. Thirty-three percent cited work demands and an unsupportive workplace culture as reasons for seeking or considering seeking a job with another company (Center for Women Policy Studies 1999).

Despite the trials and annoyances, African American professionals continue to hold positions in primarily white organizations. Their presence suggests that many remain reasonably satisfied. They are reaping intrinsic and extrinsic rewards and know the "perfect" job does not exist. Characteristics of such resilient personalities include flexibility and accommodation. Historically, an internalized strengths perspective has been a part of the survival repertoire of African Americans, who are adept at teasing out the positives in an adverse situation.

Developing Resiliency in the Family and Community

The majority of African American professionals come from middle class backgrounds. Middle class values can be found in most African Americans whether they come from the streets or from "decent" families. The family may have been poor, but the family lifestyle and values were the commonly accepted American values: being employed, obtaining an education, taking care of the family, ownership of some economic resources, being a responsible citizen, and having civic pride. A family might be poor but rich in goal oriented, socially acceptable behavior (Anderson 1984). One study of successful African American males reported that success could be attributed to encouraging parents who set rules for behavior in the home, set high expectations of academic achievement, developed consistent and strong communication, emphasized preparation for life, and served as strong positive role models (Hrabowski, Maton, and Greif 1998).

Every person evolves from his or her life experiences as a unique individual. Most African American professionals share similar early influences that shaped the core of their resiliency. These earlier experiences are identifiable in the adult's response to life's challenges and in the manner in which the person navigates the workplace. To understand the cognitive make-up of the resilient African American, it is necessary to tease out common significant experiences that coalesce into resiliency.

The family is the primary unit for providing the foundation of resiliency. Significant members of the extended family, caretakers, or individuals outside the family unit may also be influential (Thompson 1998; Hrabowski, Maton, and Greif 1998). The child learns that others consider him or her a valuable and worthwhile person. In spite of future workplace perceptions by others, the adult individual continues to know for a fact that he or she is a worthwhile person. High expectations of the child, and his or her achievements in school and the community are celebrated and rewarded. The adult expects to achieve and duly reap rewards in the adult workplace (Bowles 1988).

Obtaining an education is a priority in the African American community, seen as an avenue to a higher standard of living. The educated person is generally regarded with esteem. Most families are not wealthy, so education becomes an investment for future security. The African American professional has successfully completed several educational levels. He/she is proud of the accomplishment and inspired to continue to learn. The resilient adult is committed to lifelong learning as one strategy for maintenance of resiliency. The parent often acts as an advocate to secure resources, defend the child when appropriate, and help the child learn self-advocacy. Parents provide support for undertaking new and age-appropriate challenges. Thus, a foundation for taking risks and advocating for self also becomes a part of the resilient person. As a professional adult, the person will have had both successes and failures and will probably have enough self-confidence to explore uncharted waters.

The child is expected to be industrious and responsible. The work ethic is strongly etched into the middle class African American ethos (Thompson 1998). Work is important for economic survival and as an extension of self-identity. The African American child is sensitized to economic issues from an early age (Gutierrez and Lewis 1999). The resilient African American professional values and takes pride in their work. Choice employment opportunities are not as available to them as to their white counterparts. Thus they are more willing than whites to endure discrimination and intimidation. This should not be construed as acceptance of oppression. It should be understood as a person's willingness to absorb the transgression until the timing is right to resolve the issue.

In the African American home there are known behavioral rules and boundaries to be respected: be in the house at dusk, do your chores, appear neat and clean in public because you are judged by your appearance. Even though such restraints can create angry feelings, the individual learns to balance such feelings and divert that energy into constructive avenues. The child does his homework, pursues hobbies, has the opportunity to practice skills such as playing a musical instrument, telephones peers to vent about restrictive parents. These responsive behaviors become a part of the person's resiliency repertoire. Success in negotiating conflict is additive. Confidence in one's ability to handle conflict enables a person to risk self in future situations that may embody conflict.

Historically, the church has been the most important and influential social institution in African American life (Poole 1993). Spiritual values permeate the African American experience, and spirituality and religious institutions have dominated the moral and ethical philosophy. Spirituality provides comfort, solace, and strength in difficult times (Ward 1998; Gutierrez and Lewis 1999). It is a major resource for empowering most African Americans. Honesty, integrity, and altruism have their base in spiritual beliefs and practices.

Masten notes that an important parental task in forming the resilient person is to provide information and knowledge (Masten 1994). Most middle class African American parents try to expose their children to cultural, artistic, and civic events. The classics may be read, and there are books and newspapers in the home. Children take music lessons, and attend or participate in lectures, theater performances, and concerts. They are taken to museums, parades, ethnic celebrations, and exhibitions. The parents discuss current events, and vote for the candidate of their choice. In the workplace, whites often do not consider that the African American has had this kind of exposure. The resilient African American often needs to consciously expend energy to penetrate a conversation. It is a maneuver to break out of the invisible state.

Nurturing children for resiliency includes steering them away from wasteful or dangerous pitfalls through advice and proactive buffering (Masten 1994). Parents teach accountability by being knowledgeable about the child's friends, whereabouts, and activities. Discipline is used to reinforce rules, teach appropriate behaviors that keep the child safe, and demonstrate consequences of choices made. The parent provides supervision and support as the child practices problem solving and conflict resolution. Most African American children are taught how to respond for the best results from the police and persons in authority. All of these tasks require time and commitment from the parent. The message received by the child is affirmation of the child's value, while learning self-discipline, conflict resolution, and problem solving.

The resilient African American professional has benefited from a wide range of experiences and exposures that result in a competent, confident individual who knows his or her strengths and limitations and is willing to confront life's challenges. In addition to the family and community experience, African American professionals in human service agencies inherit a rich legacy of professional ancestors as competent role models.

African American Professional Pioneers

In the early part of the twentieth century African Americans were legally excluded from the benefits of organized social welfare (Gutierrez and Lewis

1999). Women's organizations (White 1999), neighbors, and white benefactors constituted an informal parallel social welfare system serving African Americans. The church has been a formidable force in the survival of children, families, and communities (Ward 1999). Black social work pioneers created and generated needed services where possible. A major target of the pioneers' work was the area of civil rights. In the latter part of the century high profile pioneers have had a dual focus on equal opportunity and culturally competent services. "Self study, race pride, mutual aid, and social debt became a part of the underpinning that guided their practice" (Carlton-LaNey 1999:313).

Examples are numerous. Eugene Kinckle Jones (1885–1954) fought racial discrimination against African American migrants and led the National Urban League in the early twentieth century. Jones was instrumental in developing and professionalizing African American social work. His work was the forerunner of the National Association of Black Social Workers, established in 1968 (Armfield 1999). Frankie Adams (1902–1979) was a social work educator who, with Whitney Young, developed a two year sequence of community organization practice. James Dumpson (b. 1909), vice president of the New York Community Trust, the nation's oldest and largest philanthropic organization, was dean of Fordham University, where he became the first African American dean of a white school of social work.

Lester Granger (1896–1976) was a professional social worker and leader of the National Urban League for twenty years. A Republican, his adherence to the principles of "scientific social work" and rational planning left him out of step with the early civil rights movement. He formed unions and set in motion integration of the military (NASW 1999; Brown 1997). Isabel Burns Lindsay (1916–1983) worked as a family welfare practitioner, agency administrator, and social researcher. She was the first dean of the School of Social Work of Howard University. Lindsay has been credited with coining the phrase "double jeopardy" in connection with her work with elderly African American women. In the 1960s, Essie Morgan developed community placement programs for psychiatric patients which served as a model for the Veteran's Administration hospital system. She was the first woman of color to hold the position of manager of the Washington, D.C. Veteran's Administration regional office (NASW 1999).

Whitney Young (1921–1971) served as executive director of the National Urban League and president of the Georgia branch of the National Association for the Advancement of Colored People. Time magazine cited Young's 1960 proposal for a domestic Marshall Plan as a major inspiration for President Lyndon Johnson's War on Poverty. Mark Battle (b. 1924) served as the executive director of the National Association of Social Workers for twelve years. He is a social worker, educator, consultant, businessman, and former government official. Under his leadership the NASW grew in membership and political strength. Ronald Dellums (b. 1935) has represented California's 8th Congressional District since 1970. He has been an advocate and community organizer throughout his career (NASW 1999).

Harvey (1999) cites several other African American social work contributors. Janie Porter Barrett founded the first settlement house in Virginia and one of the first settlements for African Americans in America. W. E. B. DuBois has been called the scholar of American sociology. He organized efforts to begin the scientific study of the problems of the African American community. From these efforts the Atlanta University School of Social Work was founded. E. Franklin Frazier served as dean at both the Atlanta and Howard University schools of social work. He is known for his contributions to family studies. In 1910, George Edmund Haynes, co-founder of the National Urban League, became the first African American to graduate from the New York School of Philanthropy. In 1912, he became the first African American to receive a doctorate from Columbia University.

There have been and are a large number of African American professionals in whom one can take pride of the contributions and accomplishments they have made. All of the social work professionals mentioned were affiliated with organizations. We can only guess at the hardships they endured. Their accomplishments were made during historically difficult times. Their lives serve as examples of wisdom, support, mutual aid, and resistance (Gutierrez and Lewis 1999).

Use of Resources by Professionals

The resilient professional must resolve a number of problems and dilemmas within the organization. There may be few persons with whom to freely communicate. There is a limited on-site support network. The few African American professionals who are a part of the agency may be placed throughout the organization in high visibility positions, known as "managed tokenism" (Steinhorn and Diggs-Brown 1998). As a result, the resilient professional often reaches outside the agency for his or her support system. African American colleagues, family, and friends provide a reality check for the professional's experiences since they have had similar encounters. When they get together, time is spent strategizing, defusing, and building up the person who has had repeated cognitive dissonance. "The Black experience is a dynamic spiritual phenomenon with invisible potency that triggers action and electrifies Blacks when they congregate together for a common purpose" (See 1998:14). The group provides support and guidance typical of the historical African American experience (Gutierrez and Lewis 1999). According to Harris (1994) African American professionals seek out their support network frequently because of incidents and politics in the workplace.

Fraternities and sororities provide support and an arena for community service, leadership development, "culture," and exposure to leading figures and issues of the times. These Greek letter organizations have drawn criticism from members and nonmembers because of exclusivity. Yet they provide a source of affirmation, support, and reference for African American professionals. There are few organizations with a more skilled and more coherent membership, or that are less dependent on outside resources than an African American sorority. Today over two hundred fifty thousand women belong to the three major college based sororities. The fact that these organizations have survived since the early part of the twentieth century and are still growing attests to their continuing importance (Giddings 1988).

Some African American professionals sustain themselves within the organization through elasticity of response to colleagues and situations. All organization members are potential helpmates—the janitor, the agency director, secretaries, administrative staff, and clients. They treat others as they wish to be treated. The resilient professional will open a working relationship with any agency member in the pursuit of organizational goal attainment.

Anger Fuels Motivation

In American society, overt expressions of anger and hostility are viewed as threatening and unacceptable behavior. The professional is expected to be disciplined and demonstrate emotional self-control. Yet the intensity and frequency of race-based perceptions and behaviors incite anger in the African American professional. Little is known about this rage. Whites are afraid to openly discuss anger. Many African Americans deny it exists, bottle it up, and turn it inward. The suppressed rage is evidenced in the high rate of hypertension and heart attacks among African Americans. Anger is the natural reaction of a persecuted group to another group's ability to act with power and authority in a hostile and prejudicial manner.

The use of anger is an overlooked cultural skill that resilient Blacks bring to the white organization. The skill is to be able to get angry quickly, then channel the energy from the anger into creative problem solutions or into attacking the problem and forcing swift resolution.

(Dickens and Dickens 1983:126)

The anger is often expressed to close friends or partners, or in physical activity. After the initial response to anger, the person is ready to use the generated energy to confront and resolve major issues and correct intolerable situations. The anger can surface in a controlled, constructive manner. The resilient person does not want to frighten people or put one's career in jeopardy. Strategically and constructively, the energy is used to resolve the situation. The anger is directed at the work and not toward an individual or an authority figure. Weighing options leads to creative problem solving. The resilient professional tries to resolve the conflict in a win-win way. For the African American, "anger and rage have been made to work as part of overall required strategic skills. These feelings get channeled into something that helps produce better results" (Dickens and Dickens 1983:184).

In emphasizing the dilemmas and requisite resiliency of African American professionals in predominantly white human service organizations, this paper has pointed the way toward a more positive appreciation of the challenges and strengths of the African American professional. The continued presence of African Americans in these organizations attests to their resiliency.

References

Anderson, E. 1984. The code of the streets. *Atlantic Monthly* 273 (5): 81–94.

Armfield, F. L. 1998. Eugene Kinckle Jones and the rise of professional black social workers, 1910–1940. Doctoral dissertation, Michigan State University.

Bellison, J. 1990. Workforce 2000: Already here? *Personnel* 67 (10): 3–4.

Biddle, B. J. 1979. *Role Theory: Expectations, Identities, and Behaviors.* New York: Academic Press.

Blau, P. 1970. Exchange theory. In O. Grusky and G. Miller, eds., *The Sociology of Organizations*, 127–148. New York: The Free Press.

Bowles, D. D. 1988. Development of an ethnic self-concept among Blacks. In C. Jacobs and D. D. Bowles, eds., *Ethnicity and Race: Critical Concepts in Social Work*, 103–113. Silver Spring, Md.: National Association of Social Work.

Brown, A. W. 1997. A social work leader in the struggle for racial equality: Lester Blackwell Granger. *Social Service Review* 65 (2): 226–280.

Carlton-LaNey, I. 1999. African American social work pioneers' response to need. *Social Work* 4 (4): 310–321.

Center for Women Policy Studies. 1999. Minority women discuss views on workplace issues. *Philadelphia Tribune* April 20, 1D.

Dickens, F. and J. B. Dickens. 1982. *The Black Manager.* New York: AMACOM.

Ellison, R. 1964. *The Invisible Man.* New York: New American Library.

Feagin, J. R. and C. B. Feagin. 1978. *Discrimination American Style: Institutional Racism and Sexism.* Englewood Cliffs, N.J.: Prentice-Hall.

Festinger, L. 1957. *A Theory of Cognitive Dissonance.* Evanston: Row, Peterson.

Giddings, P. 1988. *In Search of Sisterhood: Delta Sigma Theta and the Challenge of the Black Sorority Movement.* New York: William Morrow.

Gouldner, A. W. 1970. Cosmopolitans and locals: Toward an analysis of latent social roles. *Administrative Science Quarterly* December: 281–292.

Gutierrez, L. M. and E. A. Lewis. 1999. *Empowering Women of Color.* New York: Columbia University Press.

Harris, S. A. 1994. A study of the internal attributes of selected successful African American scholars in predominately white American colleges and universities in New England. Doctoral dissertation, University of Lowell.

Harvey, A. R. 1999. Brief notes on African Americans' contribution to social work. http://www.naswdc.org/PiecesNASW/Diversity/blackSW.htm

Hrabowski, F. A., K. I. Maton, and G. L. Greif. 1998. *Beating the Odds: Raising Academically Successful African American Males.* New York: Oxford University Press.

Joint Center for Political and Economic Studies. 1997. *1997 National Opinion Poll: Race Relations.* Washington, D.C.

McDaniel, C. O. and P. Balgopal. 1978. *A Three Dimensional Analysis of Black Leadership: Theoretical, Historical, Empirical.* Houston: University of Houston Press.

Masten, A. S. 1994. Resilience in individual development: Successful adaptation despite risk and adversity. In M. C. Wang and E. W. Gordon, eds., *Educational Resilience in Inner-City America,* 14. Hillsdale, N.J.: Erlman.

NASW. 1999. Social Work Pioneers: A Centennial Presentation by the NASW Leadership Academy. http://www.naswdc.org/PiecesNASW/piopeop/pioneers.htm

Parker, G. M. 1999. *Trespassing: My Sojourn in the Halls of Privilege.* Boston: Houghton Mifflin.

Poole, T. G. 1993. Black families and the Black church: A sociohistorical perspective. In H. Cheatham and J. Stewart, eds., *Black Families: Interdiscipli-nary Perspectives*. New Brunswick, N.J.: Transaction Publishers.

See, L. A. L. 1998. Human behavior theory and the African American experi-ence. *Journal of Human Behavior in the Social Environment* 1 (2/3): 7–29.

Steinhorn, L. and B. Diggs-Brown. 1998. *By the Color of Our Skin: The Illusion of Integration and the Reality of Race*. New York: Dutton.

Thompson, G. L. 1998. Predictors of resilience in African American adults. Doc-toral dissertation, Claremont Graduate University.

Ward, N. T. 1998. The African American church as service agency. In A. Carten and J. Dumpson, eds., *Removing Risks from Children: Shifting the Paradigm*, 269–282. Silver Springs, Md.: Beckham House.

White, D. G. 1999. *Too Heavy A Load: Black Women in Defense of Themselves, 1894–1994*. New York: W. W. Norton.

13 Introducing a Strengths/Resiliency Model in Mental Health Organizations

Robert Chazin, Shari Kaplan, and Stephen Terio

There is a growing literature arguing the value of the strengths perspective/resiliency enhancement paradigm in clinical practice. Many authors applaud the usefulness of this approach as a means of counterbalancing the traditional clinical emphasis on illness and dysfunction. While certainly not a new concept in social work, the more recent literature explicitly presents and further develops basic theoretical concepts underlying this approach (Cowger 1994). Beyond the theoretical, the current literature applies this model to diverse client populations. The paradigm is applied when helping people address problems at various junctures: clinicians are using this model in their work with homeless children (Felsman 1984; Douglass 1996), adolescents and young adults (Rosenbluth 1986), homeless women with children (Thrasher and Mowbray 1995), and the elderly (Perkins and Tice 1995).

Despite the strong case made for the usefulness of this approach, its actual utilization in practice remains limited. As Saleebey (1996) notes, clinical practice continues to focus on pathology and dysfunction. There is strong resistance to the strengths/resiliency model both on the part of social work practitioners and the systems in which they practice.

> The system — the bureaucracies and organizations of helping — is often diametrically opposed to a strengths orientation. In both formal and informal venues and structures, policies, and programs, the preferred language replaces the client's own lexicon with the vocabulary of problem and disease.
> (Saleebey 1996:297)

There is virtually nothing in the literature describing efforts to overcome organizational and practitioner resistance, nor methods of introducing this approach to agencies and clinicians. With rare exceptions (Kaplan et al. 1996), the problem remains. We here present examples of clinicians introducing the strengths/resiliency approach to the staff of two traditional social service agencies.

Both clinicians doing the training were employed by their respective agencies as staff, one full time, the other part time. The basic consultation principles outlined by Caplan (1970) were followed, especially the need for sensitivity to their colleagues' feelings about their work with clients. Respect for and acceptance of the work of their colleagues, and a commitment to avoid criticizing colleagues, was an essential part of the work. The trainers did not have any administrative or supervisory responsibility for the trainees' work with clients. In addition to being agency employees, their only additional role was that of educator.

Agency 1

Agency 1 offers a wide array of services to mentally retarded children, adolescents, adults, and their families or caregivers. Services are primarily long-term and include individual, family, marital, group therapy, and support groups. Psychiatrists, psychologists, social workers, and rehabilitation counselors serve their clients in clinics, homes, and at work sites. The agency seeks to facilitate clients' independence and integration into the community, to encourage self-esteem, dignity, and productivity and to protect clients incapable of self-protection. It provides clients with individualized programs, services, and supports, with particular sensitivity to cultural differences.

The agency requires that clinicians relate service goals to presenting problems and to state goals in behavioral, measurable ways. Examples of treatment goals from the agency's orientation manual are "Mother will report significant decrease of fighting at home" and "Client will report making at least one new friend over the next six months." While the agency's treatment goals aim at enhancing clients' functioning while recognizing their limitations, the agency's focus on problem and diagnosis may limit its effectiveness. The agency's staff orientation manual emphasizes problem and diagnosis, and decreasing clients' symptoms, ignoring the clients' existing abilities. The agency provides no literature to clinicians during its staff orientation that discusses assessment of and working with clients' strengths.

The Training

The training, while addressing problems and diagnosis, sought to expand the participants' perspective on treatment by introducing the strengths/resiliency model into their treatment repertoire. Specifically, the trainer hoped that participants would accept this model as a primary treatment approach.

This training was part of a weekly staff development program with staff members taking turns presenting their chosen topics. At this agency, attendance at staff development meetings is voluntary. In this case, a supervisor invited the trainer to introduce agency staff to the strengths/resiliency model so that they could expand their treatment repertoire by including this model in their assessment and treatment of clients. Staff, however, were under no obligation to use this approach in their work.

THE TRAINEES

The trainees included eight psychologists and social workers, ages 28 to 62, who had worked in the mental health profession between two and twenty-six years. These clinicians utilize psychodynamic, cognitive, cognitive/behavioral, humanistic, supportive, and psycho-educational methods in their treatment.

CONTENT AND FORMAT

During the training the following key concepts of the strengths perspective/resiliency model were introduced. The therapist should:

1. respect the clients' strengths and maintain a profound awareness of their capacities, talents, competencies, possibilities, visions, values, hopes, knowledge and abilities, and of the resources existing within and around the individual, family, and community;
2. be curious and empathic, listening to and understanding the clients' survival techniques;
3. be aware of the clients' strengths and foster these and contribute to the clients' motivation;
4. collaborate with clients in achieving the clients' desired goals;
5. help clients avoid a victim mindset;
6. view any environment as possessing valuable resources.

Two handouts were distributed. One was an assessment guideline which included categories of human attributes and positive strengths to look for under each attribute (Cowger 1992).

ASSESSMENT OF CLIENT STRENGTHS HANDOUT

A. Cognition

1. Sees the world as most other people see it in her culture
2. Has an understanding of right and wrong, from her cultural, ethical perspective
3. Understands how one's own behavior affects others and how others affect her; is insightful
4. Is open to different ways of thinking about things
5. Reasoning is easy to follow
6. Considers and weighs alternatives in problem solving

B. Emotion

1. Is in touch with feelings and is able to express them if encouraged
2. Expresses love and concern for intimate others
3. Demonstrates a degree of self-control
4. Can handle stressful situations reasonably well
5. Is positive about life; has hope
6. Has a range of emotions
7. Has emotions congruent with situation

C. Motivation

1. When having a problem, doesn't hide from, avoid, or deny it
2. Willing to seek help and share problem situation with others she can trust
3. Willing to accept responsibility for her own part or role in problem situation
4. Wants to improve current and future situations
5. Does not want to be dependent on others
6. Seeks to improve self through further knowledge, education, and skills

D. Coping

1. Is persistent in handling family crises
2. Is well organized
3. Follows through on decisions
4. Is resourceful and creative with limited resources

5. Stands up for self rather than submitting to injustice
6. Attempts to pay debts despite financial difficulty
7. Prepares for and handles new situations
8. Has dealt successfully with related problems in the past

E. Interpersonal

1. Has friends
2. Seeks to understand friends, family members, and others
3. Makes sacrifices for friends, family members, and others
4. Performs social roles appropriately (e.g., parent, spouse, son or daughter, community)
5. Is outgoing and friendly
6. Is truthful
7. Is cooperative and flexible in relating to family and friends
8. Is self-confident in relationships with others
9. Shows warm acceptance of others
10. Can accept loving and caring feelings from others
11. Has sense of propriety, good manners
12. Is a good listener
13. Expresses self spontaneously
14. Is patient
15. Has realistic expectations in relationships with others
16. Has a sense of humor
17. Has sense of satisfaction in role performance with others
18. Has ability to maintain own personal boundaries in relationships with others
19. Demonstrates comfort in sexual role/identity
20. Demonstrates ability to forgive
21. Is generous with time and money
22. Is verbally fluent
23. Is ambitious and industrious
24. Is resourceful

It was stressed that this assessment tool might be utilized to (1) stimulate thinking about strengths and their importance in the clinical process; (2) assist in identifying strengths that otherwise would not be considered; (3) assist in identifying and selecting positive and supportive content to be shared with clients; (4) provide a foundation for a case plan that is based on client competency and capability rather than inadequacy; and (5) bolster worker confidence and belief in the client.

The second handout presented guidelines for defining a problem from a strengths perspective.

DEFINING THE PROBLEM FROM A STRENGTHS PERSPECTIVE HANDOUT

1. Develop a straightforward, simple summary of the identified problem situation, which is mutually agreed upon between team members, or clinician and client.
2. Who (persons, groups, or organizations) is involved, including the client/person seeking assistance?
3. How or in what way are participants involved? What happens between the participants before, during, and immediately following activity related to the problem situation?
4. What meaning does the client/person ascribe to the problem situation?
5. What does the client/person want, related to the problem situation?
6. What does the client/person want or expect by seeking assistance?
7. What would client's/person's life be like if the problem was resolved?

Using the above handouts, the training alternated between the didactic presentation of content and group discussion of participants' questions. These clinicians questioned how realistic a strengths/resiliency approach would be with their clients. They noted that their clients not only experienced serious mental and emotional limitations but suffered extreme deprivation in their homes, relationships, and neighborhoods. In short, they viewed their clients as lacking the strengths and resources under discussion. The trainer responded with examples of the utility of this approach, using her own clients, who were drawn from the same population. One illustrative case example is presented below.

The Case of Michael

Michael is a 13-year-old African American boy who is diagnosed with Attention Deficit/Hyperactivity Disorder. He resists taking medication because he views medication as a drug and his mother is actively abusing drugs. Within the first several sessions, Michael states that he is a very good baseball player and that he plays on a school team. Michael also reports that he is not doing well in school, having difficulty paying attention in class and staying in his seat during the class period.

The clinician explores with Michael the qualities which make him such a good baseball player and teammate. Michael states that he is a good hitter because he keeps his eye on the ball, listens to the coach, and supports the other players on the team when he is not on the field. The clinician assists Michael in further defining his skills in more specific terms, i.e. Michael can concentrate, focus, follow directions well, pay attention for extended periods of time, and sit in one seat (the bench) for extended periods of time while he is involved in a baseball game.

The clinician suggests that Michael try applying these skills in his classroom and supports Michael in creating for himself an image of his teacher, classmates, and classroom as being another version of his baseball team. The teacher is to be seen as his coach, the classmates as teammates, and his chair and desk as the bench. Michael speaks to his teacher regarding this approach, requesting that she participate by giving him verbal cues when she recognizes that he may be inattentive. Over a period of three months, Michael is able to significantly improve his grades and his behavior in the classroom.

With further discussion the training participants were able to identify their clients' strengths and resiliency and to include these attributes in their treatment plans. The group discussion focused on applying this approach to practice and on the participants' views as to its potential usefulness.

TRAINING EVALUATION

Time was scheduled at the end of the training for the participants' evaluation. This evaluation included a discussion of the pros and cons of using the strengths/resiliency paradigm in their agency. The participants' reaction to the training generally was very positive. One participant said "the training was inspirational and a motivating approach to treatment." Others credited the trainer's enthusiasm for this model as motivating them to use this approach in their own work. The participants found the content to be informative and presented in a clear and thorough manner. They considered the handout listing guidelines for assessing clients' strengths and the use of illustrative case examples from the trainer's and participants' practice most helpful. They found that the combined teaching and group discussion strengthened the presentation. Some participants were less enthusiastic, noting this was not a new approach but had been the cornerstone of the profession since its beginnings.

Participants also observed that practicing therapy from this perspective would feel more rewarding. It would enhance their hopefulness and effectiveness regarding achieving goals. They also noted that this approach is the new trend in treatment. Even those participants who felt the training repeated what they already knew as clinicians, observed that their practice had lacked the consistency and depth described.

In addition to commenting on the content, the participants also acknowledged the usefulness of the training format. They stated that the didactic presentation of new information interspersed with their collaborative discussion of this approach contributed to creating an interesting and motivating presentation. They felt they had gained a clear and manageable vision of how to work with their clients.

Along with the positive comments cited above, participants noted some limitations in the presentation and some problems in implementing the approach. One clinician recommended evaluating each clinician's knowledge of this approach at the start so that the training could be more closely tailored to the trainees' level of knowledge. Another suggested that using a visual tool, such as a flip chart, along with the handouts, would have enhanced their learning through a visual connection with the material.

Some participants observed that this approach requires more clinician creativity, since it is more difficult to apply the strengths/resiliency model than the more familiar pathology/problem-focused treatment model. They expected difficulty in identifying client strengths and in integrating strengths in a treatment plan. They commented, however, that the "guidelines" handout and the discussion helped with these concerns.

Also significant were their comments about the difficulty of integrating the strengths/resiliency approach into the agency's system. These clinicians identified possible sources of agency resistance. Since third party reimbursement focuses on diagnosis of disease, shifting attention to strengths might create a problem in payment for services. These clinicians were also concerned that the more rapid improvement in client functioning would produce higher client turnover and increased case openings and closings, creating more paperwork for clinicians. They noted the need for an agency reward system to compensate for the additional paperwork likely to result from the use of a strengths/resiliency model. Understandably, these clinicians felt that this treatment approach would be particularly valuable and appropriate in short-term inpatient facilities where high turnover and accompanying paperwork are acceptable elements of job responsibility.

TRAINING FOLLOW-UP

This training led to no formal organizational changes. However, two months later, in unrelated discussions with the trainer, six participants voluntarily informed the trainer that they had been applying the strengths/resiliency approach in their work with clients. Two of the respondents were supervisors and four were line staff workers. They found the assessment tool that listed basic categories with questions under each category aimed at identifying clients' strengths to be extremely useful. They acknowledged that despite their clients' individual and social limitations, some clients who previously had shown little improvement in treatment now showed significant gains in functioning.

Agency 2

This agency is a health maintenance organization with a long history of service. Like other HMOs, it is comprised of an elaborate network of doctors and other professionals who are listed as providers. However, it also includes a number of medical and mental health centers in three specialty areas: mental health, alcoholism treatment, and a child and adolescent program.

The Training

The agency provides mandatory in-service training, rotating staff members through the year to present topics of their own choosing. The training aims at advancing the knowledge and clinical expertise of the staff. The training relationship is collaborative: debate and controversy are anticipated and welcomed as they draw out contributions from each staff member's individual expertise.

The training discussed here included the basic tenets of the strengths/resiliency approach, exercises involving a mock case vignette, and a discussion of various applications of this approach. The goals were to impart theory and clinical application of this perspective, to inspire professional staff to incorporate the strengths/resiliency perspective within their respective clinical orientations and thereby shift away from pathologizing patients, and to change the agency's delivery of services to include this approach as part of its intake with new clients.

THE TRAINEES

Nineteen staff members, including the clinic director, participated in the training. The mental health staff who participated represented various ethnicities, theoretical orientations, and years of clinical experience (ranging from ten to twenty). These clinicians typically practiced within specialty areas; for instance, some worked primarily with children, others with substance abusing clients.

CONTENT AND FORMAT

The strengths/resiliency content presented here was drawn from the same sources used at Agency 1, although the training format was somewhat different. Each of the nineteen participants was given a mock case vignette of a fictitious patient. The vignette was designed to illustrate a significant number of problems as well as strengths such as coping mechanisms, adaptive responses, and resources.

Case Vignette

Shante, a 31-year-old, divorced, bi-sexual, HIV positive African American male, came to the mental health clinic shortly after the death of his male lover with whom he had shared a five-year relationship. He has lived with the virus for well over two years and was asymptomatic without taking any retroviral medications. He was healthy and employed full-time.

At the age of 17, Shante had joined the Nation of Islam and converted from Catholicism (which he considered an oppressive "white man's" religion) to become an extremely devout Muslim. He kept his sexual orientation hidden for fear of ostracism because, as he explained, homosexuals "would be cast into the lake of fire by Allah come judgment day." He not only converted from one religion to another, but also attempted to change his sexual identity, even going so far as to committing to a heterosexual marriage arranged by the Iman (head priest) of his mosque, the Islamic place of worship. This marriage lasted for several years until he met a fellow Muslim who also was living a secret homosexual lifestyle. The two fell in love and Shante's marriage quickly ended in divorce. Shortly after, his lover discovered that he was HIV positive.

Shante and his lover managed to continue their relationship in secret, but Shante admitted that all that while he felt like a hypocrite.
The guilt of his heresy actualized when his lover died of AIDS, and he
discovered he too was HIV positive. He believed his fate was a just and
fitting punishment visited upon him by Allah. Unable to grieve the loss
of his lover, or reconcile with his faith, Shante isolated himself socially.
He remained a devout Muslim, but no longer attended the mosque
services or functions, completely dissociating himself from family and
friends. He was resigned to a life of obscurity and became extremely
depressed. It was in this condition he presented at the mental health
clinic.

Participants were asked to read the vignette and were instructed to discuss the
case from a positive, optimistic perspective. As much as the vignette could be
used to make a case for assessing pathology, it also clearly delineates a wealth
of personal strengths and resources. The first two sentences alone indicate
that the patient was more than capable of sustaining a romantic relationship
for five years, and that despite his HIV status, he was healthy. Shante was also
gainfully employed full-time, ensuring his ability to access a variety of social
systems and maintain some reasonable standard of living. Even his religious
beliefs, although used by him in self-punishment, were strengths containing
the curative properties of spirituality and connection to a community of
worship.

Almost all of the participants pathologized the patient and resisted the notion of considering strengths. They echoed many of the same criticisms of
this approach raised by other traditionally trained professional clinicians.
They viewed the strengths/resiliency perspective as overly optimistic and potentially harmful to the client in that it de-emphasized problem areas and
pathology.

However, one participant reviewed the vignette from a completely
strengths based perspective, but later acknowledged that she would probably
not use this prism with an actual client: First, the absence of pathology and
diagnosis meant an absence of admission criteria and, second, pathology
should not be overlooked even in assessing strengths.

Participants noted that often patients are manipulative and intentionally
minimize the damaging effects of their pathology. Examples were given by
members of the alcohol treatment team. They cited patients with a substance
abuse background who often resisted treatment initiatives through denial,
and sought the approval of therapists by minimizing their pathology. These

clinicians thought they would be remiss in their obligation not only to protect the patients from themselves, but also to protect society from active addicts, if they were to consider the manipulative abilities of such patients as strengths.

Another reservation was offered by a child psychologist who cited many cases in which children are referred by the school because of behavioral problems. Parents often interpret such referrals as an insult to their parenting abilities. This coupled with the fact that parents do not wish to view their children as deficient or lacking in significant developmental areas often leads parents to shift blame for their children's aberrant behavior onto teachers and other school officials. Thus parents will minimize their child's problems and seek a clinician's validation that their child is normal and that medication or special education is unwarranted. Again, the clinician would be remiss in his or her responsibility by focusing on strengths/resiliency and ignoring the parents' resistance to treatment. This could lead to a delay in accessing needed help for the child.

In response to these criticisms, the trainer referred to Saleebey's explanation that a clinician's use of the strengths/resiliency approach is neither Pollyanna-like nor does it ignore reality. Clinicians are encouraged to accurately assess pathology. But they are also called upon to assess with equal vigor the adaptive natures of patients who have survived and even learned from living with their afflictions. The trainer suggested that to exclude this perspective would be remiss in one's professional obligation and commitment to the treatment of the client. In addition, omitting this perspective can lead to a sense of helplessness or hopelessness in the clinician.

Using the writings of Saleebey and Cowger, the strengths/resiliency model's theoretical underpinnings and clinical applications were explained. To highlight the differences between the pathology and the strengths/resiliency perspective the trainer presented Saleebey's comparison of the two models (1996:298).

This led to a discussion of key terms in this perspective, such as resiliency (individual skills and abilities), membership (social connections or social resources), and cultural diversity—all tools for understanding the patient. Each item in Saleebey's comparison was discussed. Some participants reacted strongly to the concept that a patient's growth is not necessarily limited by his pathology. Many joined in echoing the sentiment that pathology undoubtedly limits an individual's capacity for growth, citing for example that "floridly psychotic patients are incapable of functioning and thus are limited in their abilities to grow even when stabilized on psychotropic medications, particularly if a personality disorder exists as well." Participants were re-minded that in a previous training session on schizophrenia given by another staff member, a film was shown in which a man had a psychotic break, was hospitalized, diagnosed with paranoid schizophrenia, and treated with med-ications. He subsequently successfully completed his Ph.D. in psychology and is now one of the most successful advocates for the chronically mentally ill. Despite this entreaty, participants remained staunchly opposed, calling this example an exception to the rule. However, they acknowledged that many clinicians, including themselves, were sometimes too dismissive of a patient's potential, especially if the pathology appeared overwhelmingly de-bilitating as is often the case with schizophrenia.

Cowger's work (1992, 1994) was also used to further present the rationale and guidelines for using this strengths/resiliency perspective. Cowger details the following important points of using assessment to unearth strengths locked within the clients' pathology, through personal and social empower-ment.

1. A focus on deficits will likely remain the entire focus of the worker and client.
2. Focusing on deficits will likely impair a worker's ability to see growth potential, reinforcing clients' self-doubts and feelings of inadequacy.
3. Strengths are all we have to work with.
4. Focusing on strengths levels the power relationship between client and worker, thereby empowering clients and liberating them from stigma-tizing diagnostic labels.

He offers guidelines for a strengths/resiliency assessment (Cowger 1994: 265), emphasizing that, regardless of their training, practitioners can use these guidelines to supplement their current assessment paradigms and thus enrich their clinical practice.

1. Give preeminence to the client's understanding of the facts.
2. Believe the client.
3. Discover what the client wants.
4. Move the assessment toward personal and environmental strengths.
5. Make assessment of strengths multidimensional.
6. Use the assessment to discover uniqueness.
7. Use language the client can understand.
8. Make assessment a joint activity between worker and client.

9. Reach a mutual agreement on the assessment.
10. Avoid blame and blaming.
11. Avoid cause-and-effect thinking.
12. Assess; do not diagnose.

Participants noted that while they already use this approach to some degree, to do so excessively would create harmful consequences. When asked about their current methods for examining patients' strengths, they offered that these were basic, elementary rapport-building skills, inherent in the counseling relationship. They viewed their encouragement of a patient's strengths as occurring almost naturally over the course of a therapeutic relationship. If a patient got in touch with deepseated pain and gained insight, this was a result of the patient possessing a capacity for emotional exploration and insight. This work demonstrated a motivation to achieve wellness that would be validated by the therapist. Participants also unanimously agreed that they generally capitalize on the talents and abilities of their patients to facilitate the therapeutic process. Rather than directing the treatment, particularly during the evaluation phase, the participants view themselves as guided by the goals and wishes of their patients.

Participants were encouraged to consider how their respective clinical orientations might accommodate the strengths/resiliency perspective. While they appeared to accept this possibility, many qualified their acceptance. They stated that given the often stressful nature of clinical work with chronic problems, therapists may cope with their frustration and validate their own sense of hopelessness by focusing on patient's pathology and using clinical labels to describe patients. Here, the use of psychological labels becomes a means of relieving the frustration of difficult work. One psychiatrist echoed this sentiment by describing how clinicians in hospitals referred to patients by their diagnosis and location on the ward ("the schizophrenic in room A may need to have his medication reevaluated"). The psychiatrist admitted that patients are reduced to diagnostic categories and the human element of practice is lost.

The absence of the strengths/resiliency perspective in the agency's current evaluation methods was noted. It was suggested that the agency begin to incorporate a section on strengths in its current consultation/evaluation form. Participants rejected this suggestion, noting the extra paperwork would add still more time to their already full schedules. Although not reflected in their recordings, participants stated that they already provided time to reinforce patients' strengths. Participants did agree to incorporate more detail on patients' strengths in the existing evaluation process. This would help them maintain a focus on patients' abilities and resources and prevent unnecessary pathologizing.

TRAINING EVALUATION AND FOLLOW-UP

Follow-up interviews were conducted with five of the participants six months after the training. Time constraints prevented a formal meeting or survey of participants. The five participants interviewed were selected because they were available and willing. The consensus was that the initial assessment of clients had not changed. All of the participants interviewed held to the belief that to satisfy admission criteria the initial consultation needed to remain a snapshot of pathology. They steadfastly maintained that quickly arriving at treatment protocols — the need for psychotropic medication, choice of individual or group treatment, the need for substance abuse treatment, or referral to other agencies — necessitates the early focus on pathology. Because of these considerations, there was little change in recording procedures.

Participants cited time pressure as another obstacle to changing procedures. Their already demanding schedules and excessive paperwork precluded adding a new section on the existing evaluation form. The interviewees agreed that the paperwork was secondary to actually treating the patients. The recording of pathology was more of an administrative rather than a clinical concern, and did not necessarily lead to pathologizing patients. They insisted that the patients' strengths would still be identified and supported over the course of treatment, even if not initially recorded.

Two of the interviewees acknowledged that they were identifying more of their patients' strengths and resiliency in their session notes. Neither was able to fully explain this change, but they agreed that it felt good to describe their patients in positive terms. They noted that they were now better able to track their patients' progress, which enhanced their clinical practice. They now focused more on progress rather than regression.

Follow-up Discussion

Subsequent discussions with training participants at both agencies indicated that training in the strengths/resiliency model had a positive impact. Although neither training effort resulted in formal organizational change, individual participants in both agencies noted ways in which the training had affected their practice. A majority acknowledged that the training reaffirmed their existing knowledge and commitment to humanistic values. While the content was not substantially new to most, it did evoke a new and heightened sensitivity to their clients' strengths. By focusing their case recordings more on a client's progress, some participants felt that they now derived more pleasure from their work. Several clinicians noted that training in the strengths/resiliency perspective had introduced them to the possibility of more creative ways of working with their clients.

Discussion with the participants at both training sites led us to several conclusions regarding recommendations for future training. These recommendations concern how the training is conducted, and how to incorporate this model into the organizational structure.

Conducting the Training

Our experience suggests several recommendations for future efforts to introduce strengths/resiliency oriented practice into organizations. In preparation, it is helpful to tailor the training to the staff. The more the trainer knows about the participants and their clients, the more the trainer can match the training to the participants' interests and needs. One should assess the participants' level of awareness and knowledge of the strengths/resiliency approach before the training so the content and format can be customized. The more knowledgeable the staff, the less a trainer needs to focus on basic concepts and the more she or he can teach application of concepts to practice. And the more a trainer knows about an agency's clientele and practice problems, the more sensitive to participants' difficulties can the trainer be, to prepare relevant case examples and join participants in formulating solutions.

To highlight the unique elements of the strengths/resiliency model it is important to contrast this paradigm with other traditional approaches, which focus on pathology. In one agency, the trainer used a visual aid to reinforce this difference — a large chart contrasting core concepts of both the strengths and pathology models. An effective way of illustrating and reinforcing the potential benefits of the strengths/resiliency approach to treatment is the use of case examples from both the trainer's and participants' practices. Case examples are particularly helpful when both trainer and participants have similar clients. We found that the handout on structured interview guidelines was another effective teaching tool. It listed questions that clinicians could ask to garner information on clients' strengths. Discussing a case vignette illuminated participants' difficulty in identifying strengths and their proclivity to see pathology.

The trainers found that interspersing didactic presentations with discussion was an effective method of training. The participants' questions often revealed their difficulty in applying this new paradigm to their clinical work. Open discussion afforded participants as well as the trainer the opportunity to elaborate on ways of applying concepts to practice. Further, it allowed participants to express and therefore lower their resistance to this new approach, resulting in an enhanced openness to new ideas.

Several reactions to the trainer at Agency 2 suggested criteria for selecting a trainer. Having a staff member present this approach to colleagues as part of an ongoing staff development program can be helpful. A trainer known to participants will elicit more openness and less resistance from colleagues than an outsider who may be perceived as imposing a foreign approach. The presenter's credibility is likely to be strengthened if she or he is a seasoned and respected clinician within the agency. If a junior, less experienced, staff member presents, it may be easier for colleagues to dismiss the strengths/resiliency model.

Regardless of the presenter's credibility, he or she should anticipate some resistance. In our experience, there is a strong preference for refracting the light of human problems through a lens of pathology rather than strengths/resiliency. Participants noted that work with severely mentally ill clients encourages a focus on pathology and clinical labels. It seems to us that by focusing on clients' pathology, clinicians seek to validate their own sense of helplessness and hopelessness as well as distance themselves from difficult clients.

Organizational Support

Our experience demonstrates clearly the necessity for organizational support in incorporating this approach into agency practice and procedures. In both agencies, participants acknowledged that they could conceivably derive satisfaction and success by using this approach. They protested, however, that this new recording method would unduly burden them and add to their already heavy workloads. For agencies to successfully incorporate the strengths/resiliency model, they must recognize that staff will resist additional recording requirements. In order to win staff support, it is incumbent upon agency administration to make appropriate accommodations.

One solution to staff resistance is offered by Consultations: A Center for Solution-Focused Brief Therapy, which utilizes only solution-focused brief treatment (Walter 1997; Walter and Peller 1992). This agency is a model of successfully incorporating a strengths/resiliency or wellness approach into therapy. Solution-focused therapy closely resembles the strengths/resiliency paradigm in that it assumes patients already possess innate or learned abilities to overcome their problems. It takes an empowerment position, using the client's own competency for healing.

This agency's support for solution-focused practice is seen in the incentives provided administrators and clinicians: the clinic has profitable formal agreements with managed care companies which automatically reimburse claims, without requiring documentation, when treatment is limited to six sessions. Thus the strengths/resiliency model need not create an additional paperwork burden for clinicians. On the contrary, to the extent that this model enhances treatment effectiveness, it can drastically reduce paperwork requirements.

Our experience suggests that the use of a strengths/resiliency model contributes to both clinicians' satisfaction and clients' progress in treatment. The successful incorporation of a strengths/resiliency model requires organizational support. It is incumbent upon administrators to understand that this model can improve clinical staffs' morale, increase treatment success, and offer financial gain to the agency. Agency administrators must invest resource dollars in training their clinicians to use this approach and negotiate funding contracts that reward effective, efficient treatment. In this era of increasing managed care involvement in mental health services this remains one clear path to agency solvency.

References

Caplan, G. 1970. *The Theory and Practice of Mental Health Consultation*. New York: Basic Books.

Cowger, C. D. 1994. Assessing client strengths: Clinical assessment for client empowerment. *Journal of the National Association of Social Workers* 39:262–268.

Cowger, C. D. 1992. Assessment of client strengths. In D. Saleebey, ed., *The Strengths Perspective in Social Work Practice*, 59–74. White Plains, N.Y.: Longman.

Douglas, A. 1996. A rethinking of the effects of homelessness on children: Resiliency and competency. *Child Welfare* 75 (6): 741–751.

Felsman, J. K. 1984. Abandoned children: A reconsideration. *Children Today* 13 (3): 13–18

Kaplan, C. P., S. Turner, E. Norman, and K. Stillson. 1996. Promoting resilience strategies: A modified consultation model. *Social Work in Education* 18 (3): 158–168.

Perkins, K. and C. Tice. 1995. A strengths perspective in practice: Older people and mental health challenges. *Journal of Gerontological Social Work* 23 (3/4): 83–97.

Rosenbluth, M. E. 1986. A study of vulnerable and resilient young adults. Doctoral dissertation, University of Chicago.

Saleebey, D. 1996. The strengths perspective in social work practice: Extensions and cautions. *Journal of the National Association of Social Workers* 41:296–305.

Thrasher, S. P. and C. T. Mowbray. 1995. A strengths perspective: An ethnographic study of homeless women with children. *Health and Social Work* 20 (2): 93–101.

Walter, J. 1997. *Solution Focused Brief Therapy*. New York: American Institute of Healthcare Workshop.

Walter, J. and J. Peller. 1992. *Becoming Solution Focused in Brief Therapy*. New York: Brunner Mazel.

14 Capitalizing on Strengths: A Resiliency Enhancement Model for At-Risk Youth

Mary Ann Forgey

A significant body of knowledge has developed on the common core of factors such as personality characteristics and dispositions, family interaction, and school and community milieu, that enable highly stressed children to maintain a sense of competence and control in their lives. Garmezy (1985) defined these factors that contribute to individual resilience in the face of adversity as protective factors. Enough is known about these multi-level protective factors to design resiliency enhancement programs for children.

Certain settings in which social workers are employed are ideal for developing and implementing programs that can enhance these protective factors to help prevent problems such as substance abuse, teenage pregnancy, HIV/STD, violence, depression, and suicide. Elementary and secondary schools and organizations like the Boys and Girls Clubs can provide prevention services to young people who are at-risk for developing a myriad of problems due to the stressors they face. Social workers are often at a loss in these preventative settings since the focus of their training has been on how to work with existing problems and pathology. Too little has been done to train social workers on how to use their specialized knowledge and skills in preventing the onset of problems through resiliency enhancement.

There is a natural fit between the orientation and training of professional social work and effective resiliency enhancement programs aimed at prevention. Prevention programs that have been highly effective have multi-level components directed at the individual, family, and community; have empirically based program designs that aim to reduce identified risk factors and enhance protective factors; and are culturally sensitive (Dryfoos 1997; Dusenbury and Falco 1997; Moore, Sugland, Blumenthal, Glei, and Snyder 1995). Social work's embrace of an ecological framework, a strengths perspective, a research-practice partnership, and culturally sensitive practice make it well suited to develop the types of programs that have been found to be most effective. The roots of social work practice can be said to lie in resiliency enhancement: the settlement house movement was an effort at increasing the resiliency of immigrant populations by delivering programs that enhanced language skills, cultural pride, and social support.

Social workers need a conceptual framework that will assist them in applying social work knowledge and skills to the development of resiliency enhancement approaches to prevention programs. The model described in this paper provides the social worker with a systematic way to approach prevention through the enhancement of resiliency. It focuses on how to develop approaches that will enhance the multi-level protective factors that have been empirically identified to promote resiliency in populations identified as being at risk. The use of this conceptual framework by social workers may result in a better understanding of the unique role social work can play in the prevention of the onset of problems and a greater appreciation of the range of social work skills involved in this work.

The Resiliency Enhancement Model of Prevention

The resiliency enhancement model of prevention is a conceptual framework utilizing the findings of resiliency research. The model is applicable to the prevention of a specific problem or for the development of more comprehensive approaches that address concurrent behaviors. The model consists of five tasks:

1. Selecting the potential problem to be prevented requires an understanding of the kinds of difficulties encountered by the population being served. Determining which problem or problems should receive priority also requires an ongoing dialogue and negotiation with the sanctioning body of the organization or agency responsible for the prevention effort.
2. Defining the target population requires identifying specific characteristics of the target population and the implications of these characteristics on the design of the intervention.

3. Identifying and refining the resiliency factors associated with the prevention of a particular problem requires an ability to apply an ecological perspective to the prevention process and to critique the existing empirical research, as well the use of other empirical methods when there are gaps in the knowledge base. The refinement of the resiliency factors to fit the defined target population also requires cultural sensitivity in understanding the implications of certain characteristics for program design.

4. Selecting the method and level of intervention, given the multi-level resiliency factors identified, the target population, and the capabilities of the sponsoring organization, requires an ability and willingness to work on the individual, family, group, organization, and community levels.

5. Developing, implementing, and using effective program evaluation assesses how well the programmatic approach has impacted on the problem to be prevented by measuring the actual reduction in the problem behavior, the reduction in risk factors, or the increase in resiliency factors associated with prevention of the problem. This step requires a basic understanding of evaluation research and the ability to connect the intervention to the evaluation process.

Examples from several prevention projects for at-risk youth will illustrate each of these steps. These projects include completed programs aimed at preventing adolescent substance abuse and HIV/STD, and a program currently in development that is more comprehensive in its approach, aiming to prevent a myriad of problems faced by adolescents.

Selecting the Potential Problem to be Prevented

The initial decision regarding the problem to focus on will provide the direction for the ensuing planning steps. Due mainly to funding streams, prevention approaches traditionally have been categorical, focusing on one type of problem to be prevented. As more knowledge has been gained about the co-occurrence of many problems, more comprehensive approaches have been recommended (Dryfoos 1997).

The problem selection process involves investigating the extent of the threat of the problem to the population the social worker considers to be the primary client group, including an analysis of the rate of the problem behavior within the primary client population. If teenage pregnancy is under consideration, some investigation should be done as to how many teenage pregnancies occurred within the past 5 years within the clients' community. Is the rate increasing or decreasing, and how does it compare to the national norm? The answers to such questions will help with the question of how much attention the prevention of this problem should receive, especially where resources are limited. The decision must also receive support from the sanctioning bodies within the organization or the community. This requires an understanding of the power structure within the organization or community and the development of a strategy to get the support of those who will play critical roles in the program's implementation. This may involve persons or organizations responsible for resource allocation as well as those who will play a critical role in engaging the target population. To gain such support the developer should have a clear vision of the entire program strategy.

Too often, for a variety of reasons, the problem selection process is not as deliberate as it needs to be. Organizations can get caught up in the "problem of the moment" for which funds become suddenly available, without giving enough consideration to whether this problem really deserves increased attention within this particular environment. Meanwhile, problems that should receive more priority go unaddressed. In addition, the lack of planning can lead to situations in which the target population receives a range of similar prevention approaches all aimed at preventing different problems.

Defining the Target Population

Specifying the characteristics of the target population to whom the intervention will be delivered is a critical task in effective prevention planning. Depending on the nature and scope of the prevention effort, this may consist of the actual definition of a target population by the prevention planner, unless the target population is already predefined based on the sponsoring agency's constituency, political factors, or funding requirements.

Where the definition of the target population is the responsibility of the program planner, a major strategy in this selection is to use the standard of who is most at risk. A great deal of research on the risk factors associated with substance abuse, HIV/AIDS, teenage pregnancy, criminality, depression, and suicide has looked at the common factors among children who later develop these problems, including characteristics of individuals, families, social contexts, and interactions between individuals and their environments. The Youth Risk Behavior Surveillance System (Kolbe, Kann, and Collins 1993) provides initial profiles of the characteristics of the most high-risk populations. The YRBSS includes three components: a national probability sample of ninth- through twelfth-graders; statewide and local school based surveys; and a national household survey.

The sample on which any risk factor research is based must be critically analyzed. Too often, the most vulnerable populations are not included. For example, in developing substance abuse prevention programs, the National Survey for High School Seniors, conducted under the auspices of the National Institute on Drug Abuse (1993), is often used. While these data are important and yield much risk factor information on in-school youth, the sample does not include dropouts or chronically truant youth, who may have the most to tell us about the risk factors for school failure and substance abuse. The YRBSS is a much richer source of data since it captures both dropouts and chronically truant youth through the household survey data.

Assigning an at-risk status and focusing prevention programs exclusively onto at-risk populations also has serious implications, particularly for ethnic or racial minorities. Since minority adolescents living in urban areas have been found to be proportionately more at risk for certain problems such as teenage pregnancy, HIV/STD, and youth violence, critics of the at-risk identification process fear that it can lead to further stereotyping, and may set in motion a self fulfilling prophecy by lowering expectations. Supporters of targeting preventative interventions at the most at-risk populations argue they have an ethical responsibility to ensure that scarce resources for prevention are spent on the most high-risk populations.

An example of how the politics of assigning at-risk status affected the prevention program design and evaluation process occurred in a federally funded HIV/STD prevention project for which the author had primary responsibility for developing the intervention. During the development stage of the project, the funding agency took the responsibility for defining the target population. The agency directed that the preventative intervention be targeted at all adolescents regardless of their ethnic or racial background, socioeconomic status, or geographic location. While it was clear from the epidemiologic evidence at that time that not all youths were equally at risk, the directive was part of an early political strategy in AIDS prevention that aimed to convey that everyone was at risk and that no group was exempt. In response to this directive, an intervention was developed that attempted to target a broad range of adolescents with a something for everyone approach. As the epidemiologic evidence mounted about the AIDS crisis among African American and Hispanic populations living in urban centers, a presidential commission recommended that the disproportionate effect of AIDS on minorities be recognized, and resources targeted to those most at risk (Leary 1993). In line with this political shift the funding agency changed its initial strategy and directed that the prevention program developed under the previous policy be implemented and evaluated only among African American and Hispanic youth living in identified epicenters. Unfortunately the program had not been designed specifically for urban minority youth. In retrospect, a more powerful intervention could have been developed if this target population had been defined from the onset.

Unexamined feelings about who "should" be the target population can also affect the process. Most child sexual abuse prevention programs have traditionally had the potential child victims as the target population and have focused on teaching potential child victims the skills to stay safe. Only recently has this limited focus on potential victims been questioned and the potential perpetrators been seen as a target population for prevention efforts. An innovative program in Vermont exemplifies this expanded focus. A community-wide media campaign is directed at potential perpetrators by highlighting the early signs and symptoms of sexually abusive behaviors and the services available to deal with compulsions to sexually abuse a child. For a long time this type of focus on prevention was not contemplated because of intense negative feelings toward this population and the consensus by many in the therapeutic community that they would not voluntarily come forward. To the surprise of many who saw this population as unreachable by efforts at prevention, the media campaign focused on enhancing the ability of potential perpetrators to ask for help has resulted in a substantial number of voluntary hotline calls for referral to services (Tabachnick 1998).

Identifying and Refining the Resiliency Enhancement Factors

Prevention research has begun to focus on the resiliency factors that are present when individuals who have been exposed to many risk factors successfully negotiate their life situations (Garmezy 1985; Rutter 1979, 1987; Werner and Smith 1982, 1992). This research on resiliency factors provides the building blocks for preventative resiliency enhancement programs.

Since social workers view problems through an ecological lens and are trained to intervene on different levels in order to effect change, it is important to identify resiliency factors to be enhanced on the individual, familial, and environmental levels. For example, to focus a school-based effort on enhancing the resiliency factor of social competence without attention to factors such as parent-child communication and school policies regarding student behavior would not be in line with the social work commitment to the person-in-environment.

Yet not all problems have been studied in the empirical literature in a way that readily informs an ecological perspective. Utilizing the practice wisdom of those working directly with the target population to find out more about the particular individual, familial, or environmental resiliency factors or to gain an understanding from focus groups from the target population are methods that can be employed to learn more.

The resiliency factors identified in empirical studies must also be scrutinized for their relevance and meaning for the defined target population. Particularly with national probability samples, it is necessary to further examine if and how the resiliency factors selected relate to the defined target population. National probability samples, while providing critical data on the demographic characteristics of the populations most at risk, are limited in the amount of information they provide for tailoring the resiliency enhancement effort to specific target populations. For example, culturally specific resiliency factors for substance abuse for African American youth, such as cultural pride (Tucker 1985) and race consciousness (Gary and Berry 1985), are not factors analyzed in national probability studies. Only population-specific studies that explore why some individuals within a group are at risk while others are not can provide this kind of information.

Data from national studies need to be considered as well. For example, early age of onset of sexual activity has been identified as a risk factor for pregnancy and sexually transmitted diseases (U.S. Department of Health and Human Services 1991). Age of onset however varies among ethnic and racial groups and for males and females. Age of onset for sexual activity has been found to be younger for African American youth than their white counterparts, and younger for African American boys than for African American girls (Centers for Disease Control and Prevention 1995; Keller et al. 1991). Understanding the specific resiliency factors of African American boys and girls who do not engage in early sexual activity would also be of great value in the refinement process, and might require the use of more qualitative methods such as focus groups or key informants within the community.

The age of the participants may also be relevant if not critical. For example, communication with parents has been found to be a resiliency factor for sexual risktaking behavior (Leland and Barth 1993). Yet what gets communicated and how it gets communicated has different implications depending on the child's age.

Gender also has implications for the selection and refinement of resiliency factors. Gender differences have been found in the ways in which boys and girls adapt and cope with stress. In general, boys are more susceptible to stress and vulnerability in the first decade of life, while girls experience more vulnerability during the second decade. Carol Gilligan, who has done the research on these differences, theorizes that boys tend to have problems earlier than girls do because they are pressured to separate earlier from their mothers (Norman 1997), while acceptable male coping responses do not allow them to feel or express this separation as a real loss. As a result, they may experience more learning problems, stuttering, and bed wetting than girls during the first decade. Girls face more of a crisis of identity when they approach adolescence and experience for the first time the need to fit into the more subordinate female role. Girls at this age have been found to experience increased levels of depression, suicide, and eating disorders. As a result of these distinct socialization and developmental experiences some resiliency factors may be different for girls than boys. For example, participation in sports has been identified as a strong resiliency factor for girls (Colton and Gore 1991). Encouraging girls to participate in sports may require specific strategies, given traditional sex role identities. For boys, the encouragement of emotional expressiveness by parents has been found to be a strong resiliency mechanism; yet the enhancement of this factor may also pose a challenge to the traditional sex role expectations for boys (Werner and Smith 1992). In order to enhance the resiliency mechanisms for boys and girls in ways that respond to their developmental and socialization differences, additional gender specific strategies need to be developed (Turner, Norman, and Zunz 1995).

The socioeconomic status of the target group must also be taken into account when refining the resiliency factors to be identified. For example, greater alienation from social institutions (Kaplan, Martin, Johnston, and Robbins 1986) and low orientation to work (Brook, Whitman, Gordon, Nomura, and Brook 1986) have been identified as risk factors for substance abuse in general population surveys. The experience of these risk factors for youth coming from impoverished environments or oppressed populations may be very different from that experienced in higher socioeconomic groups. In order to enhance the resiliency of more economically oppressed populations in relation to substance abuse, the accessibility of social institutions and the opportunities for work may need to be taken into account.

The cultural context is also a factor to be considered. Assertive communication has been identified as a resiliency factor for youth at risk for substance abuse. A focus group of inner-city African American and Hispanic pre-adolescents conducted by this author identified the need to learn how to assertively resist involvement with the inner-city drug culture as more relevant than learning how to resist the actual use of substances. According to the participants, getting involved as lookouts and drug runners was the first step, eventually leading to drug use. For this target population, developing strategies that would assist them to resist the lure of the drug culture and its monetary enticements, was identified as more important than learning how to resist drug use (Forgey 1994b; Forgey, Schinke, and Cole 1997).

Selecting the Method and Level of Intervention

Preventative interventions can be delivered on the individual, group, family, organization, or community level. Depending on the characteristics of the defined target population and the specific resiliency factor to be enhanced, certain methods and levels of intervention will be more applicable than others. Social competence in youth has been identified as a resiliency factor for a myriad of problems. Increasing social competence through the enhancement of certain social skills can be effectively and efficiently delivered on a group level using a cognitive behavioral method of intervention since this level affords multiple opportunities for the techniques of modeling, behavioral rehearsal, and feedback (Cartledge and Milburn 1980; Bandura, 1986; Barth, Leland, Kirby, and Fetro 1992). Reinforcement of these social skills can be further enhanced by providing a similar cognitive-behavioral group level intervention to peer leaders, school staff, or parents.

Environmental level resiliency factors require intervention on an organizational or community level. In a teen pregnancy prevention program aimed at promoting the teens' other options, a major community level component involved the development of community service projects and linking student volunteers with these projects. Students involved in this type of community level intervention were found to have lower pregnancy rates and lower drop out rates than students in a comparison group (Philliber and Allen 1992).

Increasing resiliency factors such as cultural pride and race consciousness for an ethnic minority population may require the development of multilevel components. In the substance abuse prevention program for inner-city African American and Hispanic youth developed previously cited, an organizational level component was included that aimed to increase the students' cultural pride through schoolwide presentation of African tales and Spanish legends by a professional storyteller. In addition, a group level component involved guided discussions within the classroom focusing on the meaning of the tales and legends in the students' current lives. On the individual level, students were given in-class and homework assignments focused on the further personalization of the stories in their lives (Forgey 1994b). When participants in this culturally focused multilevel intervention were compared to participants in a generic skills-based group level intervention at two year follow-up, they were found to drink less alcohol and have lower intentions to drink than the comparison group (Botvin, Schinke, Epstein, Diaz, and Botvin, 1995; Forgey, Schinke, and Cole 1997).

The mandate and capability of the sponsoring organization must also be analyzed in deciding the most effective intervention method and level. School systems often do not have the resources to address resiliency factors beyond the individual student or group level and often have restrictions on the family level of service they can provide. Social service agencies often have more of a capability to intervene on the individual or family level but may have more difficulty organizing and maintaining a group level intervention than a school system. Funding of prevention efforts also limits the level on which the preventative intervention can be launched. More collaboration and linking of services needs to occur among agencies and organizations with different capabilities in order to increase cost effectiveness. Creative ways of reaching beyond one level of intervention need to be developed. Within school systems that often do not have the resources to go beyond the individual or group level of intervention, developing training booklets for parents or involving parents in the student's homework assignments are ways of involving the parent and family. In an HIV/STD prevention program developed by this author, the extensive parent training component aimed at increasing parent-child communication was eliminated due to funding cutbacks. In its place a parent home video program was developed in which the students took turns bringing home selected prevention videos on HIV/STD and participating with their parents or significant adult in a guided discussion following the viewing of the video (Forgey 1994a).

Developing, Implementing, and Using Effective Program Evaluation

The measurement of the effectiveness of resiliency enhancement efforts requires a commitment to systematic research evaluation. Only with concrete evidence that these activities had an impact on the reduction of the selected problem will public support for these efforts be maintained.

There are two major objectives in evaluating the effectiveness of a planned prevention effort. The first and most obvious is to test how effective the program was in preventing the onset of the selected problem. The second purpose is to test the theoretical underpinnings of the program. If the program is shown to be effective, did the selected intervention method and level make the difference?

Not all evaluations are designed to meet both objectives equally. Often the evaluation design focuses more on measuring the outcome. The evaluation may show that the program was effective compared to a control group, but the processes within the intervention that effected these results remain mysterious. The practitioner is provided with little information to draw upon in order to replicate or build interventions that may have the most impact on behavior.

This problem typically occurs in situations in which there is insufficient communication between the evaluator and the program developer. The different training backgrounds of those involved leads to each working separately on their areas of responsibility. Evaluators focus on design issues such as the use of a control group, sample size, power analysis, and the validity and reliability of the measures. Program developers focus on the development of interventions that correspond to the characteristics of the at-risk target population and that will enhance the identified resiliency factors. Often the evaluator and program developer spend too little time discussing the interventions planned and the evaluation design. As a result the evaluation does not sufficiently measure the input (the interventions utilized)or the outcome (the effect of those interventions).

Another reason why evaluations may focus more on the problem outcome is the lack of adequate measures for the variety of resiliency factors upon which interventions are built. An example of this arose in the culturally focused substance abuse prevention program discussed earlier. Behavioral outcome measures for substance abuse were selected by the evaluation team, along with some existing measures on the mediating variables of substance abuse knowledge, social skills, peer norms and perceived peer norms. However, measures for cultural pride, race consciousness, and bi-culturalism, which were also resiliency factors to be enhanced in the program, were not developed: at the time the study was conducted, measures did not exist for these factors. While the intervention was found to be effective at two-year follow-up on certain behavioral outcomes and mediating variables, nothing could be said about the importance of these culturally specific resiliency factors in relation to the findings (Forgey 1994; Forgey, Schinke, and Cole 1997).

Some evaluation designs do focus on measuring the program's ability to enhance identified resiliency factors or decrease identified risk factors, often in prevention program evaluation where it is not feasible or realistic to get outcome data on actual problem reduction. In a program for fifth graders developed by and currently being evaluated by this author, the effectiveness of the program in delaying the onset of sexual activity cannot be measured due to lack of resources to do a sufficiently long longitudinal study. The impact of the interventions on resiliency factors such as parent child communication, aspirations for the future, assertiveness, and problem solving skills are the only variables that can feasibly be measured.

There may also be tension between the evaluators' preference for stronger experimental design (involving randomly assigned experimental and control groups) and practitioners who do not see this type of design as feasible or ethical. This tension can often be resolved by using a quasi-experimental design in which subjects are not randomly assigned to experimental or non-experimental conditions but there is a control group. The control group is often given the "traditional" intervention rather than none at all, to allay ethical concerns. In addition, the experimental intervention can be offered to the control group following the evaluation period if some level of effectiveness is found.

The last issue in prevention program evaluation involves utilization. What is learned from the evaluation is frequently not used to build up and refine the program. Practitioners too often see evaluation as a necessary evil required to receive or maintain funding. To maximize its usefulness, evaluation needs to be perceived as an integral part of the intervention itself. Every conceptual and practical step in the design of the preventative intervention needs to be integrated with the evaluation design and measurements. When intervention and evaluation fit together practitioners will more clearly see benefits and be more likely to use the evaluation results in any redesign of the intervention.

Future Directions: Implications for Social Work Education and Practice

More emphasis is being placed on the development of prevention programs in such areas as AIDS, teenage pregnancy, substance abuse, and youth violence. Social workers are well positioned to lead in the development of the kinds of prevention programs that have been found to be most effective. In order to do so, the profession must continue to strengthen its emphasis on the ecological framework, research data, the strengths perspective, cultural sensitivity, and empirically based practice, overcoming current obstacles in each of these areas.

Social work training programs continue to struggle with teaching an eco-logical framework for practice. Work with the individual and, to some extent, the family outweighs the curriculum devoted to groups, organizations, and communities. More of a balance is needed for social workers to become more adept at creating prevention programs that are grounded in the eco-logical multi-systems framework.

Developing and implementing prevention programs also requires an abil-ity to utilize and interpret the research data on at-risk population character-istics and resiliency factors. There remains a reticence on the part of social workers to really incorporate research training into clinical work. Social workers must be able to effectively utilize research knowledge to build re-siliency enhancement approaches, and to participate in the evaluation de-sign of these approaches.

The strengths perspective in social work education places social workers in the proper framework for utilizing resiliency factors. However, the strengths perspective is primarily used in clinical situations when a problem has already been recognized and resiliency factors or strengths are seen as a way of ameliorating the existing problem. The strengths perspective needs to be expanded conceptually within social work practice for use in developing strategies to prevent the onset of problems.

The profession's commitment to oppressed populations has made cultural sensitivity and competence a central part of its training. As a result, social work professionals are well equipped to understand and deal effectively with cultural differences such as race, ethnicity, gender, and sexual orientation. Social work must use this capacity not only in situations where a client pres-ents with a problem but also in the prevention of problems. Cultural sensi-tivity and competence are critical to the selection and refinement of the re-siliency factors chosen for enhancement, to the development of resiliency enhancement strategies that respond to the cultural context of the target pop-ulation, and to the development of more culturally and contextually sensitive measures to evaluate the efficacy of prevention efforts.

More opportunities to design, implement, and evaluate prevention pro-grams are also needed for students in graduate social work training programs.

In the early years of the social work profession, it was acutely aware of its uniqueness and its capacity to intervene in a preventative way. It took the lead in the settlement house movement that focused on the prevention of social ills by strengthening the capacities of new immigrants to deal with the stressful transition to a new homeland. Somewhere along the way, social work's commitment to the area of prevention became diluted, perhaps as a result of the profession's increased focus on achieving professional status by developing more clinical expertise on the individual level of intervention. Despite this divergence, social work knowledge and skills remain unique and have grown even more valuable to the current prevention movement, which recognizes the need for empirically based multi-component preventative interventions that respond to the needs of culturally diverse populations. It is time for the social work profession to once again capitalize on its strengths and move to the forefront in designing, implementing, and evaluating resiliency enhancement efforts at prevention.

References

Bandura, A. 1986. *Social Foundations of Thought and Action*. Englewood Cliffs, N.J.: Prentice Hall.

Barth, R. P., N. Leland, D. Kirby, and J. V. Fetro. 1992. Enhancing social and cognitive skills. In B. C. Miller, J. J. Card, R. I. Paikoff, and J. L. Petersen, eds., *Preventing Adolescent Pregnancy*, 53–82. Newbury Park, Cal.: Sage.

Botvin, G., S. Schinke, J. Epstein, T. Diaz, and E. Botvin. 1995. Effectiveness of culturally focused and generic skills training approaches to alcohol and drug abuse prevention among minority adolescents: Two-year follow-up results. *Psychology of Addictive Behaviors* 9 (3): 183–194.

Brook, J. S., M. Whitman, A. S. Gordon, C. Nomura, and D. W. Brook. 1986. Onset of adolescent drinking: A longitudinal study of intrapersonal and interpersonal antecedents. In B. Stimmel, ed., *Alcohol and Substance Abuse in Women and Children*, 91–109. New York: Haworth Press.

Cartledge, G. and J. F. Milburn. 1980. *Teaching Social Skills to Children*. New York: Pergamon Press.

Centers for Disease Control and Prevention. 1995. U.S. HIV and AIDS cases reported through June 1995. *HIV/AIDS Surveillance Report* 7:1–34.

Colton, M. E. and S. Gore. 1991. *Gender Differences in Stress and Coping Behaviors Among Late Adolescents*. Washington, D.C.: National Institutes of Mental Health.

Dryfoos, J. 1997. The prevalence of problem behaviors. In R. P. Weissberg, T. P. Gullotta, R. L. Hampton, B. A. Ryan, and G. R. Adams, eds., *Enhancing Children's Wellness*, 17–46. Thousand Oaks: Sage.

Dusenbury, L. and M. Falco. 1997. School based drug abuse prevention strategies: From research to policy and practice. In Weissberg, Gullotta, Hampton, Ryan, and Adams, eds., *Enhancing Children's Wellness*, 47–75.

Forgey, M. 1994a. Healthy and Alive: 7th and 8th Grade HIV Prevention Program Curriculum Guide and Student Workbook. Contract 200–91–0977, Division of Adolescent School Health, Centers for Disease Control and Prevention, Atlanta.

Forgey, M. A. 1994b. Substance abuse prevention approaches for inner-city African-American and Hispanic youth. Dissertation Abstracts International 55 (6). University Microfilms No. 9424069.

Forgey, M. A., S. P. Schinke, and K. Cole. 1997. School based interventions to prevent substance abuse among inner-city minority youth. In D. K. Wilson, J. R. Rodriguez, and W. C. Taylor, eds., *Health Promoting and Health Compromising Behaviors Among Minority Adolescents*, 251–268. Washington, D.C.: American Psychological Association.

Garmezy, N. 1985. Stress resistant children: The search for protective factors. In J. Stevenson, ed., *Recent Research in Developmental Psychopathology*, 213–233. Oxford: Pergamon Press.

Gary, L. E. and G. L. Berry. 1985. Predicting attitudes toward substance use in a Black community: Implications for prevention. *Community Mental Health Journal* 21:42–51.

Kaplan, H. B., S. S. Martin, R. J. Johnson, and C. A. Robbins. 1986. Escalation of marijuana use: Application of a general theory of deviant behavior. *Journal of Health and Social Behavior* 27:44–61.

Keller, S. E., J. A. Bartlett, S. J. Schleifer, R. L. Johnson, E. Pinner, and B. Delaney. 1991. HIV-relevant sexual behavior among a healthy inner-city heterosexual population in an endemic area of HIV. *Journal of Adolescent Health* 12:44–48.

Kolbe, L. J., L. Kann, and J. L. Collins. 1993. Overview of the youth risk behavior surveillance system. *Public Health Report* 108:2–9.

Leary, W. E. 1993. Commission says racism contributes to AIDS spread. *New York Times* January 11: A14.

Leland, N. L. and R. P. Barth. 1993. Characteristics of adolescents who have attempted to avoid HIV and who have communicated with their parents about sex. *Journal of Adolescent Research* 8:58–76.

Moore, K. A., B. W. Sugland, C. Blumenthal, D. Glei, and N. Snyder. 1995. *Adolescent Pregnancy Prevention Programs: Interventions and Evaluations*. Washington, D.C.: Child Trends.

National Institute on Drug Abuse. 1993. *National Survey Results on Drug Abuse from the Monitoring the Future Study, 1975–1992* vol. 1: secondary school students. Rockville, Md.: NIDA.

Norman, M. 1997. From Carol Gilligan's chair. *The New York Times Magazine* November 9: 50.

Philliber, S. and J. P. Allen. 1992. Life options and community service: Teen outreach program. In Miller, Card, Paikoff, and Peterson, eds., *Preventing Adolescent Pregnancy*, 139–155.

Rutter, M. 1979. Protective factors in children's responses to stress and disadvantage. In M. W. Kent and J. Rolf, eds., *Primary Prevention of Psychopathology, Vol. III: Social Competence in Children*, 49–74. Hanover, N.H.: University Press of New England.

Rutter, M. 1987. Psychosocial resilience and protective mechanisms. *American Journal of Orthopsychiatry* 57 (3): 316–331.

Tabachnick, J. 1998. Preventing child sexual abuse: Vermont public health campaign has positive results. *The Interdisciplinary Report on At-Risk Children and Families*, 1. Kingston, N.J.: Civic Research Institute.

Tucker, M. B. 1985. U.S. ethnic minorities and drug abuse: An assessment of science and practice. *International Journal of Addictions* 20:1021–1047.

Turner, S., E. Norman, and S. Zunz. 1995. Enhancing resiliency in girls and boys: A case for gender specific adolescent prevention programming. *The Journal of Primary Prevention* 16 (1): 25–38.

U.S. Department of Health and Human Services, Public Health Service. 1991. *Healthy People 2000: National Health Promotion and Disease Prevention Objectives*. DHHS Publication No. PHS 91–50212. Washington, D.C.: Government Printing Office.

Werner, E. and R. S. Smith. 1982. *Vulnerable but Invincible*. New York: McGraw Hill.

Werner, E. and R. S. Smith. 1992. *Overcoming the Odds: High Risk Children from Birth to Adulthood*. Ithaca, N.Y.: Cornell University Press.

Index